MAN, The Universal

MAN, The Universal:

A Socio-Cultural Exploration of Tagore's Creative Vision of Humanity

Volume - I

Santi Nath Chattopadhyay

GYAN

First Published, 2017

Published by

Gyan Publishing House
5, Ansari Road
Daryaganj, New Delhi-110002
Phone: 9811692060
E-mail: books@gyanbooks.com

Printed at: G. Print Process, Delhi.

Cataloging in Publication Data—DK
Courtesy: D.K. Agencies (P) Ltd. <docinfo@dkagencies.com>

Chattopadhyay, Santinath, author.
Man, the universal : a socio-cultural exploration of Tagore's creative vision of humanity / Santi Nath Chattopadhyay.
pages cm
Includes bibliographical references.
ISBN 9788121213516

1. Tagore, Rabindranath, 1861-1941. 2. Philosophical anthropology. 3. Humanism. I. Title.

B5134.T34C43 2016 DDC 144 23

Contents

Dedicated to

Gurudev Rabindranath Tagore,

In celebration of His 150th Birth Anniversary

and

Centenary Celebration of His 'Gitanjali' (Song Offerings)

Preface

The present work on 'MAN–The Universal' is a humanistic analysis of Indian thought and culture, in the background of the philosophy of Man as visualised by Rabindranath Tagore, in his idea of the religion of Man. The work is expository, comparative and critical.

This idea of the religion of Man as the expression of the potential universality in different creative states of human existence, leads to the growth and development of the philosophy of Universal Man.

In the introductory note on this work, I have discussed the objects and the main principles of the theme and the entire work on the subject is divided into eight chapters, dealing with different possibilities of human life that contribute to the comprehensive development of the philosophy of Man as the socio-cultural exploration of *Universal Humanism.*

In the examination of this idea, I have collected the humanistic views of Tagore from his numerous English and Bengali works. So far as Bengali writings are concerned, I have tried to quote from authentic English translations; failing which same have been translated by me with utmost humility and caution. With regard to the use of Bengali and Sanskrit terms, the diacritical marks have been avoided for obvious reasons and these are expressed in *italics* for simplicity and easy understanding. Inspite of my best efforts some errors have crept in, which are deeply regretted.

In the development of the theme in the intercultural context, I am happy to record my sincere gratitude to eminent Ideologist Dr Archie J. Bahm, distinguished Professor Emeritus of Philosophy, New Mexico University, USA, who was much interested to write a

Foreword from a different socio-cultural point of view, projecting a programme for making intercultural relations more effective and fruitful.

I am deeply indebted to Swami Lokeswarananda, Former Secretary, The Ramakrishna Mission Institute of Culture, Golpark, Kolkata, Dr Kalidas Bhattacharyya, Former Professor of Philosophy and Vice-Chancellor, Visva Bharati, Santiniketan, Dr Adhar Chandra Das, Dr Saroj Kumar Das, Dr Pritibhusan Chatterjee, Dept. of Philosophy, University of Calcutta, Professor Amiya Kumar Majumdar, Former UGC Professor, Rabindra Bharati University, Dr J.N. Mohanty, Former Professor of Philosophy, Temple University, USA, Dr Anil Kumar Sarkar, Former Professor of Philosophy, California State University, USA, Dr Sudhir Kumar Nandi, Former Professor of Aesthetics, Rabindra Bharati University, who inspired me and gave constructive guidance from several perspectives.

I take the opportunity to thank my publisher Gyan Publishing House, New Delhi for bringing out this work.

My relationship embarrasses me to express formal thanks to my wife Professor Chhanda Chattopadhyay, my son Dr Sudipto Chattopadhyay, Smt Somdutta Chattopadhyay, Master Somdipta (My Pentu Babu) and Sri Ram Krishna Mondal in helping me in different possible ways. In relation to it I express my thankfulness to Professor Gobinda Chandra Bandyopadhyay and Professor Maniklal Bandyopadhyay for their guidance and co-operation.

I would like to submit that I would be richly rewarded if this work stimulates the readers who are to be inspired in entering into intercultural studies for cultivation of intercultural relation and understanding for Peace.

Dr Santi Nath Chattopadhyay

'Uttoran'–22, S.K. Deb Road
(4th bye lane), Kolkata–700 048
Phone: 091 33 2521 5753/2534 3782
E-mail: cal.isisar@gmail.com
Web: www.isisar.weebly.com

Foreword

Santi Nath Chattopadhyaya's stimulating work on 'MAN, The Universal: A Socio-cultural Exploration on *Tagore's creative vision of Humanity*', is an attempt to interpret the philosophy of man in the background of the humanistic outlook of Rabindranath Tagore as revealed in his idea of the religion of Man. I have gone through Chattopadhyay's total programme which he has developed in the intercultural context, expressing its humanistic and universalistic relevance. This, I think, is a thorough and convincing research work, containing eight chapters on different problems and prospects of human life and existence, with a critical and comparative study of Eastern and Western religions, philosophies and cultures.

I

Many years ago I was introduced to the philosophy of Rabindranath Tagore by reading his *Sadhana, The Realisation of Life.* Its opening page significantly initiated my awareness of comparative philosophy, the philosopher's chief interest in intercultural studies : "The civilisation of ancient Greece was nurtured within city walls.... These walls leave their mark deep in the minds of men. They set up the principle of 'divide and rule' in our mental outlook....We divide nation and nation, knowledge and knowledge, man and nature.... In India it was the forests that our civilisation had its birth...it included the world with the man as one great truth. India put all her emphasis on the harmony that exists between the individual and the universal."[1]

As I take up again my well-marked copy of *Sadhana,* I welcome an opportunity to express my admiration of and appreciation of one of the world's greatest visions of "The Individual to The Universe" (the title of his opening chapter and the central problem of his lifetime of work).

His conclusion expresses his life-long immersion in Indian cultural heritage permeating his daily practices as well as his intellectual convictions. His vision emphasising the unity of the individual human being with the being of the total universe naturally begets a *Universal Humanism.* The universe manifests itself by embodying itself in each particular person; and each person exists as a particular embodiment of the universe. The more fully each person becomes aware of his identity with the universe, the more fully humanistic he becomes. "The more we realise the World-consciousness in all, the better for us." "In fact, the only true human progress is coincident with the widening of this range of feeling."[2] This is the central teaching of his religion of humanity, his *Universal Humanism.*

Although emerging primarily from the integrative tendencies inherent in Indian cultural heritage, Tagore tested his view, sharpened his insights, and confirmed his convictions by earnestly encountering and exploring the visions, i.e., philosophies, of other cultures. He was constantly aware of antithetical preferences expressed by many Western thinkers, and of mistaken interpretations of Indian ideas. He had warned "them against the idea that the teachers of India preached renunciation of the World and of self which leads only to the blank emptiness of negation. Their aim was the realisation of the soul, or gaining the world of perfect truth."[3]

"Tagore is a non-dualist, but not like Samkara. He thinks that the Absolute in its perfection, living away from all that happens in the world, is of no interest to man."[4] Yet "Man must realise the wholeness of his existence, his place in thee infinite."[5] When we devote ourselves to the details of daily living involving conflicts with other persons or with nature; we encounter crops of "interminable difficulties."[6] "When man's consciousness is restricted only to the immediate vicinity of his human self, the deeper roots of his nature do not find their permanent soul."[7] "We can look at ourself in its two different aspects. The self which displays itself, and the self which transcends itself."[8] Each self has two poles, the one individual, the other universal. At one "pole of my being I am separate from all. There I have broken through the cordon of equality and stand alone as an individual. I am absolutely unique, I am I, I am incomparable. The whole weight of the universe cannot crush out this individuality of mine." At the other pole, "I have to acknowledge the rule of universal law. That is where the foundation of my existence lies, deep down below. Its strength lies in its being held firm in the clasp of he comprehensive world, and in the fullness of its community with all things."[9]

"Tagore gives a higher place to love than to knowledge. He says that in knowledge the distinctions are either kept separate or completely dissolved in bare unity. But in love, the terms, the lover and the beloved, are distinguished and yet united. The consciousness of love retains both unity and difference."[10]

All our egoistic impulses, our selfish desires, ... only indicate our narrow self. When we are conscious of our soul, we perceive the inner being that transcends our ego and as its deeper affinity with the All. ...It can find out its truth by unifying itself with others, and only then has its joy."

"Man's cry is to reach his fullest expression. It is this desire for self-expression that leads him to seek wealth and power. But he has to discover that accumulation is not realisation." "What is goodness, what does our moral nature mean? My answer is that when a man begins to have an extended vision of his self, when he realises that he is much more than at present he seems to be, he begins to get conscious of his moral nature....For good is that which is desirable for our greater self. Thus, the sense of goodness comes of a truer view of our life, which is the connected view of the wholeness of the field of life, and which takes account not only of what is present before us but what is not, and perhaps never humanly can be." "This moral sense of man gives him the power to see that the self has continuity in time, but it also enables him to see that he is not true when he is only restricted to his own self....He truly belongs to individuals who are not included in his own individuality, and whom he is never even likely to know. As he has a feeling for his future self which is outside his present consciousness, so he has a feeling for his greater self which is outside the limits of his personality."[11]

Tagore's philosophy of the relation of the individual and the universal has implications for political philosophy and for religion.

Although some patriots find idealised nationalism as a most powerful force for producing feelings of unity among citizens, Tagore regarded nationalism as more divisive than unitive. "The truth is that the spirit of conflict and conquest is at the origin and in the centre of Western nationalism; its basis is on social cooperation." "For the sake of humanity we must stand up and give warning to all, that this nationalism is a cruel epidemic of evil that is sweeping over the human world of the present age, eating into its moral vitality."[12]

II

In developing the creative outlook of the philosophy of man, in the context of Intercultural Studies, Santinath Chattopadhyay has intended to support and expand the philosophy expressed by Tagore which explicitly advocates growth. Tagore opens his essay on *Man* by saying that "The road is ever extended to the outside and has no meaning within itself". Man "feels that he exists more truly in that unarrived future. The major aspects of the Supreme Man are yet unrevealed. The hope of revealing him extends continually into the future".[13] Thus, Chattopadhyay's efforts to promote intercultural studies and my proposals regarding more holistic explanation, as these presented here, are intended to serve as extensions of Tagore's ideal. We believe that Chattopadhyay's endeavours for "lifting man from an inherited past to a prospective future where the primary interest of people will be to foster the processes of cooperative and coexistent society" continue to promote Tagore's interests.

One step taken by Chattopadhyay in pursuing intercultural studies relevant to Tagore's *Universal Humanism* is to invite me, a person obviously from a different culture, to offer suggestion toward some modest explanation. The shaping of my mind began with Christian fundamentalism, revolting against its contradictions, and acquiring understanding through studying physical, biological, psychological and sociological evolution, supported methodologically by British Empiricism as a philosophy of science, and coming to maturity through ideas of emergent evolution and pragmatic methodology. Because my studies extended throughout the philosophies of the world's major civilisations,[14] my present ideas and ideals have ingredients from many cultures.

For example, having studied and taught courses in Indian philosophy for more than thirty years, I have become part Indian by adopting ideas from Indian philosophies. Although obviously less immersed in Indian cultural heritage than Tagore or Chattopadhyay, my own views have been influenced by it in at least four ways: 1. I needed ideas in Advaita Vedanta to complete my theory of the nature of polarity and its Diagram of Types.[15] 2. I needed the Hindu idea and name, *ananda,* blissful feeling of contentment, to complete my understanding of the four kinds of intrinsic value.[16] 3. I needed the enlightenment (*bodhi*) obtained from studying the philosophy of Goutama, the Buddha, in the *Vinaya* and *Sutta Pitakas* to provide conviction about how to reduce unhappiness.[17] 4. I recognised that a "both-and logic" essential to my organicism had already been developed in Jaina *Syadvada,* doubtless from debates with Buddhist logicians.[18]

But my views have also received influences from Chinese culture, and I have endeavoured to rise above my culture in quest of more comprehensive understanding, even if, as pointed out by to me in 1963 by a sharp observer in my Visva-Bharati University audience: "Your long list of differences between Asian and Western culture is itself evidence of a Western (pluralistic) approach and conclusion that fails to embody the spirit of Indian (monistic) philosophy." So, although my intentions are clearly intercultural in their aims and sources,[19] my contributions here must be regarded as expansions having their directions originating more in Western than in Asian cultures.

Chattopadhyay pursues his quest for increased intercultural understanding hereby focusing upon the nature of religion as conceived by several different thinkers and by comparing them with Tagore's conception as something embedded in and transcending all cultures. Religion, as conceived by Tagore, is a "natural expression of human existence". Hence, Chattopadhyay cites from other sources, "Man is incurably religious" and "The history of man is the history of Religion". My own conception agrees with this: "Religion consists in man's concern for his ultimate values and how to attain it, preserve it, and enjoy it."[20] Surely nothing is more central to human concerns than the ultimate values, the intrinsic values of life itself, both whenever they are endangered or when they appear as foundation bases for one's life as a whole. "The needs in man that gave rise to his religious experiences and expressions in the first place remain inherent in his nature".[21] So I must agree that "religion may be treated as a universally present phenomenon". In spite of all of the many cultural differences, concern for what is ultimate in the nature of human value is common to all.

Two ingredients in the nature of religion receive special emphasis in Chattopadhyay's account of Tagore's views: spirituality and love.

Spirituality involves unity. "The ideal of unity…can only be realised in one's own inner spirit."[22] But also unity of self with others in a "brotherhood among men" and unity with the universe are involved in fuller understanding of unity and spirituality. Tagore's problem of the religion of the individual and the universal is one of how to recognise the ultimacy and perpetuity of unity in the midst of obvious pluralities and conflicts in life, including those coming naturally with change. "Our self to live must go through a continual change and growth of form, which may be termed a continual death and a continual life going on at the same time. It is really courting death when we refuse to accept death; when we wish to give the form of self some fixed changelessness; when the self feels no impulse which urges it to grow out of itself." But it also "must merge in the universal time after time". "Whenever the part, spurning the whole, tries to run a separate course of its own, the great pull of all gives it a violent wrench, stops it suddenly, and brings it to dust."[23]

Love involves unity and more. Although Tagore regards love (love of the universe as love of ultimate unity) as a mystery, I regard love, like existence itself, even if still somewhat mysterious, as no longer a complete mystery. Whereas Tagore's emotional embodiment of love for others and the universe as a concrete feeling is poetically conceived as an unanalysable supreme value, I find the multiplicities of kinds and intensities of human love so common place that they are available for scientific observation and generalisations that may supplement both the poetic and merely erotic expressions with knowledge that is somewhat reliable. Just as I have treated goodness and oughtness (in axilogy and ethics) scientifically, so I advocate promoting a science[24] of love.

The ultimate locus of love is intrinsic value which is apprehended as feeling of enjoyment. I agree when Tagore says, "This joy, which is another name for love, must by its very nature have duality for its realisation." [25] Any mystery of mere unity is missing here; the mystery is how what is one can also be dual or many, or how what is many or two can still be united. "Love must be one and two at the same time."[26] By interpreting such dualities as lover and beloved, and lover who is also loved, as polar opposites, their union in concrete polarities need no longer be regarded as very mysterious. My own view is that polarity involves not only some identity of differing existences but also when involved in temporal process as partly interexisting as well.[27]

"The ideal of love", interprets Chattopadhyay, "elevates all to a transcendent and superhuman[28] process of religious and philosophic consciousness, which provides a ground for an advanced order of humanity in international contexts." Tagore's founding of educational opportunities in Shantiniketan exemplifies a practical effort to support Indian "processes with a further prospect of varied alternatives". Chattopadhyay's active interest in stimulating others from different cultures of the world to develop the 'International Society for Intercultural Studies and Research' is another practical endeavour not only to explore ideals of love inherent in man and in religion in other cultures but also for the purpose of expressing his own love, and the love expressed by his fellow workers, through earnest search for evidences of the universality of love foundational to *Universal Humanism* and the Religion of Man.

III

The problem of "the one and the many" has troubled mankind the beginning of his efforts to explain the nature of things. Tagore tackles the problem in many ways, but focuses especially its exemplification in the relation of the individual to the universal. Mankind will continue to struggle with the problem, and no satisfactory world philosophy will be achieved until this problem has been solved with some degree of satisfaction. My own efforts to deal with the problem have been lifelong and gradual emergence of more satisfactory insights have encouraged me to report and propose some features of an explanation intended in that direction. Re-examination of the Philosophy of Tagore provides an opportunity for a summary expression of these ideas in comparison with his magnificent vision of *Universal Humanism.*

Although my work has been long in developing, my recent explorations in systems theory connected with the Society for General Systems Research provides me with a current language in terms of which to express ideas: Western materialists have become increasingly dissatisfied with traditional mechanistic interpretations of nature and have developed "cybernetics" by adding a "feedback mechanism"[29] to account for processes regaining "stable equilibrium" needed for retaining such unity and stability as is needed before proceeding. But even cybernetics failed to satisfy growing demands for "more holistic explanations", which then resulted in a series of theoretical development, initiated by Ludwig von Bertalarffly and sketched in my article, "Five Systems Concepts of Society", appearing in the journal of the International Federation for Systems Research.[30] Hence the title to this section of my contribution to Chattopadhyay's study of Tagore's philosophy.

For me now, the problem of the one and the many occurs most centrally in the problem of a whole and its parts. Since spirituality has been identified with the unity of wholeness and materiality with plurality of parts, problems pertaining to a spirit-matter polarity may be worked out simultaneously with those pertaining to the whole-parts polarity, which has received "extended attention" in my efforts to achieve a more adequate kind of "more holistic explanation".

Although I feel at home in much of Tagore's writing and share his ideals of a *Universal Humanism* and religion of Man, his "inauguration of Man" (i.e., superman) as an existing cosmic consciousness appeals to me as succumbing too much to traditional ideals of unity, eternity, and infinite, and, in spite of his seeming rejection of any absolute divinity, permits his poetic visions to carry him away (or back) in that direction. Of three solutions to the problem of the one and the many, those favouring the-one-in-the-many, those favouring the-many-in-the-one, and those favouring the-one-and-the-many more equally, Tagore seems to favour the first, although, as I shall how, he vacillates between the first and the last in which he also feels at home. Since my own views favour the latter, some differences result. The reader may make his own judgment about whether views extend Tagore's or extend beyond them.

A central characteristic of may conception of the nature of is that opposites exist as complementary rather than contradictory and thus participate in polarity which involves some unity (and thus holeness) as well as some duality (and thus partness). The central concept of this explanation called "organic unity", that unity or whole which is inclusive the whole as opposed to its parts and the parts as opposed the whole (and each other) and all of these oppositions. My thesis is that the whole which includes both whole and parts and their polar interdependencies is "more holistic", i.e., more concretely wholistic, than the wholeness of a whole opposed to parts. Involved here is a decision to regard the view that a whole and its parts are opposed to each other in such a way that increase in wholeness involves decrease in partness and that increase in partness involves decrease in wholeness is less holistic than the view that organic unity varies with increase or decrease of the strength of the harmonious cooperation of the whole and its parts in ways inclusive of their complementary oppositions involving embodiment of interdependencies, inter actions and interexistences functioning entitively.

That Tagore was at least somewhat aware of the issues involved in this more holistic explanation may be observed in quotes from *Sadhana.* "We have what we call in Sanskrit *dvandva,* a series of opposites in creation; such as, the positive pole and the negative, the centripetal force and the centrifugal, attraction and repulsion. These are also mere names, they are no explanations. They are only-different ways of asserting that the world in its essence is a reconciliation of pairs of opposing forces. These forces, like the left and the right hands of the creator, are acting in absolute harmony, yet acting in opposite directions."[31] He explains the nature of self as involving two poles.[32] He opposes the individual and the universal and then identifies them. He distinguishes between the finite and the infinite and then envisions them as identical. Narvane interprets Tagore as a persistent harmonizer of views: "Tagore remains faithful to the point of view of the middle path; he seeks to build a bridge between the two extremes of monism and pluralism. He asserts that the many are real, and yet the organic unity of the whole is not destroyed."[33] But when Tagore asserts explicitly, "The underlying principle must be unity, not opposition."[34] I find my own claim that the underlying, or rather more inclusive, principle is ("must be") that unity which includes polar opposition provides a somewhat differing emphasis. Hence, also, I regard it as a somewhat "more holistic explanation".

My contribution to the religion of man may be exemplified by my membership in the American Humanist Association since before its beginning,[35] when I was a student in the University of Michigan under Roy Wood Sellers, chief originator of the first Humanist Manifesto.[36] I too find understanding the nature of self a central problem in philosophy, ethics and religion, made devote fifteen chapters to it in my *Why Be Moral?* I emphasise "the multifarious ways is which a self has its origin, its nature and its riches in the social and cultural aspects of life."[37] Each self exists and functions in terms of self-concepts. So "the nature, complexity and size of an individual depends on the number and kinds of things with which he feels identified. One index for measuring feelings of identification is expression of feelings of opposition. For example, the thought of yourself as a patriot had little significance until you became aware of some opposition by other nations to yourself.... But also, the size of a person is determined: in part by the number of kinds of oppositions he has overcome. The conception of yourself as an humanitarian can come, significantly and consistently, only when you can feel yourself identified with all human beings, including those to whom you felt opposed as patriot."[38]

"Religion is man's concern for the goal of life. When achieved; the goal, to be enjoyed, must be appreciated as present." Such appreciation "is aesthetically complete when life itself as a whole is experienced as being an intrinsic value (and) is cosmically complete when life is experienced as having its fullest, i.e., widest, deepest and most inclusive, extent in the universe."[39] I accept Tagore's ideal as one option, namely, that "all of your possessions have their only significance for you, not in themselves but in the relation they establish with the infinite."[40]

But I prefer to regard religion as including multiplicities of options regarding most valued depictions of life as a whole, each person either adopting a single most beautiful vision or retaining an ability to appreciate several kinds and levels of personal identification. "Some feel identified with the earth, some with our solar system, some with our galaxy, and some with the whole universe.... Persons who identify themselves too narrowly tend to neglect some of the most enjoyable values of life."[41] "If there are several levels of complexity with which he is acquainted, then a person may have a duty to consider with how many of them it is to his interest to feel identified. ...And he may need to fluctuate in his conceptions, and feelings of identification, at different times, ...including in it as much as one can of the whole of his universe."[42]

Before closing, I wish to reflect on Chattopadhyay's suggestions for developing love in a disinterested form in widening social relations. I conceive selves as inherently social in nature, from before birth, through all social extensions of its interests, and even, following Confucius, interest in being respected after death. If "disinterested" means "fair," or "just," or "universal", then recognise that religious, philosophical, cultural or creative attitudes often include them. But I also think with Tagore and Chattopadhyay that love of others and of mankind, even of nature and the cosmos, is a fundamental kind of human interest that is to be expanded through socio-cultural communications.

So I welcome Chattopadhyay's attitude in achieving peace through the cultivation of love as selfless service for others. I think that persons may have less ability to promote peace in others when they fail to be at peace within themselves. But I also believe that world peace cannot be achieved without organisation, even without multiplicities of organisations. I am acquainted with many peace societies, each pursuing its own efforts as an exercise in futility even though pursued eagerly. What is needed today therefore is a "Peace Union", an organisation uniting the disparate, even conflicting, efforts of the many societies in cooperative actions, hoping that uniting such endeavours may produce results when independent activities fail.[43] I see this proposal as consistent with Tagore's interest in unity and as a practical technique for more effectively promoting universal love, and also supportive of Chattopadhyay's inter-cultural interests since an effective "Union" will involve harmonious cooperation of people and institutions in many cultures.

November 27, 1986
Albuquerque, N.M. 87131,
USA.

Archie J. Bahm
Professor of Philosophy, Emeritus
University of New Mexico, USA.

Notes

1. Rabindranath Tagore, 'The Realisation of Life', *Sadhana,* pp. 3, 5, Macmillan Company, New York, 1913.
2. *Ibid.*, pp. 21, 18.
3. *Ibid.*, p. 31.
4. P.T. Raju, *Structural Depths of Indian Thought,* p. 564, South Asia Publishers, New Delhi, 1985.
5. *Sadhana,* p. 10.
6. *Ibid.*, p. 10.
7. *Ibid.*, p. 11.
8. *Ibid.*, p. 86.
9. *Ibid.*, p. 69.
10. Raju, p. 546.
11. *Sadhana,* pp. 40, 45, 55.
12. Rabindranath Tagore, Nationalism, pp. 33. 28, The Macmillan Company New York, 1917.
13. Rabindranath Tagore, *Man*, pp. 3, 15, Kitabistan, Allahabad, 1937.
14. See my *The World's Living Religions,* New York, 1964; *Philosophy of Buddha,* New Delhi, 1982; *Yoga: Union With The Ultimate,* New Delhi, 1978; *Bhagavad Gita: The 'Wisdom of krishna,* Bombay, 1970; *Tao Teh King by Lao Tzu,* New York, 1958 ; *The Heart of Confucius,* Tokyo, 1960; *Comparative Philosophy,* New Delhi, 1977.
15. See my 'Vedantic Contributions to Organicism', The Philosophical Quarterly, Vol. XXXIV, 1963; Philosophy: An Introduction, Ch. 20, New York, 1953; Polarity, Dialectic, and Organicity, Ch. 2, Springfield, 1970.
16. See my Axiology; The Science of Values, Albuquerque, 1980.
17. See my *Philosophy of the Buddha* and *The World's Living Religions*, pp. 98-119.

18. See my 'Jainism and Organicism', *The Voice of Ahimsa,* Vol. V, 1955; *Philosophy East and West,* pp. 127-30, Vol. XII, 1957-58.
19. As evidenced by my *The World's Living Religions* and *Comparative Philosophy.* See my 'Philosophy and Interdisciplinary Research', Spectrum, Djakarta, 1978.
20. *The World's Living Religions,* p. 16; *Philosophy: An Introduction, Ch. 25.*
21. *Ibid.*, p. 14.
22. Rabindranath Tagore, *The Religion of Man,* p. 66.
23. *Sadhana,* pp. 81-82, 87, 90.
24. Not materialistic or mathematical science, but empirical (inductive) science evolved into using pragmatic method.
25. *Sadhana,* p. 104.
26. *Ibid.*, p. 114.
27. See 'Wholes and Parts of Things', *Contextos,* Vol. 2, 1984, and 'The Nature of Existing Things', Systems Research, Vol. 3, 1986.
28. I interpret this as super-individual, but not beyond the human.
29. *Behavioral Science,* pp. 204-18, Vol. 28, 1983.
30. *Systems Research,* pp. 145-50, Vol. I, 1984 and Vol. III,1986, pp. 177-85.
31. *Sadhana,* p. 96.
32. *Ibid.*, pp. 69, 76.
33. V.S. Narvane, *Modern Indian Thought,* p. 130, Asia Publishing House, Bombay, 1964.
34. *Sadhana,* p. 96.
35. i.e., when it was caned. 'The Humanist Press Association'.
36. See: 'Why Humanism is a Religion', *Free Mind,* Vol. XXIV, 1981; 'Ecumenical Humanism', *Religious Humanism,* Vol. XV, 1981; 'Humanism', *The World's Living Religions;'*
37. *Why Be Moral?,* p. 37, Munshiram Manoharlal, Delhi, 1980.
38. 'What is self? The Organicist Answer', *Darshana,* Vol. II, 1962.
39. *Why Be Moral* 7, pp. 434-5, 445.
40. *Sadhana,* p. 148.
41. Sec my, *Ethics: The Science of Oughtness,* p.138, Albuquerque, 1980.
42. *Why Be Moral* 7, pp. 455, 466.
43. 'Peace Union', *Journal of Peace Studies,* 1986.

Introductory Note

The present work on 'MAN, The Universal: A Socio-Cultural Exploration of Tagore's Creative Vision of Humanity', is a humanistic analysis on philosophy of Universal Man, as developed by a noted contemporary Indian thinker, Rabindranath Tagore. The fundamental object of this work is to evaluate the social, material, spiritual nature of man as his creative existence, presented form or model of the religion of Man as the natural expression of man in manifesting potential universality.

In the context of this analysis, the term religion is used for proper examination of human nature and existence, not as the imposition of ideas or values on man but as the natural explanation of creative socio-cultural and humanistic values, presented in different systems of Indian thought and culture.

Religion, in this sense, is essentially related with man as the natural expression of his creative potentiality, manifested in different stages of his existence, in a transcendent–experiential sense. The meaning of this process is nothing but the expression of potential universality of man, as essentially related to the highest value of universality, as gradually manifested in different degrees through a disinterested love and service for mankind. With reference to this analysis of the human nature and value of human existence, there is an explanation of the programme of the religion of Man, developing the philosophy of Universal Man which is to be evaluated in the context of a critical and comparative study of both Indian and Western philosophy and culture.

This type of comprehensive approach examines the essential universality in man in all times and in all societies, which may be treated as the evolution of creative values in society and culture, developing the philosophy of Socio-cultural Humanism.

In the background of this analysis, Tagore's idea of the religion of Man is to be evaluated properly. The proper meaning of the idea of the religion of Man stands on the development of the nature of religion as the essential or the fundamental basis of human life, which, finally is taken as the natural expression of the human existence. Rabindranath, the poet-philosopher and a contemporary Indian thinker, takes the meaning of religion in the sense that has the inmost relation with human life and society. This view of Tagore thus inspires him to establish the unity between man and religion, which is the foundation of religion on man and man on religion. The introduction of this comprehensive outlook leads one to the establishment of a new idea of the religion of Man.

In developing the new and comprehensive idea of the religion of Man, Tagore firstly explains the nature of religion as existing potentially in the evolution of human life in the history of human existence. Then, on the basis of the true nature or meaning of religion he explains the proper nature and existence of man as divine human being, which is recognised by Tagore as 'the divinity of man' as the universal consciousness to be realised in human nature.

Thus, for the development of Tagore's idea of Universal Man, his universal presence in all societies in all times are to be discerned, which is nothing but the evaluation of religion in historical evolution in the history of human beings. If religion is explained in this dynamic sense, it is found that it occupies an important place in human life and society. In different forms and symbols it exists and functions in every society of the world. From the earliest stage and throughout different modern stages of the developed society, the presence of religion can be found in different forms. In this context religion may be treated as universally present phenomenon.

This universal form of religious experience is explained by Ducasse thus: "Religion, of one kind or another seems to a nearly universal feature of the life of mankind."[1] This 'universal feature' of religion supplies a comprehensive view of life that includes the essential nature, character and existence man. Galloway rightly observes, "It is the problem of final meaning of religion as a constituent element in human life and development."[2] Different human needs and desires, like growth, existence, self-development, etc., and faith in a supreme or superhuman power on whom a finite human being can depend for his well-being, are reflected in religion and it involves initially different ritualistic procedures for obtaining the favour of supreme power or for the development of inner life through the realisation of infinite or higher values which are manifested through different human activities in a social and institutional form. In the opinion of Cunningham, it may be said, "Mankind is incurably religious. Wherever the face of the earth man is found and at whatever level of civilisation he may happen to be, he commonly has his religious beliefs and practices."[3]

The study of man and human society becomes incomplete if it does not include the study of religion. If a comprehensive survey of the human experience and society can be made, it will be found that from the earliest times and throughout the ages, religion is intimately related with human life that reveals a complete view of the history of man from a humanistic perspective. For this, Comte, a positivist, recognises that religion the whole of human existence. Max Muller also repeats the same opinion that the true history of man is the history of religion. This writer's vision is an acceptance of their positions only as a process towards a further development will be evident in this discourse.

Indian spiritualism, which is not divorced from the human life and existence, centres round the idea of religion or Hindu view of life which is the establishment of spiritual brotherhood among men through the eternal bond of love. This ideal of religion is interpreted by Radhakrishnan: "A spiritual fellowship is the meaning of history. The purpose of the cosmic process is the city of God in and out of time. Earth is the seed ground of the new life and spirit. Earth and heaven are intermingled."[4] The foundation of this spiritual outlook of the interrelation among men in the world is the fundamental object of Indian outlook on religion which has its roots in the *Vedas,* the *Upanishads* and other systems of Indian Philosophy, and can also be revealed in different thoughts and works of contemporary Indian thinkers. Dr Das rightly points out, "If one wants to get the core of Hinduism as a religion, one must understand the theistic movements which has its roots " in the *Vedas* and *Upanishads,* and has its periodic fruitions, chief among the latest being Sri Ramakrishna, Swami Vivekananda, Mahatma Gandhi, Sri Aurobindo and Rabindranath."[5] This work supports these processes with a further prospect in varied alternative lines.

Of these contemporary Indian thinkers the religious outlook of Rabindranath Tagore is to be discussed, for Tagore has developed philosophic and humanistic outlook which is present in his idea of the religion of Man. The religious views of Tagore centre round the idea of man, and the development of man's nature and existence lies in the realisation of a dynamic religious process in activity. This ideal of Tagore, finally reveals the total nature of his existence as a man, where his multiple nature as a poet, philosopher, politician, social reformer, nationalist, internationalist, etc., are manifest in novel ways. This integral attitude in evolution and development inspires him to open his heart and feeling for the interpretations of the *Vedas,* the *Upanishads,* and other traditional views about life, both Eastern and Western, through a comprehensive perspective in manifesting one's intellect and emotion, mind and heart, reason and feeling, in relation and prospect. This dynamic outlook of Tagore expresses the spirit of non-duality with an integrality in and through the processes of the nature. So Tagore does not deny differences, separateness, limitations, contradictions, finiteness of life, but all of them according to him, reveal an integral feeling of oneness or non-duality in everfresh manifestation.

This comprehensive outlook of Tagore establishes man on religious currents where man's religion is taken as an expression of human nature which is religious, finally developing spirit of unity of values, as reflected in different religious thinkers and philosophers, throughout the ages in mankind general.

This ideal of Tagore's religious experience of man expresses innate and essential nature of man which is the root of religious experience. Tagore thinks that just as the nature of fire is to burn, so the nature of man is inextricably bound with his religious consciousness as a potency. This essential nature of man finally develops the idea of Man in him, who crosses all limitations, contradictions or finiteness of life, due to material '*ego*'. '*Ego*' in man satisfies material interests, but the 'Universal Man' in him inspires man to overcome limitations and contradictions through the development of his integral spirit of unity or synthetic outlook. Tagore observes with a profound sentiment, "Someone lives in our heart, who is Man, but who crosses individual man. *Sada Jananam hridaye sannivishtah.* He is a Man for all and for His attraction introduces universality in thought, feeling and action of man. Great Man feels Him in all men, sacrifices life easily through His love. Through the feeling of that Man, a man crosses the individual limitation, and reaches the boundary of Man."[6]

The inauguration of Man in man is the fundamental end of man's religious experience, where an individual tries to develop his infinite nature and existence, crossing all limitations and contradictions of life. So according to Tagore, all contradictions owing to the desire for the satisfaction of material interests and necessities of life in this mundane world, are reals to be confronted but man's eternal of infinite power revolts against this process, which, is the truth of man.

The realisation of this truth, is the self-realisation of man's true self. He realises his own self or nature as unity or identity through the development of his personality in its completeness and progress. So to know one's own self as a process towards universal unity, it is to become a Universal Man, who realises *'So 'ham'* that is 'I am He' or 'I am in all'-the truth, a vedantic vision. This is the realisation of a complete man, who according to Tagore, is *Manava Brahma* where a man, through the realisation of a universal consciousness or infiniteness, becomes 'divine', and God as infinite potentiality, also becomes 'human' through His perfect manifestation and realisation in human life. In this final state of human life, Tagore's fundamental end of religion of Man as 'the divinity of Man' and God's manifestation in humanity is established.

This final state of human life, according to Tagore, is the highest state of salvation through unity, when all contradictions, limitations or finiteness are merged into an infinite process which is *"Brahmavihara,* or travelling or 'living in the infinite'."[7] In this state of process with a completeness, all contradictions of life are got rid of through the effective realisation of infiniteness in life and world. To explain this state Tagore says, "To be dwelling in such contemplation while standing, walking, sitting or lying down, until sleep' overcomes thee, is called living in Brahma".[8] In this state of life, man reaches the highest mental equilibrium when his narrowness or limitation does not touch him and then he can realise the prospects beyond contradictions and diversities. To realise this final state of integral experience is to develop the highest state of human existence as infinite, which, according to Tagore, is to become Infinite through a mergence with the Infinite. He points out, "Our union with a Being whose activity is worldwide and who dwells in the heart of humanity cannot be a passive one. In order to be united with Him we have to divest our work of selfishness and become *Vishvakarma* 'the world worker'."[9]

In this process of becoming, or in the development of the highest state of integrality, Tagore introduces a process which is manifested in love; because, firstly, it helps a man to develop his infinity of existence through the realisation of the highest value of life: "The infinite is love itself-the eternal spirit of joy."[10] So God or Absolute in this context is *Upanishadic* in spirit to be taken as the realisation of the absolute or infinite value, as manifest in the integral consciousness of love.

Secondly, the ideal of love elevates all to a transcendental and superhuman process of religious and philosophic consciousness, which provides a ground for an advanced order of humanity in international contexts.

Finally, this humanistic outlook of integrality through love and action, develops a comprehensive method of realisation of infinite through a disinterested feeling, and a programme of selfless service for mankind. This method of love develops the infinity in the finite life and existence, which goes so well with Tagore's following statements; "the infinite was not the idea of a spirit of an unbounded cosmic activity, but the infinite whose meaning is in the positive ideal of goodness and love, which cannot be otherwise than human."[11]

Thus, the humanistic outlook of Tagore's religion of Man inspires an individual to solve all contradictions of moral and social life through the development of selflessness in love and action. The contradiction between individual interest and collective or social interest creates the fundamental problem in moral life and in social life of man. But a man, through the development of the spirit of infinity, can overcome this finite contradiction and finally he can establish for himself a humanist ideal of unity in love, through selfless service for others.

This is the advent of *Humanism* in Tagore's philosophy of Man through the introduction of the human ideal of love in man and society. Ordinarily man may work for his own self, but the ideal of love as indicated, develops a disinterested feeling, for others that inspires him to work for other human beings in society. In this way a man is intimately related with others in an eternal and continuous process of life in society and thus finally he is united with all. This is the final end of Tagore's Humanism from a universalist international perspective, when man realises *So 'ham* as universal unity, that leads to the Inauguration of *Manava Brahma* or Universal Man, in the human existence.

This ideal of *Universal Humanism,* introduced by Tagore's religion of Man, thus finally establishes man on a comprehensive religious platform fostering a novel Humanism in the sociocultural form, spelling out a new Society for Man, which is the spirit of an integral consciousness of man as Man from different points of view in expressing Man's diversity of interests and prospects. Tagore observes, "...to study the mind of man in its realisation of different aspects of truth from diverse points of view."[12]

In order to cultivate this universalist attitude of humanity in its progress, Tagore founded *Visva-Bharati* as a platform for training or education centre. His Santiniketan, an abode of peace, is the home for Mankind in general, as the *Auroville* of Sri Aurobindo or *Sabarmati Ashram* of Gandhiji. This outlook of Man as Universal in spirit and aspiration is the way towards the development of an eternal unity of man. It may be compared and critically evaluated in the background of the traditional outlook of religion and philosophy, both of the East and the West. It is an institutional procedure of Tagore which can be compared with the alternative programmes of different contemporary

Indian thinkers like Vivekananda who established *Ramakrishna Mission* and Sri Aurobindo who founded *Aurobindo Ashram*, at Pondicherry, as already mentioned. But it is to be pointed out that this institutional procedure of Tagore, does not follow any rigid religious principle that suppresses the potentiality in man, but it tries to emancipate religion from its restrictive aspects of superstitions, orthodoxy, and other conflicting modes and contradictions or limitations that spoil the flow of life in its mystic directions. This emancipation from intellectual and emotional contradictions paves the way for the realisation of religious as the dynamic religion of man that helps a man to manifest one's perfection or infinity, the potentiality of Man's divinity and infinity in progress. The manifestation of this religious consciousness leads to the development of essential relation among men through which man becomes truly Man through the development of His Infinite Personality. Tagore writes, "...the relational world of ours is not arbitrary. It is individual yet it is universal. My world is mine, its element is my mind, yet it is not wholly unlike your world. Therefore, it is not in my own individual personality that this reality is contained, but in an infinite personality." So Tagore explains this situation of "...the relational world of ours" in his rhythmic ways of a poet of the world singing an eternal song which reveals one's individual personality in an infinite personality.

The development of this infinite personality in different stages, means a gradual unfolding of an international Man the world in different forms that finally leads one to the establishment of the highest state of human freedom in love as the final character of Man to be realised in this confronted life process.

So the final end of Tagore's religion of Man is the essential development of man towards Man, as starting in common, Universality of feeling and consciousness through the human procedure of love that introduces infiniteness in finite and thus overcoming all limitations and contradictions through an integral consciousness and through diversities.

This entire scheme of the religion of Man, developing the philosophy of Universal Man, according to Tagore, has been divided into eight chapters. The object of the first chapter on 'Philosophy of

Man, The Universal: Its Growth and Development in a Comprehensive form' is to deal with the evolutionary progress and the development of the comprehensive outlook through the evaluation of different ideals of religion and philosophy as prevalent in general among Mankind. The second chapter on 'The Religion: The Realisation of Man, The Universal', deals with the expression of an integral outlook in the life of man, who is potentially religious or divine, and the religion of Man is the expression of the infinite nature and the divine spirit of man in transcending his confronted limitation or finiteness. In the third chapter on 'The idea of *Jivandevata*: A Creative Expansion of The Humanity of God', it is observed that the absolute spirit or the infinite ideal of life in the form of *Jivandevata,* appears as the guiding principle for the expression of the infinity or divinity of man which is manifested in human life in different forms. Through these manifestations in different stages in human life, God or Absolute as potentiality in manifestation appears in varied situations involving human values in development in life. The fourth chapter on 'God and Man: An Examination of Goodness as Universality of Man and Humanity of God', deals with the proper relation between God and Man, that appears initially as dual but finally it is manifest as a non-dual integral process. In this spirit of non-dual prospect of the significance of Man's existence as divine becomes manifest and complete. In this context the end of the fifth chapter on 'Good and Evil: Social Contradictions and Reconciliation in Unity', is to explain the nature of all contradictions of life or evils in society and the reality of goodness becomes conspicuous as the highest expression of value in the world of changing values. Thus, in the sixth chapter on 'Freedom in Unity: The Humanistic Processes of Realising Universality', it discusses that how the role of man in society becomes possible through a disinterested love and selfless service, which establishes an interrelation among men in this world. This intimate relation in love, finally leads to the highest state of human freedom, the optimum goal or prospect of Mankind in the full internationalist context.

The seventh chapter on 'An Evaluation: A Socio-Cultural Exploration of Universal Humanism', the Theory of Creative Man', presents the critical and comparative estimate of an overall outlook, end or ideal constituting the code of Tagore's religion of Man towards the establishment of human situation that prepares a ground for *Humanism* in universalist context when a man becomes truly human through the development of his infinite personality that leads him to expand the completeness of life.

In eighth chapter on 'An Epilogue: Final Observations on the Expansion of the Theory of Creative Man, The Universal', it is concluded thus development of this universal outlook through the inauguration of the spirit of cooperation of man and society should be the guiding principle of our culture and civilisation. The advancement of human civilisation through this cooperative process and understanding of the different nations and states, will lead to the emergence of a novel sociocultural process in and through diversities to a tolerable social peace and prosperity of Mankind as a whole. To justify this broad-based outlook of Tagore and its application in society through the development of the spirit of the religion of Man as a universally acceptable consciousness, matches well with Dr Radhakrishnan's insigthful statements as below: "...Tagore believed in the unity of the human race, a unity enriched by diversity. co-operation fertilisation are necessary for the complete and harmonious development of the human race. He wrote: As the mission of the rose lies in the unfolding of the petals which implies distinctiveness, so the rose of humanity is perfect only when the diverse races and nations have developed their distinct characteristics to perfection yet all remain attached to the stem of humanity by the bond of brotherhood."

East and West have the same goal but have their respective missions to fulfill. Peace cannot be achieved by organisations. It can come only when our minds become undowed with generosity and goodwill towards all. We must be filled with the moral power of love and the vision of spiritual unity. We have to solve our problems through the help of our higher nature"[13],——which has to be constructed through our creative nature breaking all cultural boundaries for a prospective goal suitable for all with a spirit of tolerance and appreciation.

In the light of this evaluation, finally, it may be said that Tagore's religion of Man is a natural and social expression of man not as it is, but as going to be, in the background of his universal coexistence in and through the development of the spirit of love as the manifestation of the divinity in humanity.

Notes

1. C. J. Ducasse, *A Philosophical Scrutiny of Religion,* p. 7.
2. Galloway, *The Philosophy of Religion,* p. 24.
3. G. W. Cunningham, *Problems of Philosophy,* p. 399.
4. Dr S. Radbhakrishnan, *Religion and Culture,* p. 9.
5. Article by Dr. A. C. Das, *Visva-Bharati Quarterly.*
6. Rabindranath Tagore, 'Introduction', *Manusher Dharma.*
7. Rabindranath Tagore, *The Religion of Man,* p. 43.
8. *Ibid.*
9. Rabindranath Tagore, *The Religion of Man,* p. 42.
10. *Ibid.*
11. *Ibid.*, p. 43.
12. Visva-Bharati, *Memorandum of Association.*
13. Dr S. Radhakrishnan, *Religion and Culture,* p. 175.

Chapter - 1

Philosophy of Man, the Universal: Its Growth and Development in A Comprehensive Form

Indian heritage–its culture and philosophy, stands fundamentally on religious experience in development from a transcendental background. So, it becomes the primary basis of Indian way of life, and thus it occupies a central position in the development of India's contemporary philosophic attitudes. Different contemporary Indian thinkers like Sri Aurobindo, Vivekananda and others, in different periods, have tried to explain the character and role of religion governing philosophy of human life. This religious consciousness thus finally stands on an integral consciousness of all aspects life, as the development of a universalist attitude of man. Rabindranath Tagore, like those contemporary Indian thinkers, tried to develop this universalist outlook that is expressed through his idea of religion of Man. This type of religion is the expression of man's nature and outlook influencing man's activity-process within a social milieu. In developing this comprehensive attitude towards life as a whole, Tagore points out that both philosophy and religion, divorced from life, become blind and useless. So the ideas of philosophy and religion are placed in togetherness as two distinct experiential processes in relation and prospect, manifesting a new order of social life with an international prospect for mankind to choose. This neo-outlook of truth in the existence of man is expressed and developed by Tagore as the eternal idea of being concretised in one's life, with international insight.

In developing this universalist attitude of Tagore, a great poet of the world, one can discern his captivating visions through his poetry, religion and philosophy - all setting up an atmosphere of cosmic unity with a possibility. This was a development of a truth, a synthetic outlook so that he was at once a poet and a philosopher. Dr Radhakrishnan rightly observes, "The poet worships God as the spirit of beauty, while the philosopher pays his homage to God as the idea of Truth… the two are not opposed, as truth is beauty and beauty is truth,"[1] dwelt together realising truthful reality or beautiful truth in togetherness. This outlook of truth as the ground for value and reality inspires Tagore to establish it in life process with elements of eternal reality, spiritual love and perfection, all running into one another and finally developing a man of universal outlook in his religious consciousness, and a ground for further possibility.

For this development of the universalist humanistic outlook in the context of religious experience, Tagore collects different ideas from different thought currents of the world, and finally tries to develop a comprehensive outlook of man's religious consciousness. So if his idea of the religion of Man is carefully examined it is found that Tagore is influenced by different thoughts of the world in the different stages of development of the form of *Humanism* in a universalist aspect wherein combined all ideas in a rationalist scientific manner. In the evaluation of this method, a famous critic Nalini Kanta Gupta writes in his *Rabindranath*[2] that the streams of *Vaisnavism* and 'pagan' became manifest in the enjoyment of beauty through the external senses where modern scientific reason or rationalism are all combined together. All these processes contribute to the development Tagore's comprehensive poetic and religious nature and consciousness.

If we try to recount the factors that built up his religious outlook, we shall find them well distributed in togetherness his family life, traditional Hindu religious scriptures of *Upanishads,* the *Buddhism* and the *Vedanta* with prospect in a social revolt of Raja Rammohan Roy and Brahmoism with a tint of the Mystic and the Christian outlook, developing a doctrine of love at work in the development of his comprehensive beautified glimpse of a spirit of compassion in development.

We may now briefly refer to the influence of different factors on the making up of Tagore's idea of the religion of Man.

Impact of Family

The influence of the humanitarian views of different members of Tagore's family and the humanist approaches of his family culture to the development of the life and the thought of Rabindranath, are very much important. In 1861, Tagore was born in an illustrious affluent family of Kolkata where he was inspired by the humanistic ideas presented through the daily prayers from *Upanishads* by his father. In *Sadhana,* Tagore writes, "the writer has been brought up in a family texts of the *Upanishads* are used in daily worship and he has had before him the example of his father, who lived his long life in the closest communion with God, while not neglecting his duties to the world, or allowing his keen interest in all human affairs to suffer any abatement."[3]

If the humanistic process of Tagore's family and the humanistic outlook of his family life are properly examined, it is found that these had a tremendous influence on the first stage of the life of Rabindranath that inspired him to reveal the eternal spirit of man. In this connection Tagore explains the cultural and humanist approaches of *Upanishads* in different manners.[4] The first mantra of the *Ishopanishad: Isavasya- midam sarvam yat kinca jagatyam jagat, Tena tyaktena bhunjitha ma gridhah kasyasviddhanam* opened the door of the spiritual life of Debendranath, the father of the poet and supplied him the eternal inspiration. Rabindranath explains, 'That mantra of the *Ishopanishad* which inspired my father has been revealed to me again and again with newer and newer significance and I have told my own self again and again: Do not have greed; Enjoy whatever is given by Him'.[5] If we know that everything is filled by Him and what we have is His gift, then we can realise the manifestation of the Infinite in us as the worldly objects what we enjoy; and thus we can express our relation with the Infinite with a loving spirit. The inspiration of the mantra extends "Our consciousness of Him in devotion, in goodness and in love."[6] This ideal is interpreted by Rabindranath in his book '*The Religion of Man*': "...this world which is all movement is pervaded by one supreme unity and, therefore, true enjoyment can never be had through the satisfaction of greed, but only through the surrender of our individual self to the universal self."[7] In the festival of the *Paus,* 1321, be delivered, '*Ma gridhah.* No imperfection no greed should come in the mind.'[8] Rabindranath learns from the *Ishopanishad* not to have a desire for possessions of other men. For desire increases greed that creates obstructions to love. The ideal of love inspires to realise the significance of the ultimate truth in life that beyond the desire of the worldly objects. Mukherjee observes, "Desire is hindrance to love. It is the movement the opposite direction of truth, towards the illusion that self is our final object."[9] So, in '*The Religion of Man*', fundamental object of the *Ishopanishad* is evaluated by Rabindranath, "The *Isha* of our *Upanishad,* the Supersoul which permeates all moving things, is the God of human universe whose mind we share in all our true, love and service, and whom to reveal in ourselves renunciation of self is the highest end of life."[10] Thus, it is observed that the fundamental end of human life is to develop the spirit of renunciation that is the sacrifice of desires, greed or poor self-interest for the development of the intimate relation with others in love that can be expressed through unconditional love and disinterested service for others. This the eternal outlook of Indian culture that is the fundamental seat of Indian family life which influences Tagore to develop the humanist view of his religion of Man.

Influence of Indian Culture and Heritage

The humanistic outlook of Rabindranath that is expressed through his idea of the religion of Man is developed under the influence of Indian culture and Indian way of life presented through the transcendental insights expressed in progressive developrnents from the *Vedas* to *Upanishads, Vedanta* etc. From his very childhood Rabindranath was influenced by the spirit of love and renunciation which he imbibed from the perennial reservoirs of the *Upanishads* that helped him to cultivate the spirit of universality and humanistic outlook on life. It is evaluated by Dr N. R. Ray as an evolutionary process towards the *Universal Humanism* through the Upanishadic thoughts and words.[11] The view of *Humanism* stands on the spirit of love and renunciation, taught in the *Upanishads.* Man can survive forever through this sacrificing spirit in continuous service to humanity. In *Santiniketan,* Tagore explains this idea, '*Upanishad* says: *Kurvanneveha- karmani jijivisecchatam samah'*—we will have to live hundred years through work. This is their message who have realised sufficiently through the pleasures of the soul.[12] This ideal of pleasure is the eternal joy of life which is manifested everywhere. In *'The Religion of Man',* Tagore explains the ideal, '*Raso vai Sah*'. "The Infinite is love itself', the eternal spirit of joy."[13] The seers of *Upanishads* realise the existence of joy or *ananda* in man, so in the *Svetasvataropanishad* man is declared as *Amritasya putrah* or the son of absolute or nectarine process. Tagore is inspired by this ideal of *Upanishad* and in *Naivedya,* he also explains man as *Amriter Putra Yata Devgan* and in *Sadhana,* he evaluates the existence of bliss in everything: "Joy is everywhere; it is in the earth's green covering of grass; in the blue serenity of the sky; in the reckless exuberance of spring; in the severe abstinence of grey winter; in the living flesh that animates our bodily frame; in the perfect poise of the human figure, noble and upright; in living; in the exercise of all our powers; in the acquisition of knowledge; in fighting evils, in dying for gains we never can share." Tagore thinks that human being proceeds gradually towards his higher life that can be explained as the evolutionary progress towards the realisation of joy or pristine pleasure. Man has no rest in this process of advancement and cannot stop anywhere till the goal is reached,-*charaiveti charaiveti.* This urge in man for the realisation of joy, is eternal. Dr Sen points out, "The call of the eternal, this dynamic urge,-all this gave shape to Tagore's thought and philosophy. He had never known he had not advocated rest. That is why he had built up no cult of his own. He has moved on and on, without rest. This being the keynote of Tagore's thought, he is of the company of those spiritual rebels of ancient India."[14] He was the post Hegelian Bergson of the East, smashing all restricted intellectual constructions to realise the *Urge (Elan)* behind cosmic and psychic processes.

Thus, if the thought of Rabindranath is properly examined, it is found that he is influenced by the wider and dynamic currents estimated of the *Vedas* and the *Upanishads* in the different stages of his life. In *Manusher Dharma,* he writes that at his age of twelve years he got *Gayatri mantra*[15] from his father as the transcendent song and spirit of life. In *Jivansmriti,* Tagore points out that firstly he could not understand the meaning of this mantra, then he gradually realised transcendent significance as the urge for life. In the article 'Bhotka' of *Santiniketan,* he explains, '*Gayatri* as the mantra of meditation to know him who lives in between the nature the world and the mind of man.'[16] This realisation of Tagore inspires him to observe the existence of an integral process within human life and society. This spirit of impenetrable identity supplied by this mantra, influences Tagore very much, as it produces a disinterested yet detached feeling in him to realise the intimate relation of Infinite with the finite and restricted external world confronting and surrounding him. In *The Religion of Man,* Tagore points out, "This produced sense of serene exaltation in me, the daily meditation upon the infinite being which unites in one stream of creation my mind and the outer world". The development of this outlook through the realisation of the significance of the *Gayatri* is evaluated by Dr Seal, "the *Gayatri* expresses Brahma as the light of light in our souls, our inspiration and impulse to all that is good, even unto salvation."[17] Thus, it may be said that the eternal inspiration of Indian spiritual life cultivates the divine values like goodness in the thoughts of Rabindranath, it is this process that makes him a true thinker about man. In an article, Pandit Kshiti Mohan Sen rightly says that Tagore had a direct contact with the *Samhitas* and many of his writings express the eternal meaning of the *Samhitas.*[18] *Atharva Veda* also speaks about the humanity and this world of man that inspires Tagore to develop the idea of the religion of Man. The development of this idea of the religion of Man through the influence of the human outlook of *Atharva Veda* is evaluated by S. K. Das very carefully. In his *Tagore and the Perennial Problems of Philosophy,* he observes, "...the word 'Surplus', dwelling in man which had an eventful career as a creative spirit in Tagore's artistry of truth about the Religion of Man that is, 'the religion of the humanity of our God and that of the divinity of

Man.'-Making no secret about it, he frankly confesses that he draws upon the fruitful conception of *"Ucchishta"* as expounded in the *Atharva Veda,* in all its meaningful exaltation and metaphysical efficacy."[19] This idea of *Ucchishta* in *Atharva Veda* influenced Tagore's idea of *Surplus* in man.

Thus, it is observed that in the development of humanist outlook, "Tagore was initially influenced by the Indian view of life specially supplied by the *Vedas* and the *Upanishads.* In this connection it may be said that Tagore was not an ordinary commentator or a common interpreter of the *Upanishads* or the ancient Indian lore. He realised the proper meanings of the *Shlokas* according to his own point of view where he did not follow any traditional commentary or interpretation, but on the other hand, sometimes new truths flashed upon him through the observation of the inner mystic significance of the verses of many of the *Upanishads* as mentioned. In *The Philosophy of Rabindranath Tagore,* Dr Roy points out, "Sometimes we find that the poet himself discovered some truths but he tried to link them up with those of the *Upanishads.* Again, we find that while expounding a particular Upanishadic *Shloka,* he adds to it some wisdom of his own."[20] Thus, the evaluation of the inner spirit of Indian thought from Tagore's own standpoint opened the door of a new outlook about man and human life. In developing this view, he collected the materials from ancient Indian views of *Vedas, Upanishads* and *Vedanta,* and then focussed all these materials to develop the spirit-of an integral consciousness in life as manifest in the advanced processes of Advaita Vedanta from *Samkara* downwards. In the development of this spirit of non-duality or *Advaitam,* Dr Mahadevan properly evaluates its significance in man that makes him complete. Evaluating the *Advaita* outlook of man, he writes, "It is as a human being that the soul acts and enjoys, enjoys and acts, and also has the competence to break through this vicious circle and gains the highest human goal which is release (moksha)."[21] This state of *Moksha;* is a state of non-duality of the individual and the Absolute, which is finally explained by *Samkara,* an *Advaita Vedantin* of the eighth century thus: 'Brahman is the only Reality and the individual soul is non-different from Brahman, *Brahma satyam....jivo Brahmaiva naparah.'* In the realisation of the absolute value of unity in human life. Tagore is influenced by the ideal of absolute Monism of *Advaita Vedanta.* But it should be mentioned in this connection that in the observation of Tagore, this type of the realisation of Absolute non-duality in life can be possible through love that makes the individual more intimate with the Absolute. In the development of this personal and intimate relation of love, Tagore also is influenced by the *Visistadvaitavada* of Ramanuja and later *Vaishnava* process of Bengal, which recognises Brahman as the Supreme Person with whom a personal relation can be established as in Jiva Goswami, Baladeva and others, after Chaitanya. In the evaluation of the relation of love between *Brahman* or Absolute and *Jiva* or the Individual, Tagore, like Ramanuja and others after him to this date, takes *Brahman* as 'the Sovereign Lord, the supreme person and who is realised in love.'[22]

In this way Tagore spans the opposite procedures of duality and non-duality for the development of a prospective outlook in life, and thus observes, "We discern two opposite currents in India's divine lore *(Brahma-Vidya)*-The abstract God, and the personal God, monism and duality. There cannot be worship unless we admit duality, and yet there cannot be devotion unless we fix our gaze on one."[23] In the evaluation of Tagore's realisation of these interconnectedness or centres of values in life, Dr Radhakrishnan rightly points out, *Iswara,* the highest manifestation of the Absolute, is the personal Lord of the universe. The distinction of the lover and loved is kept up till the last point, when in perfect love the two become one."[24]

In Tagore's poetic emotion, he is very much influenced by the ideal of love and joy, which is taken by *Upanishads* as pure principle or *tatva,* and *Vedanta* takes this idea as Absolute Truth. These ideas of *Upanishads* and *Vedanta* are again evaluated by Tagore, and he takes Absolute or God as the underlying and inspiring substratum of pleasure and love who manifests himself in this world through a social interpersonal process of love or pleasure. In the thoughts of Tagore, it finally appears as the inextricable relation between diverse processes in manifestation. *Brahman* is not taken Tagore as the primary principle or efficient cause of the world, but he thinks in the sense of a relational whole from which the Absolute is expanded in the whole world. Dr Radhakrishnan rightly observes, "To Rabindranath God is not a being seated high up in the heavens, but a spirit immanent in the whole universe of persons and things. Rabindranath's love is a spiritual love...which losses itself in the sea of the Absolute."[25] The realisation of Absolute in love is a very source of his idea of *Jivandevata,* that creates in him thirst for peace beyond the diversities and the differences of the world. Dr Radhakrishnan again writes, "We can say that the Absolute, which is above the pairs of opposites beauty and ugliness, truth and error, good and evil, still appears for the sake of man as perfect Beauty, perfect Truth, perfect Goodness."[26] This realisation of the values of Truth, Beauty and Goodness in Tagore, are expressed the different stages of thoughts in *Kheya, Chitra, Gitanjali, Gitimalaya* and *Gitali.* In these writings, it is observed that Truth or Reality appears in life as the personal God, through the appreciative manifestations of love that makes a personal or intimate relation between God and man. This idea of personal God in Tagore in its prospect for beauty is explained by Dr Radhakrishnan, "If Rabindranath is viewed as the worshipper of a personal-God, he may be looked upon as a living example of long and noble succession of religious devotees of whom India is justly proud." In this connection the influence of the idea of personal God presented by the *Gita* may be referred to; as the *Gita* observes God or Absolute as positive or personal,-*Vasudevah sarvamidam.* But, for the realisation of God, the *Gita* prescribes ways of *Jnanayoga; Karmayoga* and *Bhaktiyoga,* Tagore, on the other hand, states firmly that love that wins over knowledge and action can lead to the realisation of God in man. In his dramatic poems like 'Gandharir Avedan', 'Karana Kunti Samvad' of *Katha O Kahini;* and lyrical dramas *Chitrangada,* 'Viday Abhishap', etc., we find the superiority of the ideal of love over the ordinary demands of life. In the development of this ideal in life, Tagore is also influenced by the humanistic outlook of *Ramayana, Mahabharata, Puranas* and many other ancient Indian lores. His was a spanning of all gulfs between austere reason and captivating emotional processes that run through every heart of man and woman, reaching the masses, orders and ages of mankind as a whole.

Mysticism and the Mystic Way of Life

On his way to the cultivation of the humanist ideal of love in life,

Rabindranath is very much influenced by the humanist views of different Indian sects, different thoughts and ways of life of mystics from Kabir and Dadu to the *Bauls* of Bengal. In this connection it may be pointed out that poetic feeling of Tagore is developed through the inspiration from the musical spirit of *Vaisnava* lyrics. In *Jivansmriti* Tagore writes, *Gita Govinda* I have read so many times and enjoyed.'[27] Regarding this influence of *Vaisnavism* on the poetic imagination of Rabindranath, Rhys observes, "It was the spirit as well as the letter and congenial forms of that poetry that helped to mould his poetic character."[28] In Tagore's *'Bhanusimhathakurer Padavali'* and in *Gitanjali,* we find the formative influence of love and beauty from *Vaisnavism* which is an advanced thought of India of the post-Samkarite period. The inner spirit of *Gitanjali* reveals the spiritual realisation of Tagore that is explained by Charu Banerjee as the perception of play of God in love, and the expression of his attitude towards the ego consciousness that is a bar to a union with Absolute.[29] According to Tagore, it is love only that destroys the blind *egoism* of man and helps him to be united with God. Here his mystic ideas reach the depths of the Islamic mystics with a difference. The eternal love between *Radha* and *Krishna,* of *Vaisnavism* is transferred by Tagore to the love of devotee and God. The devotee opens his heart towards God and God also accepts his deep through his eternal love.[30] In *Santiniketan,* Tagore writes, 'Love has no other means except love. For this purpose the day when the devotee renounces his *egoism*, and unites voluntarily his own will with the divine will, then on that day, the manifestation of his joy in man becomes complete.'[31] So Tagore thinks that the ideal of love in the different procedures or ways, helps us to realise in life the eternal or divine love that should be the only way to salvation. In *The Religion of Man,* he expresses, "Love for whom comprehends love for all creatures and exceeds in depth and strength all other loves, leading to difficult endeavours and martyrdoms that have no other gain than the fulfilment of this love itself."[32]

So love is the only medium through which man can realise intimate relation of unity in everything and this realisation, according to Tagore, is nothing but the realisation of love in everything, with an utter forgetfulness of one's restricted self. In this connection it may be observed that the ideal of love in *Vaisnavism* is related to the purified faith or devotion to God beyond this material world. But in Tagore's idea of divinity this type of implicit devotion is absent as he unites the ideal of love with joyous attitude that is the expression of perfect bliss and can be realised in this sensible world which is not denied or rejected by Tagore as unreal and illusory. But *Vaisnavas* think that this complete realisation of love will be possible in the transcendental world, *Vaikuntha.* So by accepting the realisation of divine love beyond this worldly life the ideas of *Vaisnavism* centre round God and His transcendental world where they try to divinise man only, but as Tagore recognises the complete realisation of love in this world, his aim is not only to divinise man but to humanise God also, so that his fundamental object of the religion of Man is the establishment of "The idea of the humanity of our God, or the divinity of Man the eternal."[33] So the establishment of the ideals of 'divinity' and 'humanity' in love is the fundamental object of Tagore's religion of Man. In developing this ideal of love, Tagore is not only influenced by *Vaisnava* doctrine of devotion, but he also gets an inspiration from the thoughts and ways of life of *Bauls,* Kabir and other Indian mystics as mentioned. In the spirit of love in the life of *Bauls,* Tagore observes the spirit of universality and for this he raises a question, 'Why should we learn the principles of universal love only from the foreigners? Can we not learn them from the *Bauls*....?'[34] According to the ideas of *Bauls,* this poor body is the temple of the living God where the union of finite with the infinite can be possible through love. This is interpreted by Tagore in *The Religion of Man:* "A popular sect of Bengal, called *Bauls,* who have no images, temples, scriptures, or ceremonials, who declare in their songs the divinity of man, and express for him an intense feeling of love."[35] God, according to *Bauls,* is Infinite, but He lives in the finite beings and manifests himself in this finite world in every heart through eternal love. This ideal of *Bauls* inspires Tagore to form the ideal of *Humanism* and he says, "It gives us a clue to the inner meaning of all religions. For it suggests that these religions are never about a God of cosmic force, but rather about the God of human-personality."[36] Regarding the foundation of the ideals of Tagore's religion of Man through the inspirations from the ideals of *Bauls,* Dr Dasgupta points out, "Through all his songs and poems Tagore sings of an Infinite Being, who is seeking His self-realisation-and the best expression of Divine Personality is through the human personality, and throughout the life-process of man there is going on this continual process of love-making between the man and the Divine. This human personality and the Divine Personality, both of which remain combined in the nature of man are the 'I' and 'you', the 'Lover' and the 'Beloved' so much spoken of by poet Tagore in his songs and poems. In singing of the 'I' and 'you' in man, between the man and the 'Man of the heart', Tagore has been the greatest of the *Bauls* of Bengal."[37] It should also be observed in this connection that in developing this novel idea of man, Tagore is also influenced by the ideals of love and non-violence of *Buddhism*. The ideals of man, presented by Tagore as the seeker of truth, lover of the poor and the neglected, are derived from the ideas of love and service for human beings as expressed by *Bauls* and *Buddhism*, that are represented by Tagore in the characters of Dhananjaya Vairagi, Thakur dada, Dadathakur and *Baul* of *Prayaschitta, Muktadhara, Sharadotsav, Dakghar, Raja, Achalayatan* and *Phalguni.*

In this way, Rabindranath in the development of the human outlook of love in his religion of Man, is very much influenced by the different mystics like *Bauls,* Nanak, Kabir, Dadu, Ravidas and others. Kabir who preceded Nanak and others, also observes that God can be realised in this world in the 'Human, bodily existence, the mud of material life'. This conception of Kabir inspires Tagore to write "He is there where the tiller is tilling the hard ground and where the path-maker is breaking stones."[38] God manifests Himself in the life and the work of man through the divine and eternal love.

In this spirit of love and eternality Kabir asks, "If you have not drunk of the nectar of that One Love, what boots it though you should purge yourself of all stains?" Love is potential in the heart of man and through its proper manifestation in life, a man becomes a real lover, who according to Kabir, "is never slow in offering his head for his Lord's service."[39] This ideal of love as developed by Kabir and other Indian mystics is explained and analysed by Sen, when he raises an important point about the Indian mystics. He writes, 'They have got an identity and equality with God through the religion of love, that is more delicious than the non-duality of *Vedanta*.'[40] This religion of love as founded by the Indian Mystics, is accepted by Tagore as the basis of his religion of Man. Here it may also be pointed out that in developing the idea of love Tagore is also influenced by the life and thoughts of Hafiz or other *Sufi* saints and many other mystics of the West. So reviewing these influences of *mysticism* in Tagore's life, some commentators and Rabindra critics recognise him as a mystic. In this context, E. Underhill considers Tagore's *Gitanjali,* as "the classics of mystical literature."[41] Dr Surendranath Dasgupta also holds the same view about Tagore and accepts him as a mystic. He observes, "...it has come upon him in poetic enlightenment as it were through the insight of a seer."[42] All these observers find the depths of mystic insight in the development of Tagore's thought and writings. In Tagore's famous novel *Chaturanga,* they also notice Tagore's mystic approaches to life. The psychological contradictions between Damini and Shachis are presented in this novel, because Damini likes sensual and material happiness and Shachis, after his initiation by Lilananda Swami, definitely leans towards the mystic or supersensuous experience. But the uniqueness of Tagore lies in the reconciliation of sensuous and supersensuous experiences through a synthesis of mystic and humanistic outlook as expressed through the relation of love.

If this type of humanistic approach of Tagore is properly examined, it is found that there is a great difference between mystical outlook and humanitarian view of Rabindranath. To observe this difference, one has to know characteristics proper to *mysticism*, presented by Underhill and their differences from Tagore are also to be evaluated. In *Mysticism,* it is characterised that "True mysticism is active and practical". Though like the mystics Tagore also does not recognise the intellectual method as the process of realisation, still the words 'practical', 'active', etc., cannot be used in discussing his spiritual realisation as he is not a saint like the mystics. About mysticism it is said, "Its aims are wholly transcendental and spiritual." Tagore's spiritual realisation of divine love does not transcend this world but it is completely possible in this sensible world. It is also observed, "This One is for the mystic, not merely the Reality of all that is, but also a loving and personal object of love; never an object of exploration. It draws his whole being homeward, but always under the guidance of the heart". Here Underhill refers to the heart or the emotion as the only source of mystical outlook; but the source of the humanist outlook of Tagore is neither emotion nor intellect but is the combination of these two. Regarding the meditation of life by the mystics one also discerns the "Living Union with this One- which is the term of his adventure- is a definite state or form of enhanced life…It is arrived at by a definite and ardous physical process–the so-called mystic way.... "It must be pointed, out that Tagore is a poet and not a saint, so in his spiritual realisation of love, he does not follow any restricted way of life or 'Mystic way…' "which was codified by the neo-platonists as Purgation, Illumination and Ecstasy."[43]

Considering these characteristics of mysticism it is already observed that there is a difference between Tagore and the mystics. In the light of this evaluation, it may be pointed out that Tagore should not be considered a typical mystic. But in the development of the ideal of the religion of Man, one will find in Tagore a mystic's humanist outlook of life so patent. In *The Religion of Man,* one will find also in Tagore, that, "perfection dwells ideally in Man the Eternal, inspiring love for this ideal in the individual, urging him more and more to realise it."[44] Thus, it is to be noted in this connection, that in Tagore there is the humanitarian view of mysticism. Thus, in the process of cultivation of the humanist outlook Tagore gathers materials from different humanitarian views of the world and the ways of life. In this progress of Tagore's thought it can be observed that the influence of the ideals of love, peace and endurance of Christianity, is very much important.

Like Christ, Tagore also cultivates the spirit of love and peace. Some commentators think that in the formulation of the idea of the religion of Man, Tagore was primarily influenced by Christianity. Saunders observes, "The God of *Gitanjali* is no impersonal, imperturable absolute of Hindu philosophy…. He is at least a Christ-like God, and the experience of…His suppliant and lover is one with the deep core of all Christian experience."[45] Thompson also finds the Christian elements in the writings of Tagore. He writes, "There are places in *Naivedya* where I think that there has fallen upon characteristically Indian thought the memory of some parable or words of Jesus."[46]

Thus, all these thinkers feel the importance of Christian element in Rabindranath. Some Christian thinkers even take him to be 'more Christian than Christians.' But on careful examination, one may observe that this statement is one sided as it does not reflect the total development of Tagore's thought.

Tagore collects the materials from different currents of humanist thoughts of the world. His *Gitanjali* and the *Bible* express the ideal of universal truth. It is possible that Tagore might have read the *New Testament* and might have been influenced by the ideals of Christianity, but these do not prove that the primary inspiration of his deliberation came from Christianity. Dr Radhakrishnan rightly concludes, "Our conclusion is that in his *Sadhana* and other work, Rabindranath, by his power of imagination, has breathed into the dry bones of the ancient philosophy of India and made it live. His teaching is in no sense a mere borrowed product of Christianity; indeed, it goes deeper in certain fundamental aspects than Christianity as represented to us in the West."[47] Thus, it is to be noted in this connection that Tagore recognised the role of the doctrine of love as developed in Christianity* but he developed deeper in the process of development of the ideals of love and humanist ideas in his religion of Man.

Brahmoism and Brahmo Samaj

In this process of development of religion of Man, Tagore was also influenced by the reformative outlook of the *Brahmo Samaj* movement of his predecessors from Raja Rammohan Roy to the stage of his father.

Raja Rammohan Roy, a well-known reformer of Bengal, instituted *Brahmo Samaj* in 1828 to save the nation and the country from superstitions of the Hindu religion. Hindu society at that time was once more in its cultural history was overwhelmed by the evils of caste system and idolatry. The idol worship and the social inequality, then prevailed created confusions. Rammohan protested against these narrow explanations of *Hinduism* and brought a revolutionary change in the religious process of the country. In his article, *The Religion of an Artist,* Rabindranath observes an important change made by Rammohan by referring to the history of his time thus: "I was born in 1861: that is not an important date of history, but it belongs to a great epoch in Bengal, when the currents of three movements had met in the life of our country. One of these, the religious, was introduced by a very great hearted man of gigantic intelligence, Raja Rammohan Roy. It was revolutionary, for he tried to reopen the channel of spiritual life which had been obstructed for many years by the sands and debris of creeds that were formal and materialistic, fixed in external practices lacking spiritual significance."[48]

In this way Tagore evaluates the contribution of Rammohan Roy in the reformation of Hindu Society, by a recast, with a further development.

Among different movements for the social change of his time, Tagore draws attention to the two of the movements, viz, *(i)* of the *Brahmo Samaj* movement of Rammohan Roy to Debendranath Tagore, his father, and *(ii)* The Ramakrishna-Vivekananda movement in the stage of formation, as a process close to the *Brahmo Samaj* process. In this complex social background, Rabindranath Tagore became operative with his epoch-making thoughts and writings. The fundamentals of which, as stated before, became operative to establish man in religion and society, on a new transcendental level with a life of social process, not evinced before.

So the introduction of humanist outlook, as the spiritual development of social and personal processes, freed from all contradictions, was the supreme end of these movements combining in his exalted spirit- the best of Sri Ramakrishna,Vivekananda and Rammohan Roy. Sri Ramakrishna and Vivekananda may be treated as religious thinkers, but Rammohan is a social reformer. Rammohan's contributions in social life were for the elimination of superstitions, orthodoxy etc. In *'Charitra Puja',* Tagore interprets Rammohan as the unity of intellectual power with the power of service, that urged him to introduce European or scientific method of education for the change of traditional educational and social customs like *Satidaha,* etc. The aim of his *Brahmo Samaj* was to draw attention to One

Universal Truth among the different ways of life of men of different religions, seeking harmony among Hinduism, Islam, Christianity, etc., and then in India. Regarding this view we get certain opinions in his books *Brahmopasana, Prarthanapatra, Anushthan etc.* In *Brahmopasana,* Rammohan explains two ideals of religion one is 'the great devotion to the all controlling Absolute', and the other is 'the decent and just behaviour among the individuals.' These two ideals according to Rammohan, will help men to establish an eternal relation among them and in this way they will realise one Universal Truth or Absolute, who is present in all men of all classes in the world. In the *Trust Deed* of *Brahmo Samaj* we find this reflection of his thought where it is said that *Brahmo Samaj* "a place of public meeting of all sorts and descriptions of people without distinction as shall behave themselves in an orderly sober religious and devout manner for the worship and adoration of the Eternal Unsearchable and Immutable who is the Author and Preserver of the Universe...."

In this outlook of *Brahmo Samaj* the spiritual unity in man is presented which is to observe the existence of universality in human life.

In this process of the development of the spirit of universality in man, Rammohan tried to establish Indian way of life as religious or spiritual unity and on the other, he also tried to re-establish formless Indian Absolutism or Universalism that influenced the followers of *Brahmo Samaj,* particularly Debendranath Tagore, the father of Rabindranath and the real successor of the idea of Rammohan. But we must mention here that there is a difference between Rammohan and Debendranath. To Debendranath Tagore, there is an admission of the compassionate mind, which is pervasively present both in Hinduism and Buddhism. For this Dr Ghosh observes: 'The religious life of Rammohan is the meditation for seeking the truth and the religious life of Debendranath is the eagerness for the realisation of truth.'[49] The realisation of Debendranath brought a new pattern of life in *Brahmoism* which was a remarkable advancement beyond the way of abstract universality, introduced by Rammohan in human life and society.

In order to understand the proper spirit of the social organisation, *Brahmo Samaj,* founded by Rammohan and developed by Debendranath, the ends or objects of this organisation, structural peculiarities, need further elucidation. Debendranath Tagore, a true follower of *Brahmoism* instituted a society known as *Tattvaranjani,* that later on became *Tattva bodhini Sabha* to work as the organisation of *Brahmo Samaj.* Under the guidance of Debendranath, the *Brahmo Dharma* spread gradually. *Adi Brahmo Samaj,* the religious School founded by him, and the religious instrument *Tattvabodhini Patrika,* expounded the views and ideals of Brahmoism that brought a new light in religion. In this light of new idea the meaning of *Brahmo Dharma* is evaluated. The proper meaning and the real significance of *Brahmo Dharma* is based on the truths derived by its *Bijmantra,* where we find an ultimate realisation of Absolute who exists in the beginning of the world and everything of the world is created by Him; *Om Brahma va ekamidamagra asit nanyat kinchanasit. Tadidam sarvamasrijat.* This mantra expresses the meaning and nature of Absolute Unity through which *Brahmoism* tries to supply a complete nature of the Absolute. According to this view, He is infinite, eternal, omniscient, omnipresent, omnipotent, non-dual, independent, all-powerful, controller, protector and *perfect-Tadeva nityam jnanamanantam sivam svatantram niravayavamekamevadvitiyam sarvavyapi sarvaniyantri sarvaasrayam sarvavit sarvasaktimad dhruvam purnamapratimamitti.* The significance of this mantra that expresses the nature of Absolute lies in its realisation in life. Realisation of the Absolute is the realisation of absolute goodness in this life or hereafter that can be acquired only by the prayer to Him,-*Ekasya tasyaivopasanaya paratrikamaihikancha shubham bhavati.* The meaning of this realisation is the accomplishment of goodness in life. For this, *Brahmoism* finally refers to some social duties of life that can please *Him,-Tasmin pritistasya priyakaryasadhanancha tadupasanameva.* This refers to some social duties and responsibilities for others that develop the social and intimate relation among men as the manifestation of Absolute as Truth, Beauty and Goodness.

Thus, the humanist outlook, present in *Brahmoism*, influenced by Debendranath very much and according to him it is developed through love and service for human beings that can establish an intimate relation between the individual and the Absolute which is the expression of divine unity in men. This humanitarian view of Debendranath is evaluated and elevated by Rabindranath as an attempt 'to realise His principle by knowledge, to love Him by character and self-surrender to Him by action'.[50] This evaluation by Tagore of the search for divinity in each man and woman is the development of the synthetic procedure of thought as influenced by the emotional spirit of Debendranath, as father, and rationalist attitude of Rammohan as the founder of *Brahmo Samaj.* The ideals of *Brahmoism* here in Tagore, reveals itself in the life of man that influenced him to see in the world of man the presence of both the rational and emotional elements in relation. Living in a *Brahmo* atmosphere Rabindranath Tagore tried to seek the One Ultimate Truth in all men, and in this way he was gradually realising in life the one, eternal, non-dual Absolute, or *Brahman,*which is *Satyam, Shivam* and *Anandam.* This realisation of Absolute in life is the manifestation of divinity in human life that represents the idea of Absolute as the substratum of human values.

This *Brahmo* outlook, ideal and way of life of this association, influenced Tagore to enter into this organisation and to take active part for the development of its humanitarian view and universal spirit through his writings and activities. In 1884, Rabindranath became the Secretary of *Adi Brahmo Samaj,* and wrote many articles on *Brahmo Dharma* which he recognised as the religion of the world. In the article on 'Rammohan Roy', he expressed, 'The world is indebted to India for *Brahmo Dharma.*[51] But some educated followers of Hinduism protested against this view and the great novelist Bankimchandra Chatterjee also criticised *Brahmoism.* Rabindranath sought to controvert this criticism of Bankim Chandra and charged him with destroying the spirit of religion.[52] Religion, according to Tagore, is the fulfilment of different ends of different individuals through its greater and wider processes. In *'Ekti Puratan Katha'*, he writes 'greatness is not limited to particular aim, thousand aims are fulfilled by it'.[53] Bankimchandra, in *'Adi Brahmo Samaj O Navyn Hindu Sampradaya'*, interpreted this opinion of Tagore as the explanation of *Adi Brahmo Samaj.* But in the essay *'Kaiphiyat'*, Tagore replied that he did not advocate *Brahmo Samaj* but expressed his attitude towards religion, universally present in every society. However, the attitudes of Bankim Chandra and Rabindranath towards religion and society were similar, as both of them tried to remove the superstitions and narrow outlook of Hinduism for the welfare of the society. So in the end their controversy resulted in a friendship between them. Tagore wrote, "Bankimchandra was brave enough to go against the orthodoxy which believed in the security of tombstones and in that finality which can only belong to the lifeless".[54] This represents the liberal and the wider view of Tagore which is not to be explained from a particular point of view and this outlook in Tagore inspired him to collect materials from the thought of any thinker which were be evaluated by him from a greater point of view for the development of his humanist and comprehensive outlook.

This humanitarian view of Tagore and the synthetic development of his thought urged him to be more active in work and writings for the reformation of society, for the elimination of superstations and ignorance in the traditional way of life and the establishment of humanist outlook for the welfare of the society. In this way he stood against the orthodoxy of Hinduism and wrote many articles to reform the practice of idolatry and religious prohibitions enjoined by Hinduism. In the article *'Sakar O Nirakar'*, he raised several arguments against idol worship. According to him if our attention and thinking concentrated on idols, we cannot come out of it. To worship an idol means to work under the imagination, but Infinite can never be an object of imagination. He can only be realised through a direct vision that prepares us for realising universal element in religion. In *'Dharmer Navayug'* he criticised the narrow practices of Hinduism,-'We talk big of the universality of religion but in practice, we narrow it down to the scope of our own acts. Like other material possessions, religion becomes the target of our vanity and sectarianism.'[55] This narrow sectarian view can create the differences in life and society and thus it introduces some kind of caste system and imposes certain restrictions or prohibitions upon people of the society, creating inequality among men and destroying universal spirit of religion. In this connection one article of Tagore *'Dharmer Adhikar'* may be referred to where he explains carefully the proper nature of man; which is the combination of two powers. 'One is his 'can' and the other is 'should'. The man can do certain action, this is the easy side of his power. But he should do certain actions, this constitutes the utmost exercise of his power'. According to Tagore, 'when our 'can' is completely assimilated by our 'should' we attain the most desired object of our life, we attain truth.'[56] But the sectarian view of Hinduism opposes this normal and natural procedure of the human life. Tagore tries to interpret the character of those persons who are responsible for raising obstructions in the world of religion: "Those important people who cannot act up to this ideal of religion try to pull it down to their own level. Thus, taboos and prohibitions arise." These limitations make a man self-interested and psychologically mean-minded. This will not help him to realise the eternal significance of religion. For this in *'Dharmer Navayug'*, Tagore appeals to the people, 'Today we are feeling the necessity of a religion that is not circumscribed to a particular seat of a particular time. Today we need a religion which is not sunk in the labyrinth of outward ceremonies, but a religion which is as wide as the skies.' This wider view of life is the fundamental basis of religion that represents the Indian way of life which cultivates a synthetic spirit of humanity and divinity in different ages. In this spirit, it is found that the religion is not an imposition of restrictions on life, but it, as observed by Tagore, rightly is the natural expression of human life.

Thus, it is to be noted in this connection, that this religious view of Tagore inspired him to write and to work for the elimination of different obstacles to maintain a universalist spirit in religious consciousness. This comprehensive spirit in Tagore inspires him to eliminate the unnecessary part of any thought and then to collect and unite its necessary elements for the synthetic development of life. Thus, it is to be noted that though Tagore stands against the orthodoxy of *Hinduism* as the unnecessary evil of society, still it must be mentioned here that this inspiration he gets from the universal spirit of *Hinduism* that is based on *Upanishadic* thoughts. So the fundamental end of Tagore is to deduce eternal spirit of *Hinduism* from the *Vedas* and the *Upanishads* and then to link it with the liberal procedure of *Brahmoism*. This method is a synthetic product of *Hinduism* and *Brahmoism*, that influences him to write in *'Atmaparichaya'* the following: '*Brahmoism* has received its spiritual inspiration from *Hinduism*, it stands on the broad basis of Hindu culture'. In way the spiritual inspiration of *Hinduism* nourishes the outlook of *Brahmoism* and this reopens the eternal of *Hinduism*. He observes rightly that, 'Today *Hinduism* needs open the sacred, secret truth of its own heart. It must preach the gospel of *Universalism* to the entire Universe. Today through the salvation of *Brahmoism*, *Hinduism* has fulfilling its own mission.'[57] This observation of Tagore proves the reorganisation of thought in a synthetic process, through which the apparent controversies among different thoughts are reconciled through the development of the spirit of Unity or Universality, present in all these thoughts.

In this light of a new ideal, if the view of Tagore is properly evaluated, it is found that his fundamental object is not to find any religious association for imposition of restrictions on natural development of human life but to introduce a synthetic, universal and humanistic outlook on life and society, which is to be established through his idea of the religion of Man. If the background of the development of this new idea is carefully examined it is observed that no particular element of any particular thought is predominant in his idea, but a synthesis of different common elements of different thoughts are very much important in the formation of his humanitarian view. So it is to be noted in this connection that neither *Hinduism* nor *Brahmoism* alone but a synthetic product of the two ideals inspired Tagore to proceed towards another new way of life. This idea of the meeting of *Brahmoism* with a reformed *Hinduism*, Tagore interprets his drama *Achalayatan,* indicating a confluence between the old conservative outlook of *Mahapanchaka* and the new revolutionary idea of *Panchaka.* Through the interchange and exchange of thoughts and ideals of the new and the old, a completely new light of knowledge can be focussed. This leads him to collect the different ideals from the different religious writings and finally enables him to establish a new form of humanist situation of his creation. Dr Dasgupta explains this new outlook of Tagore thus: "Though Rabindranath was from his childhood initiated to the *Brahmo* faith of his father, as reflected in many of his early songs, we gradually find him discovering a religion of his own, of which we find but little trace either in the writings of ancient India or in the writings of the West."[58]

This novel form of the religion of Man of Rabindranath is an establishment of the *Universal Humanism* with the ideals of knowledge, love and action derived from the traditional Indian outlook, insightfully matched with the advanced writings of the West. It is also to be observed here that, Tagore, in this process of reorientation develops the idea of harmony in all ideals and methods, in the spirit of eternal love, in its process aspect of active participation with foreign nationalities, as formed between him and C. F. Andrews among others.

Thus, when the different stages of the influence of different ideals on the life and thoughts of Tagore are properly examined it is found that there is a gradual progress of his idea in international and interpersonal contexts, resolving the gulf that is among the peoples of different countries, religions, cultures and cults. He became the minstrel of whole humanity a poet laureate in actualising the process later.

The Development of Comprehensive Outlook

Thus, finally it may be pointed out that Tagore's idea of the religion of Man is a comprehensive development of his thoughts and ideas in a manner to focuss the processes of unity or harmony in the human life, and among peoples, countries and cultures of the world.

For the development of this cosmopolitan outlook, Tagore introduces a process of welcoming mankind as a whole in his universality. In this process, firstly, his attempt is to collect different ideas from different thoughts and writings of great thinkers of the Asian and European countries and then to emphasise common elements of all these ideas for the development of a comprehensive idea representing a perspective for mankind as a whole where the universal absolutistic idea of *Vedas, Upanishads, Vedanta, Brahmoism* and the ideals of love, service and sacrifice or *Sufis, Vaishnavas, Bauls, Buddha, Christ* and of other thoughts of the world flow into one another and thinkers of the world in their meetings and exchanges build up a process of the religion of Man, which man has to share commonly and communicate as a colossal family, losing their restrictiveness.

Regarding the growth and the development of Tagore's world outlook in and through his focussing process of developing the idea of the religion of Man, Prabodh Chandra Sen explains that the significance of this thought lies in the participation and exchange of different ideals, ridding human minds from the tensions, conflicts and confusions. Evaluating this idea in this manner, Sen rightly points out, 'Rabindranath wanted that religion, where knowledge, love and action are assembled, where the truth realisation of the *Upanishads,* the cooperation and kindness of Buddhism and love and reverence of Vaishnavism and Christianity are placed together to be shared and enforced as the healthy food for progressive healthy attitude. That mind is solely opposed to sectarian differences, scriptural rules and ritualism.'[59] Thus, it is observed that the comprehensive idea, in its adventure forward is developed through the humanistic outlook of Tagore as his religion of Man that can introduce harmony in the differences of human life and human society of the world as a whole.

After a careful observation of the significance of the comprehensive outlook of Tagore, as introduced in his idea of religion of Man, its importance in the human life can also be explained. This importance lies in the gradual progress of human life in and through the development of different ideals towards the inauguration of unity, leading to Tagore's Universal Unity as Truth in man. Regarding this progress of human life, Tagore, in *The Religion of Man,* observes, "Progress means that there is an ideal perfection which the individual seeks to reach by extending his limits in knowledge, power, love, enjoyment, thus approaching the universal."[60] The development of the universal existence, crossing all the limits of life in society, is the final and fundamental progress of human life. This comprehensive social consciousness is the universal spirit of Tagore. In his *Man, The Religion of Man, Personality, Creative Unity, Manuser Dharma, Dharma, Sanchaya, Sadhana, Santiniketan* and in other writings, Tagore reveals the eternal and universal existence and personality of Man. This universal existence of man is to be expressed through his many-sided personality as the manifestation of different creative elements representing Universality as Truth. To evaluate this idea of Truth, according to Tagore, is "to study the mind of man in its realisation of different aspects of truth from diverse points of view."[61]

To realise the Truth in human existence from different standpoints is to understand the significance of the universal personality of man, which, according to Tagore, is expressed through his different creative activities. For the development of harmonious human personality beyond differences and contradictions, Tagore emphasises the growth of an intimate relation of man with others through one's thoughts and activities. Tagore, in the *Memorandum of Association* of Visva-Bharati, seeks the "cooperation between the thinkers and scholars of both Eastern and Western countries, free from all antagonisms of race, nationality, creed or caste, and in the name of one Supreme Being who is *Santam, Sivam, Advaitam*." The realisation of transcendent consciousness as 'One Supreme Being', is the accomplishment of man's own universal existence that is to be manifested and developed in and through different work in love for mankind.

So, finally it may be noted in this connection that a careful observation of the development of Tagore's thought and life proves that he is influenced by the different thoughts and ways of the world in his different stages of life. This process leads to a continuous progress of his humanist outlook that explains the nature and existence of Man as Universal.

Notes

1. Dr S. Radhakrishnan, *The Philosophy of Rabindranath Tagore,* p. 160.
2. Nalini Kanta Gupta, *Rabindranath,* p. 97.
3. Rabindranath Tagore, *Sadhana,* 'Preface,' p. vii.
4. Sarasilal Sarkar, *Rabindra Kavye Trayi Parikalpana.*
5. *Rabindrarachanavali,* 1st Part, 'Introduction'.
6. Rabindranath Tagore, Art 'Realisation of the Infinite', *Sadhana.*
7. Rabindranath Tagore, *The Religion of Man,* p. 14.
8. Rabindranath Tagore, *Santiniketan, 'Dikshar Din'* Vol. II, p. 416.
9. A. K. Mukherjee, Upanishad in the Eyes of Rabindranath Tagore, p. 5.
10. Rabindranath Tagore, *The Religion of Man,* p. 15.
11. Dr Nihar Ranjan Roy, 'Rabindranather Manavikata', *Rabindranath,* edited by Dr D. Bhattacharya.
12. Rabindranath Tagore, *Santiniketan,* Vol. II, p. 172.
13. 'The Spiritual Union', *The Religion of Man,* p. 42.

14. Dr Sachin Sen, *The Political Thought of Tagore,* pp. 13-14.
15. *Rig Veda Samhita, 'Om Bhurbhubah Sva Tatsaviturvarenyam Bhargo Devasya Dhimahi DhiyoYoNah Prachodayat.*
16. Rabindranath Tagore, *Santiniketan,* Vol. II, p. 4.
17. Dr Bojendranath Seal, *Comparative Studies in Vaishnavism and Christianity,* pp. 85-86.
18. *Visva Bharati Quarterly,* Tagore Birthday Number.
19. Dr S. K. Das, *Tagore and the Perennial Problems of Philosophy*, p. 51.
20. Dr Benoy Gopal Roy, *The Philosophy of Rabindranath Tagore,* p. 4.
21. Dr T. M. P. Mahadevan, 'The Vedanta Concept of Man'. *Religion and Society,* Vol. vii. Nos. 3 and 4.
22. Article of H. N. Dutta, *Visva-Bharati Quarterly,* Tagore Birthday Number.
23. *Modern Review.*
24. Dr S. Radhakrishnan, *The Philosophy of Rabindranath Tagore,* p. 55.
25. Dr S. Radhakrishnan, *The Philosophy of Rabindranath Lagore,* p. 54.
26. *Ibid*, p. 56.
27. Rabindranath Tagore, *Jivansmriti,* p. 79.
28. Ernest Rhys, *Rabindranath Tagore : A Biographical Study.*
29. Charu Banerjee, *Rabi Rasmi,* Vol. II, p. 87.
30. Rabindranath Tagore, *Gitanjali,* poem 34, *Amar Milan lagi tumi ascha kave theke or poem 121 Tai tomar ananda amar par...*
31. *Rabindra Rachanavali,* Vol. XII, p. 368
32. Rabindranath Tagore, *The Religion of Man,* p. 12.
33. Rabindranath Tagore, *The Religion of Man,* p. 11.
34. *Rabindrarachanavali,* 'Achalita Samgraha', Part II, p. 134.
35. Rabindranath Tagore, *The Religion of Man,* p. 12.
36. Rabindranath Tagore, *The Religion of Man,* p. 12.
37. Dr S. B. Dasgupta, *Obscure Religious Cults,* pp. 214-15.
38. Rabindranath Tagore, Eng. *Gitanjali,* Poem No. 11.
39. Rabindranath Tagore, *One Hundred Poems of Kabir,* No. LV.
40. Kshitimohan Sen, *Bharater Samskriti,* pp. 75-76.
41. *The Nation.*
42. R. Chatterjee (ed.), *The Golden Book of Tagore,* pp. 67-68
43. Evelyn Underhill, *Mysticism* (4th edn.), p. 112.
44. Rabindranath Tagore, *The Religion of Man,* p. 11.
45. *International Review of Mission,* p. 149.
46. E.J. Thompson, *Rabindranath Tagore : Poet and Dramatist,* p. 193.
47. Dr S. Radhakrishnan, *The Philosophy of Rabindranath Tagore,* p. 119.

*In this context Dr Moriz Winternitz observes that Rabindranath, though not a Christian, still different elements of Christianity enter into his analysis of philosophy and religion. (Ref: *Rabindranath Tagore: Religion und Weltanschauung des Dichters).*

48. Radhakrishnan and J. H. Muirhead, *Contemporary Indian Philosophy,* p. 25.
49. Dr T.K. Ghosh, *Rabindranather Dharma Chinta,* p. 20.
50. *Rabindrarachanavali,* Vol. XV, p. 502.
51. P.K. Mukherjee, *Rabindrajivani,* Vol. I, p. 159.
52. Article, *Bharati.*
53. P.K. Mukherjee, *Rabindrajivani,* Vol. I, p. 158.
54. Dr S. Radhakrishnan and J. H. Muirhead, *Contemporary Indian Philosophy,* p. 25.
55. Rabindranath Tagore, 'Dharmer Navayug', *Sanchaya.*
56. Rabindranath Tagore, 'Dharmer Adhikar', *Sanchaya.*
57. P.K. Mukherjee, *Rabindrajivani,* Vol. I, p. 500.
58. Dr S. N. Dasgupta, *Rabindranath, the Poet and the philosopher,* Vol. I, p. 32.
59. Prabodh Chandra Sen, 'Rabindranather Dharmachinta', *Visva-Bharati Patrika.*
60. Rabindranath Tagore, *The Religion of Man,* p. 15.
61. Visva-Bharati, *Memorandum of Association.*

Chapter - 2

The Religion: Realisation of Man, The Universal

Meaning of Tagore's Idea of Religion as the Religion of Man

The comprehensive and universal humanist outlook of Tagore, as developed through the influences of different human aspirations and ideals of the world, finally inspires him to explain the existence of man in a natural form. This natural expression of human life, according to Rabindranath, is the proper religion of Man that, firstly, explains his material existence in his material world and secondly, evaluates his essential human spirit to overcome the material contradictions of life towards the development of unity or harmony. This harmonious development of human personality, in the opinion of Tagore, is the fundamental basis of human existence, that, on the one hand, relates the idea of religion with the expression of human nature and thus makes human life free from the supernatural influences like dogmas, orthodoxy, etc., and on the other hand develops the idea of the *religion* of Man of his own which is the inauguration of Universal Man in and through the contradictions of the material existence of man in this world. It may be said thus that man's spiritual nature is expressed initially in human's naturalist situation then by the enlightened spiritual consciousness man goes beyond his basic nature.

In order to develop the idea of man's religious consciousness, Tagore explains the significance of the term religion in his own way. Religion, according to him, is the recognition of man's natural basis of life. So all thoughts and activities of man centres round his life in naturalist situation. So man's religion in this sense is explained by Tagore thus: 'It is like the morning light, immense and simple. It is god's gift of himself and hence it is eternal and great...Religion surrounds us, permits us to get it, we have only to open our hearts.'[1]

So simplicity in life or clearness in mind is 'to open our hearts', to Nature and other minds. But man, due to different complexities in this material life, creates different contradictory processes in the natural way of life or in simple procedure of religion. Religion is used in this sense for the satisfaction of material interest or poor demands of life and thus it can exploit the natural sentiment of common men and in this way different contradictions like orthodoxy, sectarian outlook, etc., are created in the normal procedure of life or religion. This view about religion, as Tagore observes, "is a perverse form of worldliness in the disguise of religion; it breeds narrowness of heart in a greater measure than the cult of the world based upon material interest can ever do."[2]

Different social evils produced by the narrowness of mind or heart caused by the material interest in the name of religion can be removed through the proper interpretation of the meaning of human life as the religion of Man which "can have no meaning in the enclosure of mere physical or material interest." The true significance of religion that lies in the human existence can be realised by an analysis of the intrinsic nature of man. Proper analysis of human nature, in the opinion of Tagore, proves that religion exists in the roots of human existence which forms the basic nature of man. So, religion being the inner nature of man is identified with human life. Thus, man does never exist without religion. In *'Dharmer Artha'*, Tagore explains that the nature of man is to fulfill religion as the nature of fire is to burn. In this connection Tagore observes that man, in this material world, has undoubtedly material demands or ordinary interests of life which can create conflicts and tensions in life. But the higher of supreme need of life, according to Tagore, is the vital need for a developed religious consciousness which is realised in a higher order through the development of universal element of religious consciousness of mankind in general.

Thus, it may be said that this vital need for religion in life inspires man to overcome different limitations and contradictions of life. It is already indicated that the self-interest or lower material demands can create conflicts and contradictions in the normal life of man. But religion, according to Tagore, "has its genesis in man's desire to be released from the limitation of what is." So religion is the only method that can remove these limitations and can also solve the contradictions by revealing the real nature of man. This, according to Tagore, is the proper function of religion. In his *Hibbert Lecture* on 'Man's nature', Tagore points out, "Religion has its function in reconciling the contradiction, by subordinating the brute nature to what we consider as the truth of Man." This is nothing but man's realisation of spiritual consciousness by a progressive detachment from the interests of lower orders of life.

Truth in man, in the opinion of Tagore, is to overcome limitations or contradictions through the realisation of infiniteness or perfection, potential in him. This perfection, that exists in the root of human nature, urges him to develop his nature through the suppression of narrow desires or animality and thus through this manifestation of perfection, an individual exists as the Man, different from animal. So awareness of perfection is the essential part of human nature, and that, according to Tagore, is the proper religion of man. He observes, 'The religion of man is his perfection as the fireness of fire and animality of animal.'[3] The development of this perfection in life in different stages, is nothing but the realisation of religion that proceeds towards the final realisation of perfection as the completeness of life.

The perfection, potential in human nature, is recognised by Rabindranath as the power of *surplus* in human life. In different essays like *'The Surplus in Man', 'The Creative Spirit', 'Man's Universe'*, Rabindranath explains the history of the development of human nature which is the evolutionary progress of developing the power of *surplus* in human life. In the different stages of evolution, man has tried gradually to realise his own nature or the nature of this inherent power, that is above all the paradoxes or the contradictions. In the article *'The Surplus in Man'*, Tagore writes, "Man has taken centuries to discuss the question of his own true nature and has not yet come to a conclusion. He has been building up elaborate religions to convince himself, against his natural inclinations, of the paradox that he is not what he is but something greater."

Human life comes along a long course of evolution, which, according to Tagore, is a gradual realisation of his inner power of *surplus* in man which exceeds the narrowness or limitation of his life. Tagore explains, "...in order to know himself truly Man in his religion cultivates the vision of Being who exceeds him in truth and with whom also he has his Kinship."[4] The power of *surplus* in man thus develops the proper significance of man's existence as 'The vision of Being', which has kinship with Truth. This idea of the creative power of *surplus,* is derived by Tagore, from the productive idea of *Ucchista* in *Atharva Veda,* that explains the completeness about the nature and existence of man. In '*The Creative Spirit*', Tagore explains this constructive nature as-"Righteousness, truth, great endeavours, empire, religion, enterprise, heroism and prosperity, the past and the future, dwell in the surpassing strength of the surplus."[5]

Thus, this power of *surplus* in man, urges him to realise the diverse aspects of life, which gradually inspires him to know and to realise the Ultimate Principle or Supreme Value of life. Tagore explains, "...men seek their own supreme value, which they call divine,...The mind,...should know that religion is not essentially cosmic or even abstract, it finds itself when it touches the *Brahma* in man; otherwise it has no justification to exist."[6] In this insightful understanding of the *surplus* in one's Nature, Tagore, in a different way returns to the perennial fullness of the *Upanishads,* and modernises the concept to baffle the process of the West which stands always for an external power.

The development of this supreme value in human existence as the realisation of Ultimate Reality as *Brahman,* is nothing but the manifestation of perfection in Man. Through this Realisation "He tries to sublimate his individual self into a manifestation which he believes to have the majesty of the ideal Man." So man becomes ideal to himself through the realisation of his potential power that according to Tagore, "is the meaning of the universal reality." Thus, through this procedure, man "becomes one with his God, for him, his God is nothing greater than power."[7] Here it should be mentioned that Tagore in his ideal of religion, conceives of religion as something which ultimately makes man identical with God and this can be possible only through the complete realisation of power or perfection in him. This idea in Tagore inspires him to interpret the proper meaning, value and ideals of religion. Dr Das observes in *The Straight Forward Ideal of Religion (Dharmer Saral Adarsha,* 1903*), Meaning of Religion (Dharmer Artha,* 1911), the nature of man is explained by Tagore as the realisation of universal reality, "which combindly furnish a simple philosophic rendering of what is meant by 're-realisation' or *'Prapta-Praptih'* of *Advaita Vedanta* Philosophy."[8] Rabindranath tries to interpret this view in different ways. In different articles of *Santiniketan,* and in many songs and writings, Tagore represents this idea of his Self-fulfilling process of religion.

Thus, it may be said that the development of the true significance of religion is the realisation of the essential nature of man or the potential power of perfection involved in man's *surplus* in the different stages of the evolution of human life. In *Atmaparichaya,* Tagore discusses all the stages of these realisations-'Santam, in the first stage of religious consciousness as man is under his nature he wants happiness, wealth, he thirsts for enjoying pleasure like a child, when his aim is love. Then a hesitation comes in his mind through the inauguration of humanity; he seeks the solution between the contradictions of happiness and sorrows, good and evil he does not avoid sorrows. He is then not afraid of death. This is the transcendent stage of *Sivam* where his aim is final salvation. But yet there is a later stage which is an ascend to love. In this supreme transcendence there is a confluence of *Ganga* and *Yamuna* of happiness and sorrow, enjoyment and sacrifice, life and death. There lies the non-dual experience from one and to the other-*Advaitam.*' So man in his first stage of life is under the limitation of nature or narrow interests. But in the final stage of love there develops in him, gradually a human outlook that helps him enter into the second stage of life where he tries to establish a relation with all other men to form an ideal order of humanity. Thus, in this process, he proceeds towards the highest realisation of the last or the final stage of his life where there will be the establishment of a complete unity or non-duality or *Advaitam* in love.

If the total nature of man in different stages of life, is properly explained, we can find the unity of religion with life that exists in the inner spirit of Man. This unity in human spirit is the unity in love, *that, according to Tagore, helps a man to transcend the limitations or contradictions of maternal life. This proves that man, as a material being, may live with material contradiction or limitation, but he also has the power to cross it or to overcome it. The ideal of love that exists potentially in the intrinsic nature or power of man inspires him to cross this narrow limitation or limited stage of life where the human wants for mere happiness, wealth, etc., can create contradictions, disunities or disharmonies. These, according to Tagore, are 'the separateness of self'. But in the article *'The Creative Spirit'*, Tagore observes, "The spirit of love, dwelling in the boundless realm of the surplus, emancipates our consciousness from the illusory bond of the separateness of self, it is ever trying to spread its illumination in the human world." In this way the ideal of love in man, inspires him to sacrifice all his individual limitations for the realisation of the eternal spirit of religion and through this process he develops an idea of universal unity and interrelationship among all disintegrations of human life. This, according to Tagore, is the best endeavour of human being that "...invokes our Supreme Being for the only bond of unity that leads us to truth, namely, that of righteousness."[9] The development of this idea gradually extends the human consciousness towards Ultimate Unity or One Universal Truth, that, according to Tagore, is identified with Man's God. In his article *'Man's Nature'*, Tagore writes, "with the extension of the consciousness of human unity his God became revealed to him as one and 'universal', proving that the truth of human unity is the truth of Man's God". Therefore, religion primarily means the cultivation or the development of the ideal of Universal Being or Ultimate Truth, what, according to Tagore, is real and eternal and he thinks that it is stable, permanent and inborn. This is expressed in Tagore's article *'Man's Nature'* as below: "Religion consists, in the endeavour of men to cultivate and express those qualities which are inherent in the nature of Man the Eternal, and to have 'faith in Him'."

Thus, the development of the real significance of religion lies in the cultivation of inner human qualities towards the eternal or universal spirit in man. In the article *'Dharmer Artha'* of *Sanchaya,* Tagore points out, 'To attain unto this plane of *Atman* and the endeavour with which we seek to be lodged therein is what we term *Dharma* itself.' So the idea of man cannot be separated from the idea of religion as man is always after the realisation of his divine life where he is always trying to realise his eternal religious nature that can be recognised by Tagore as the 'Truest endeavour' of human being. Thus, in *'Dharrmer Artha'*, Tagore again established his view, 'Just as the essential property or the virtue of a hero is called 'heroism', that of a king is termed his 'kingship', even so is the virtue of *Atman* called 'virtue' itself...' This virtue in the inner spirit of man as Self or *Atman* is the virtue of unity of life with religion that finally develops a universal unity in human existence when individual self is identified with Universal self. In *Manuser Dharma,* Tagore expresses this idea, 'This is the message that is being born along the corridors of history- *So'ham* I and my father are one.' This is the inauguration of universal unity in the human existence.

The Essential Development of Universality in Man

The ideal of unity or universality in man develops the idea of the identity of individuality and universality, that can be expressed through different human and social relations; when a man tries to be conscious of his own existence and he is also conscious of this spirit of unity in him that develops his universal nature. In *The Religion of Man,* Tagore writes, "From the time when Man became truly conscious of his own self he also became conscious of a mysterious spirit of unity which found its manifestation through him in his society. It is a subtle medium of relationship between individuals, which is...for its own ultimate truth,...a value of life." The development of this higher value of life helps a man to enter into the second stage of life as *Sivam.* This stage of *Sivam* is the stage of overcoming the limitations or contradictions of life due to self interests and the basic needs of life and thus develops the ideal of humanity, manifested through the human relations of love. The ascent to love in this stage of *Sivam,* finally leads to the development of final unity in life. In *Atmaparichaya* Tagore points out, 'In that stage of *Sivam* his aim is final Salvation.' The ideal of humanity as the highest value of life, manifested through the relation of love, makes men more intimate and finally develops a spirit of unity in life and society. This, according to Tagore, is the expression of universality. Tagore also points out that the idea of God, is the substratum of the highest values of love, goodness, etc., it is manifest in human life through human processes of love and service. In this stage of life, God, in the opinion of Tagore, is not exclusively transcendent, but becomes immanent in human situation also. Here Tagore introduces the ideas of 'the divinity of man' and 'the humanity of God' as the core of his religion of Man. In the development of these ideals, man is taken by Tagore as the representative of a universal spirit who realises this universality in his life through a union with the *Divine* which is the perfection or completeness of human life. Tagore again tries to perceive *Brahman* or the Universal Reality in the human personality. Human life is the only medium through which we can know Him and can please Him through human actions. In 'Man's nature', Tagore observes, "...man feels that truth finds its body in such perfection, and when he seeks for his own best revelation he seeks a medium which has the harmonious unity, as has music. Our impulse to give expression to Universal Man produces arts and literature."[10] Different human actions, through creative art, literature, etc., inspire individual man to proceed towards the Universal Man; where a harmonious unity among all men can be established through a divine union with Ultimate Reality or God. This has been recognised by Tagore as the expression of God in man and the eternal effort of man for the realisation of God in him becomes complete through their perfect union. In a *Vaisnava kavita* of *Sonar Tari,* Tagore expresses this outlook; 'I offer to the dear ones whichever I can offer to God and give those to God whatever I can offer to the dear ones.... I make God dear and the dear as God.'[11]

This idea of creative unity of humanity and divinity as perfectly realised and manifested through the creative personality of man, is properly evaluated by Dr Sinha in the following manner. He writes, "As to the nature of man himself, Tagore focused on what he characteristically terms 'the surplus in man'. The glory of human nature lies in self-transcendence in man's movement of surpassing himself. The true meaning of living is outliving, it is ever growing out of itself. To the animal belongs the unimaginative repetition of the vital processes and habits within a safe restriction imposed by nature. But to man belongs the privilege and responsibility to live in the dimension of freedom and truth. When the demands of biological and physical levels are met, when his immediate needs of living are satisfied, there would still remain a surplus storehouse, as it were, of creative consciousness. And that is the source of all his creative self-expression in the forms of art, religion, philosophy, poetry and so on. In such creative activities man realises a deep-lying sense of reality, making itself felt in the self-expression of human personality. The spiritual superfluity in man invokes in us the Universal Man who is 'the seer and doer of all times and places'. The Super-personal Man, 'the Universal Spirit of Man-the Eternal', as Tagere prefers to express it, finds its meeting ground within the individual being of the human person".[12]

This type of humanist outlook that invokes religious consciousness develops a new spirit of *Universal Humanism* of Rabindranath. This ideal of *Humanism*, according to Tagore, is universal in character as it develops harmony in the world through the cultivation of humanity in the life of man and society. *Man, Humanity, The Religion of Man,* etc., are used by Tagore only to express this universal humanistic outlook that, according to him, is a harnessing of different ideals like love, knowledge, action, truth, beauty, pleasure, good, sacrifice; etc. Man realises these universal ideals in the different stages of the evolution of his religious life that has been interpreted by Rabindranath in his book *The Religion of Man:* "My religion is the reconciliation of the Superpersonal man, the universal human spirit in my own individual being."

Humanism, according to Tagore, is the, unity or harmony in human life, which is the truth of man. This truth as universal unity, potential in man, is to be realised in the intrinsic nature of man. In the article '*Spiritual Union*', Tagore writes, "This truth of realisation is not in space, it can only be realised in one's own inner spirit." The realisation of this ideal in the inner spirit or nature of man, leads gradually to the universal unity or 'the deeper relatedness', through the manifestation of absolute pleasure in him. Dr Mitra observes, "The pleasure of which he has said again and again seems particularly to be an expression of this worldly, human, social mentality".[13]

This worldy, humanist and social outlook, manifested in the idea of the *Universal Humanism* of Rabindranath is to be realised in inner or intrinsic nature of man, which is explained by Tagore in different ways. In *Manuser Dharma,* Tagore observes, man has two necessities in life, one is for the external world and the other is for his own inner spirit and these needs of life develop two views: 'one is his individual idea or *Jivabhava* and the other is universal outlook or *Visvabhava'*. The inspiration from the inner spirit of man compels him to be free from the individual idea or *Jivabhava* and to proceed towards a higher or universal ideal, that, according to Tagore, is beyond the ordinary necessities of food, clothes, etc. Through the realisation of this universal ideal in the inner nature he advances towards the completeness of his life; '...where he is not separated, where is his completeness where the Universal Man moves by crossing the individual limits'.[14]

In this connection Tagore tries to explain the history of Man. This history, according to Tagore, is the history of the development of the ideal of *Humanism* as the representation of humanist outlook. Thus, the history of human life proves that a man can overcome different contradictions in different periods and gradually realises his universal nature towards the development of unity in contradictions. In this way man learns to become Universal Man, that is nothing but the inauguration of universal consciousness in him beyond all contradictions caused by his self-interest or 'ego'. The realisation of this universal consciousness, according to Tagore, is the self-realisation of man which connects the individual self with the Universal Self. In *Manuser Dharma,* Tagore interprets this concept thus, 'In the history it is found that the self realisation of man proceeds naturally from the outer to the inner mind...where he has reached the universal mental world crossing the material limits'. In this world, a man completely realises the true nature of his own self which is perfectly united with the Universal Self. This realisation is possible through the evolution of consciousness in man that proceeds towards

Universalism through the different stages of its realisation in human life. These stages of self-realisation mean the attainment of three different positions in three places in the process of evolution. In the article '*Manavsatya*', Tagore explains, 'we have three mother lands which are interrelated. The first is the world. Men live in all the places of the world....The second dwelling place of men is the world of memory or *Smritiloka*....All men are united in the world of memory...Men are born in the whole world and are born again in the history of the whole universe. His third dwelling place is the spiritual world. That can be said as a continent of universal human mind. This spiritual world is a place for the union among all men through the inner mind.' Thus, in the different stages of self-realisation, man realises an interrelation with all men of the world; and the development of this idea gradually unites man with Universal Man. Through this divine or eternal union, the perfection or completeness in man is manifested as the flame of a lamp manifests itself, man also manifests himself naturally through this union with Universal Man'...where individual man wants to realise the Universal Man, removing a veil of his egoism.'[15] Tagore thinks that this perfect realisation of self inspires man to see the existence of other's spirit in him and in this way he realises the universal spirit. This is the truth consciousness of man which is developed through the realisation of the Universal Self. Tagore explains, 'The man who knows other's self in his own self, he knows the truth.'[16] Realisation of this truth is the realisation of the spirit of non-duality with the Universal Man.

In the process of the evolution of religious consciousness, man gradually realises the truth potential in him and thus expresses the ideal of divinity that finally unites him with all men through the realisation of Universal Man. Expression of divinity in man makes him complete, that is the development of the highest ideal of humanity. This, according to Tagore, is a process of human life where an individual human being always tries to become a Man towards perfection. This dynamic procedure towards perfection or completeness, according to Rabindranath, is *life* and the opposite of this is *stagnation* or *death.*

In the evolution of human life Tagore, in the true spirit of the *Upanishads,* thinks that Man in his adventures crosses the stages of darkness as untruth, and death, and realises the light of truth, perfection or infinity in him. Tagore observes, 'In the vast evolution of the world we come across the first meaning in life-particles, then in animals and finally in man. The outer doors begin to open one after the other, till we come to the innermost region of man. Here we find the finite soaked in the Infinite.'[17]

The realisation of this highest state of life or infinity, according to Tagore, is possible in this life and world that needs the suppression of poor or narrow interests of life. In the religion of Man, Tagore observes that this process is very much normal and natural in human life, the function of which is to open the door of the human heart through love in knowledge and service for others. Tagore points out, "In our life we have one side which is finite, where we exhaust ourselves at every step, and we have another side, where our aspiration, enjoyment and sacrifice are infinite. This infinite side of man must have its revelations in some symbols which have the elements of immortality. There it naturally seeks perfection. Therefore, it refuses all that is flimsy and feeble and incongruous. It builds for its dwelling a paradise, where only those materials are used that have transcended the earth's mortality."[18]

Man has an eternal power or potentiality to transcend all the limitations or contradictions of life that expresses 'earth's mortality' and thus finally finite man becomes Infinite. In art, science, philosophy and different disinterested work for others man expresses his potential divinity. In *The Religion of Man,* Tagore points out, "The individual man must exist for Man the Great, and must express him in disinterested work, in science and philosophy, in literature and arts, in science and worship. This is his religion which is working in the heart of all his religions in various names and forms". In this way Tagore repeatedly explains the proper significance of religion of Man where he tries to prove that the essential nature or fundamental religion of Man is the expression of his potential divinity through his disinterested activities for others.

Tagore, like all other thinkers, tries to realise the proper nature of man. In *Sadhana* (1912), *Personality* (1917), *Creative Unity* (1922), *The Religion of Man,* Hibbert lecture at Manchester College, Oxford (1930), *Religion of an Artist* (1933), etc., he evaluates the essential feature of man. In *The Religion of Man,* when Tagore explains the eternal or divine nature of man that transcends all contradictions of human life, his explanation of the nature of the religion of man occupies a unique position in all religions of the world. He thinks that fundamental ends of all religions should stand on the explanation of the religion of man and for this he includes all his religious discussions under *The Religion of Man* which is a new addition to the philosophy of religion. This is explained by Tagore in a letter to Pramatha Chaudhuri where he writes, 'To realise a new thing in a new form in Bengali language is not too easy...'[19] The religious explanation concerning this new form of realisation of the religion of man, according to the commentators, is a unique explanation which is recognised by Prabhat Mukherjee as a *Kaustuvamani.*[20]

The uniqueness or the significance of the religion of Man stands on the explanation of human nature which is a controversial issue. Human civilisation starts with this question that centres round the nature and existence of man. Different thinkers have tried to evaluate the nature of man from different points of view. Some put an importance on the animal aspect and others emphasise on the rational aspect of man. This type of emphasis on a particular aspect ignoring the total nature of man creates a confusion about the analysis of man. For this Alexis Carol takes man as 'Man the unknown'. But all these confusions may be removed in the light of Tagore's religion of Man, where man is taken as a potentially universal being. The universality in man, according to Tagore, can transcend all confusions and contradictions about his life and existence.

Tagore's idea of the divinity of man supplies a complete view about all human beings. Man according to him, is a complexity of animality or *Jivabhava* and humanity or *Visvabhava.* The animality of man, inspires a man to work for his own interest or enjoyment that creates limitations or contradictions in life. But man is not satisfied with this limitation as his divine nature inspires him to transcend all limitations.

So Tagore's outlook on man as a complex of two elements creates a coherency in human nature. Thus, through his explanation of coherent nature of man, Tagore, on the one hand, explains the totality of man, and this satisfies the requirements for the development of religious consciousness. The proper English meaning of religion is coherency and the Sanskrit term *Dharma* is originated from *Dhri dhatu* that means acceptance. Religion accepts all the elements of human life for the betterment of life and society, a coherency among all elements at the background of highest unity is necessary. For this Tagore also introduces a divine unity for the realisation of completeness or perfection of human life and society.

Tagore observes that divine nature of man transcends all limitations and finally realises his completeness which is the realisation of universal Man in him. In *Manuser Dharma,* Tagore explains, 'Someone lives in our heart, who is Man, but transcending individual *man-sada jananam hridaye sannivistah.* He becomes Universal Man for all times and persons.' The realisation of this Universal Man in the life of an individual is the final end of Tagore's religion of Man, where an individual man crosses all his limitations and individualities in this life and world through the development of the spirit of unity with all other human beings. The development of this spirit is the extension of his infinite personality that includes all human personalities and thus an individual realises that he is 'Man the Great'. Tagore says, "Through the realisation of that Man, a man reaches the stage of Man crossing has own individual limitations."[21] This, according to Tagore, is man's self-realisation, which is the realisation of potential infinity in him.

Realisation of self as Infinite as the unity of finite with Infinite in the finite existence of man is the fundamental end of Tagore's religion of Man where a man becomes divine in and through his life and activities in this world. This view of Tagore expresses a proper knowledge of a complete man that has a similarity with the idea of Hegel when he observes; "Religion is the knowledge possessed by the finite mind of its nature as absolute mind." To know finite mind as an absolute mind is the proper meaning of realisation which is to realise man's own infinite nature through his disinterested love, knowledge and service for others as this can produce a divine unity with all human beings. Regarding this feeling of unity Tagore writes again 'That man who can know other's self in his self and also knows his own self in other's self, can know the Truth.'[22] This idealist-transcendentalist process as developed by Tagore is essentially *Upanishadic*, in contrast to Hegel's abstract idealist attitude of the Western traditions.

Truth, according to Tagore, is one and eternal in transcendent mystic sense of India, and the realisation of truth in human life to Tagore is the realisation of the *infinite nature of man* as a perennial expression. Tagore feels the expression of this truth consciousness in everything of the world. But all objects of the world have no relation with our heart and good activities. The exchange of thoughts and actions, according to Tagore, is possible in man only when placed in a basic transcendental order, in that alone we can realise a complete manifestation of Truth as God or Absolute. Tagore writes, "*Brahman* or the Ultimate Reality can be perceived only through human personality. We can know Him and can please Him only through this medium. In this world, our actions amidst human surroundings are the best prayers to the Almighty. We care for human personality and human personality is the divine personality."[23]

Transcendentally placed a man, through love and service of humanity, can develop his divine personality that helps him to realise 'Man the Great' or Universal Man in him. According to Tagore, the religious process in a piece of meditation on humanity. In *Manuser Dharma,* Tagore explains the nature of this ideal, 'The animal in man enjoys everything on the way of the ordinary religion but the spirit in man meditates on the way to develop the religious consciousness of man.'[24] Man, on this way of meditation in the progressive transcendent direction, can acquire the knowledge of Universal Man in finite individual and finally realise the identity of the confronted Man, with the basic meditative-Infinite Man. Regarding this type of realisation which is not merely conceptual as introduced by Hegel in Western thought outmoded by Tagore in his

Upanishadic transcendented setup of religious process, as has been attempted in this dissertation, in tune with Hegel also observes, "Religion is the divine spirit's knowledge of itself through the meditation of the finite spirit." So the inauguration of divine spirit or universality in finite life is the final end of meditation, that helps a man to transcend all his confronted conceptual limitations and thus developing his infinite meditative personality.

Thus, it may be said that meditation on the religion of Man, according to Tagore, is the development of potential infinity in the individual, that is a gradual realisation of divinity through the confrontation of all limitations and contradictions of human life and society. In this way a man learns to become divine or 'Man the Great' in a transcendent meditative set up through a gradual unfolding of highest ideal of humanity. Thus, he becomes a complete or perfect Man when he observes, "I shall become *Brahman* for I am He." This is the final realisation of perfect or Universal Man that, according to Tagore, is *Manava Brahma;* it is a state where unity with Infinite in finite is possible and finite here becomes Divine or Infinite. In the *Upanishadic* transcendent-experiential setup, always there is a dual self in togetherness or connectedness, in which the dependent confronted self has a role to be perfected.

Like Bosanquet and Green, Tagore also puts an emphasis on the finite-infinite nature of the individual and through the activity of the divine principle in man, whereas to the above post-Hegelians, neo-Hegelians the Absolute is transcendentally super-sensuous and super-conceptual by a contrast from the conceptual Absolute of Hegel. Tagore's meditative transcendental Absolute is the inspiring sustaining basis to overcome man's finiteness and finally help Man to become Infinite. Evaluating this ideal of infinity in finite, in the milieu of a transcendent-confronted process, Tagore says; 'yes I shall become *Brahman.* I cannot think of any other idea but this.

I will definitely say I shall become the Infinite.'[25] This is not possible in the Western setup of a conceptual Absolute followed by a supra-intellectual process by contrast as in either Bosanquet or Green.

Realisation of 'I am He' or 'to become the Infinite' through the union of the finite with the Infinite finally makes a man Divine in a meditative-transcendental sense of the *Upanishads.* So traditional religious explanation about the realisation of God as a transcendental concept is not the true explanation of the idea of the realisation of God which is introduced by Tagore in his religion of Man in the neo-*Vedic* current of India beyond Ramakrishna-Vivekananda Vedantic process. Realisation of God according to Tagore, is the manifestation of divine ideal in human life when God as a cosmic process in a meditative-transcendental setup becomes Man and man through the realisation of divinity, becomes God. This according to Tagore, is *A tmanam biddhi* of *Upanishad* or realisation of man's own self when he observes, *So' ham* or 'I am He'.

Introduction of this divine union of finite with the Infinite in the transcendent-experiential sphere as suggested in the religion of Man, expresses Tagore's synthetic outlook in which he, like all other contemporary Indian thinkers, tries to synthesise the dualism or *Dvaitavada* and non-dualism or *Advaitavada.* As Tagore accepts the finite-infinite nature of man, he observes that a man, so long as he lives in limitations of life and society, lives under difference or duality; but his infinite nature inspires him to transcend this duality and thus he finally realises divine unity or non-duality and says, *So'ham.*

We may profitably compare Tagore's stand with that of Samkara in this context as post-Samkarite Thinker, giving a new meaning to Samkara's *Maya,* where the realist element of Man is brought modifying the Samkarite implication of *Maya* further. In this connection it should be mentioned that Samkara denied the existence of this finite life and material world as the product of *Maya* or illusion for he finally wanted to be free from limitations of human life and world through a complete or perfect knowledge of non-duality or *So' ham.* Tagore, as a poet-philosopher, wants to realise the revelation of Infinite Truth in everything of the world in different degrees and in man this realisation becomes complete; as he, though living in limitations of the world, can also transcend these limitations through the development of his infinite nature and thus finally realise transcendent-experiential process of non-duality as the highest state of divinity. So Tagore does not ignore the importance of human life in this world, because the highest ideal of divinity, according to him, is completely manifested in man. In this connection Tagore takes man as the representative of creator, as the human life, in the highest state of creation, represents divinity in the form of unity or coherency. Tagore observes, "Man as a creation represents the creator and this is why of all creatures it has been possible for him to comprehend this world in his knowledge and in his feeling and in his imagination, to realise in his individual spirit a union with a spirit that is everywhere."[26]

It may be noted *enpassant* that both Samkara and Rabindranath- believe in the philosophy of *So' ham* or non-duality, but seeks the final salvation from human life and world a complete knowledge of this ideal. Tagore, on the one hand, wants to realise the highest ideal of non-duality the process of the confronted universe of day-to-day life where a man can transcend the limitation of this life in this very world through the development of his infinite nature of possibilities and thus tempting oneself with a complete process of man in this universe. Completeness or perfection of human life is more real and more true to Tagore as it expresses the highest state of divinity in a transcendent-experiential sense where a man becomes Universal Man or 'Man the Great'.

Thus, Tagore's religion of Man is a unique form of religion among all other religions of the world. But the importance of its uniqueness lies in the explanation of human nature as the expression of divinity through the realisation of universality or 'Man the Great' in him. Here man does not worship God as transcendent, but he himself becomes God or Infinite through the experiential process of concrete realisation of his divinity or infinity and thus God or Infinite is completely manifested in human life as the expression of the highest state of divine unity in life. For this the humanisation of God through His complete manifestation in human life, and divinisation of man through a complete realisation of divinity in human life, as the fundamental principles of the religion of Man are established, where Tagore observes, "I felt that I had found my religion at last, the religion of man, in which the infinite became defined in humanity and came close to me so as to need my love and cooperation. This idea of mine found at a later date its expression in my poems, *Jivandevata,* the Lord of my life." According to Rabindranath, the infinite ideal of love in man inspires him to transcend his finiteness and thus in the highest state of human life a divine unity in the form of humanity is established in love. In this connection Tagore points out that the ideal of love in the form of *Jivandevata* becomes the guiding principle or creative spirit of the development of human outlook that guides a man to proceed towards completeness when he develops his full divinity and becomes a Universal Man.

Notes

1. *Rabindrarachanavali,* Vol. XII, p. 19.
2. C.F. Andrews (Ed), Thoughts form Tagore, p. 73.
3. 'Patradhara', *Prabasi.*
4. Rabindranath Tagore, *The Religion of Man,* p. 38.
5. Rabindranath Tagore, *The Religion of Man,* p. 27.
6. *Ibid.*, p. 38.
7. Rabindranath Tagore, 'The Surplus in Man', *The Religion of Man,* p. 35.
8. Dr S.K. Das, *Tagore and the Perennial Problems of Philosophy,* p. 53. *Tagore took his cue while formulating his doctrine of totality from Buddhism. We may further suggest that the Buddhistic ideal of *Maitri* and *Karuna* inspired Tagore to explain the totality of human nature in love, developed through the universal brotherhood.
9. Rabindranath Tagore, *The Religion of Man,* p. 30.
10. Rabindranath Tagore, *The Religion of Man,* p. 94.
11. *Devatare Yaha Dite Pari......Devatare priye kari priyere Devata.*
12. 'Rabindranath Tagore: The Poet of Universal Man', Inaugural Lecture by Prof. Dr. Debabrata Sinha, Rabindranath Tagore Lectureship Foundation, Toronto.
13. Dr Haraprasad Mitra, 'Rabindra Manase Manusyatva O Dharrnadharana' *Prajna.*
14. Rabindranath Tagore, *Manuser Dharma,* p. 10.
15. Rabindranath Tagore, *Manuser Dharma,* p. 83.
16. *Ibid.*, p. 10.
17. Rabindranath Tagore, *Manuser Dharma,* p. 97.
18. Rabindranath Tagore, *Personality,* p. 30.
19. P.K. Mukherjee, *Rabindrajivani,* Vol. III, p. 854.

20. A precious stone that God Narayana wears on his bosom.
21. Rabindranath Tagore, *Manuser Dharma,* 'Introduction'.
22. *Ibid.*, p. 10.
23. Rabindranath Tagore, 'Dharma', *Rabindrarachanavali,* Vol. XIII, p. 383.
24. Rabindranath Tagore, *Manuser Dharma,* p. 53.
25. Rabindranath Tagore, *Santiniketan,* Vol. II, p. 336.
26. Rabindranath Tagore, *The Religion of Man,* p. 133.

Chapter - 3

The Idea of Jivandevata: A Creative Expansion of the Humanity of God

Religion of Man, which is above all the limitations of different religions and orthodoxy or conservatism, expresses Tagore's humanist and comprehensive outlook and establishes man as a divine being that is a perfect form of expression between God and man as dual yet non-dual processes in this confronted universe, manifesting the unity of divinity and humanity in human being. Through the realisation of this perfect nature as unity, a man tries to be related with other human beings, and this realisation finally forms a unity between individual man and Universal Man. Universal Man, the Ultimate Reality of Tagore's religion of Man, can be known or realised through the human personality. In '*Dharma*', Tagore observes, 'The ultimate reality can be perceived only through human personality. We can know him and please him only through this medium'. For this, man is accepted by the poet as the representative of Universal Spirit and through the realisation of this spirit in him, man becomes one with the Universal Reality or God.

So the realisation of universal or eternal spirit in man is the accomplishment of God in him. The idea of God, thus, in the observation of Tagore, is the substratum of the highest value of human goodness. God, in this sense, as the ontological essence of man, removes all his evils of life and thus he tries to realise his perfect goodness as God. This is the realisation of eternal humanity. Tagore says, 'Man has reached his own God on the basis of his own feeling of divine humanity'.[1] According to Tagore we can come to the "idea of God from the idea of perfect goodness or divine humanity. Tagore observes: God is *Manava Brahma* that means 'Reality is human'. This idea of God is received by Tagore from the idea of *Ucchistasukta* of *Atharva Veda.* The spiritual or eternal quality of goodness exists in man's nature of *'surplus'*. The realisation of this nature helps him to realise in him the unity with the Universal Man. This unity is the final realisable objective for Man. Roy evaluates this view: "This unity is supersensual unity. This universal human existence or *Manavik Bhuma* is *Manava Brahma.*He is Universal Man. In this context of the feeling of harmony with Universal Man, the self-realisation of individual man becomes possible.'Reality is human'."[2]

In this perfect state of unity man realises the supreme value as the Ultimate Reality of life and this Reality as the idea of God is manifested in human life as the human God in the form of perfect goodness or humanity. In this procedure of manifestation, man gradually becomes divine and God becomes human. The establishment of this idea of God in man and the idea of man in God is the fundamental end of Tagore's religion of Man. In a *Vaisnava kavita,* Tagore presents this idea: 'I make God dear and the dear as God'.[3]

Vaisnavism puts an emphasis on the relation between God and man. God exists in everything and to find God in every thing is to find God in man's own self, which also is God: *Sarvabhutesu yah pasyet bhagavadbhavamatmanah, Bhutani bhagavatyatmanyesha bhagavatottamah.*[4] Tagore expresses this Vaisnava outlook in his idea of *Sarvanubhuti* or 'at-homeness' in all and in 'Vasundhara' of *Sonar Tari,* the poet expresses a feeling of intimate relation with his own self and all other human beings, nature and God. Love is the only eternal medium through which the idea of *Sarvanubhuti* can be manifested in human life.

In *'Ananta Prem'* of *Manasi,* Tagore explains, love is eternal and man and God are also eternal. In eternal love finite man as lover and Infinite God as beloved becomes intimate or one, and thus in truth, love makes God human and man Divine. The Infinite manifests itself in the finite where lies the fundamental ideas of truth and beauty.

Now with reference to the beauty of nature it is to be mentioned that nature also like the lover of the beloved plays a game of life with man. So the eternal ideal of love establishes a relation of unity among man, nature and God. This idea of eternal or intimate relation of love between lover and beloved, is expressed by Tagore in his different writings where he tries to establish his idea of *Jivandevata.*

Tagore's idea of *Jivandevata* expresses both the personal and impersonal aspects of Reality. In love we find the manifestation of this two aspects of Reality; sometimes He is manifested in man and nature, and sometimes He stands as distinct from the supreme ideal that is to be realised by man. Both nature and Absolute *Jivandevata* play the game of love with man. But man's object of love is not two, as *Jivandevata* being Absolute and perfect being, is both immanent and transcendent. If nature is taken as man's object of love, then *Jivandevata* as nature, is immanent in nature and then both *Jivandevata* and nature are taken as identical. But *Jivandevata* also is transcendent or impersonal, and hence distinct from both nature and man. He creates man and nature for his own self-manifestation in love. So God, nature and man are the three essential factors of Tagore's religion of Man, where man and nature are treated as the end and not the means. Nature being potentially divine helps man to develop his true and perfect nature which is the divine personality. Thus, man in nature tries to develop his divine personality through the realisation of the highest idea of *Jivandevata* and Absolute *Jivandevata* also realises Himself in absolute love through man and nature.

While developing the idea of *Jivandevata* as Tagore often lapses into the idea of absolutism, some commentators like S.N. Dasgupta, and Radhakrishnan, took him to be an absolutist. But referring to the personal aspect of God and the theistic element in the idea of *Jivandevata,* some others called him a theist. Dutta pointed out "Rabindranath was temperamentally opposed to puritanism, asceticism and impersonal absolutism. He rather chose to emphasise like the Vaishnava those aspects of the *Upanishads* which taught that the finites were created by the Infinite out of Its own endless joy of love, and they are, therefore, not illusory but real".[5] Here one has to distinguish the transcendent as the ground for the confronted apparent reality mentioned earlier. Viewed from this prospect, Tagore's religious experience cannot be categorised either as Absolutistic or Theistic.

So with reference to this idea of Rabindranath the opinions of critics are divided and we find a controversy about theism and absolutistic interpretations of Tagore's view. But after a careful examination of the idea of Tagore's philosophical speculations of religion of Man we find that in the development of the concept of *Jivandevata,* Tagore runs the two processes of theism and absolutism together as two realisable prospects for Man's personal and impersonal orders of experiential process. Regarding this process, Dr Srivastava rightly observes, "Along with his philosophy we find that the characteristic of the great contemporary Indian philosophers, viz., Dr Radhakrishnan, Mahatma Gandhi, Swami Vivekananda and Sri Aurobindo lies in accepting both the theistic and the absolutistic aspects of God as real, and in evolving synthetic system of Philosophy. They all develop different systems of thought but they incorporate both the aspects of the infinite. One takes the theistic aspect as merely empirical and the absolutistic aspects as real, the other conceives both the theism and absolutism as real, and still some others conceive the Reality to be a concrete universal or a positive being".[6] So in support of this view it may be said that in the writings of different contemporary Indian thinkers we find the same element of synthesis as alternative transcendental modes. Swami Vivekananda, Sri Aurobindo, Mahatma Gandhi, and Dr Radhakrishnan develop a comprehensive philosophical attitude on the basis of a perfect unity of the absolutistic and the theistic aspects of God which also is present in Rabindranath.

In the development of the idea of *Jivandevata* Tagore was firstly influenced by the absolutism as transcendent-meditative process of *Upanishad* where *Brahman* was recognised as the pure ground of reality and consciousness that includes *everything,-Sarvam Khalvidam Brahma tajjalaniti.*[7] He is immanent in this universe, there is nothing beyond Him and the existence, birth, death of finite beings, are included in Him. This pantheistic and impersonal absolutism of

Upanishad influences Tagore, but this aspect is not unconditional or abstract Reality of Samkara, as he denounces the idea of void or empty Absolute of *Advaita Vedanta.* With reference to the pantheism or all inclusive and impersonal Absolute of *Upanishad* it may be pointed out that it can satisfy our intellect but not our heart. Tagore is a great poet who is not satisfied with mere knowledge of Reality; his longing is for the realisation of Reality in love. In this connection we may point out that Tagore, in his realisation of Reality in love, was very much influenced by the ideas of *Vaisnavism.* But he interprets Vaisnavism in his own way where we get both personal and impersonal aspects of God in love. P.T. Raju rightly observes, "Tagore is much influenced by *Vaisnavism*, and he is a Vaisnava in his own way. He calls His Supreme person *Advaitam* and his philosophy is a sort of *Vaisnava Advaita* or an *Advaita* in which *bhakti* or love plays the chief role".[8]

In *Bhaktitattva* or the theory of love of *Vaisnava* religion uses the term *Rasa* that determines the relation between God and man or devotee in different ways. In *Chaitanya Charitamrita,* Krishnadas Kaviraj explains four types of *Rasa* e.g., *Dasya, Sakhya, Vatsalya* and *Sringara.*[9] God is taken as master in *Dasya.* He is treated as friend in *Sakhya* and in *Vatsalya* He is father or mother. In *Sringara* He is lover. This last relation of *Sringara* makes the circle of relation complete. This, according to *Vaisnava* thinker, is *Madhura Rasa* or the sweet relation between lover and beloved.

In the religious life of Tagore we find different stages of the relationship between God and man, which is not very different from the *Vaisnava* process of religion. In the article *'Namastestu'* Tagore writes, "The relations through which we can realise God, are not always the same. We can adopt him either as father, or as master or as friend".[10]

In the different religions of the world we find different interpretations of this relation between God and man. In Christianity, Islam and in other religions of India, God is treated as father and in *Shakta Sadhana* and in the ideas of Ramakrishna and Ramaprasad, God is accepted as mother. To realise the goodness of God as father and to seek the affection of God as mother, we find different procedures of meditations in these religions.

Regarding the mother-concept of God, Tagore writes god as 'Mother looks after the happiness and comfort of her child, satisfies his appetite, consoles him in mourning, serves him in disease'.[11] But father-concept of God does not serve the above particular needs of man. So, Tagore writes, 'Father does not arrange for our happiness only. He directs the goodness also'.[12]

But these two relative aspects of God are transcended in the *Vedas* and the *Upanishads* where 'There is a difference between father and mother in the material world, but both these ideas of father and mother are identified in the idea of Father, who is saluted by the *mantra* of *Veda'*.[13]

So this idea of the Supreme Father is One or Absolute (*Tad Ekam*) who is the transcendent consciousness beyond all relational experiences.

In the final development of Tagore's idea of *Jivandevata* we find this idea of God who is One in many and many in One. When God is manifested through this world as transcendent process, He is One. But when He is confronted in a concrete form, He is human in nature. Here man tries to realise Him in love where the sense of superiority of the father and inferiority of the son is gone; and God becomes realised by man as his *Sakha* or friend. Some *Vaisnava* thinkers also accept God as *Sakha* or friend. In this connection Tagore points out that in the final stage of life man tries to establish his friendship with God and thus an intimate relation between man and God as lover and beloved becomes established. In this way man also realises the existence of God in him as the Supreme Person or the Universal Man. Tagore observes, 'This God is *Visvakarma* who has expressed himself in innumerable forms through innumerable activities of the world; but He is *Mahatma sada jananam hridaye sannivistah.* He is inserted always in the heart of men as great-in his own form, in the form of Supreme One'.[14] So the realisation of God in love, or the establishment of god as the manifestation in human life as a Supreme Person etc., of *Jivandevata* in different forms becomes realised.

In '*Atmacharit*', Tagore evaluates the different stages of expressions of *Jivandevata* in human life. In the idea of *Jivandevata* the personal aspect of God is very much important and throughout *The Religion of Man, Personality, Creative Unity* and *Gitanjali,* Tagore explains the human character of God. He is taken as Supreme Person who is the ultimate ground of all powers, qualities and existence. In this connection Tagore uses the term *'Personality'* which in reality is the substratum of infinite will, power, bliss and goodness. Infinite Personality refers to One, who as Infinite, includes finite. Merz rightly observes, "Personality, always impresses us as the most powerful instance of individual existence". So with reference to this idea it may be said that Tagore apparently like Hegel, speaks of God's personality as the transcendental unity of all finite existences when God as the divine personality becomes human through his manifestation in the human existence and human personality in love. But Tagore's God is the transcendent *Vedic* principle sustaining the entire manifest process as mentioned beyond all conceptual modes.

Thus, ideas of 'the divinity of man' and 'the humanity of God', as established in Tagore's religion of Man, are developed through Tagore's idea of *Jivandevata.* Tagore points out, "I felt that I had found my religion at last, the religion of man, in which the infinite became defined in humanity and came close to me so as to need my love and co-operation".[15] Through the intimate relation of love with God man becomes divine and tries to establish an oneness with him. So Tagore's idea of *Jivandevata,* as the eternal inspirer of human life, is treated by him as 'Lord of my life'. Tagore observes, "This idea of mine found at a later date its expression in some of my poems addressed to what I called *Jivandevata,* the Lord of my life".[16] In the poem 'Jivandevata'.[17] Tagore tries to explain the nature of this eternal spirit in man, that inspires him to realise the divinity in life. All through the writings concerning *Jivandevata* Tagore evaluates this innermost spirit which is developed in his life in different forms in different ways. In different places Tagore interprets this pervasively present spirit differently, e.g., *'Jivandevata', 'Manasa Sundari', 'Abhisarika', 'Manasi'*, etc.

So if we explain the creative life of Tagore, we shall find the expression of this idea of *Jivandevata* in different forms where Tagore's life proceeds towards divinity and his idea of God in the form of *Jivandevata* appears before him either as individual man or us Universal or Supreme Person. From the early stage of life, Tagore tried to trace the significance of this idea and tried to realise its perfection. In *The Religion of Man,* Tagore expresses this process with profound feeling the following: "When I was eighteen, a sudden spring breeze of religious experience for the first time came to my life and passed away leaving in my memory a direct message of spiritual reality. One day while I stood watching at early dawn the sun sending out its rays from behind the trees, I suddenly felt as if some ancient mist had in a moment lifted from my sight, and the morning light on the face of the world revealed an inner radiance of joy. The invisible screen of the common-place was removed from all things and all men, and their ultimate significance was intensified in my mind; and this is the definition of beauty. That which was memorable in this experience was its human message, the sudden expansion of my consciousness in the super-personal world of man".[18] Thus, the gradual realisation of Infinite in finite life removes all limitations of finiteness and gives rise to a transcendent process of 'the super-personal world of man'.

According to some thinkers, this transcendent-experiential process as the realisation of this universal idea is the realisation of Tagore's own self, when Tagore, like Hindu monk or *yogin,* tries to realise the existence of God or universality in him. In *'The Religion of an Artist*', Tagore expresses this eagerness, "I had a vague notion as to who and what it was that touched my heart's chords, like the infant which does not know its mother's name or who or what she is." This *Tattva-jijnasa* or the eternal question about 'who or what she is' inspires him to realise the Universal Self or *Bara-Ami* in his own individual self where the narrow or poor ego meets the Universal Self as the Lord of his life. So this idea of *Bara-Ami* or Universal Self, according to Tagore, is the creative personality or the 'Lord of my Life'. In *Atmaparichay,* he explains this idea as *Jivandevata* as below: 'I have written about my inner creative power which is supplying unity and significance to all pleasures, sufferings and all events of my life, relating my form and transformation, birth and rebirth in a thread, and through which I am feeling an unity in the universe, is called *Jivandevata*....'[19]

In different stages of life Tagore realised this creative power or *Jivandevata,* through which his life is related with nature and world*. Tagore says, "...the first stage of my realisation was through my feeling of intimacy *with* nature."[20] This feeling of Tagore was gradually developed and it established a unity with the external world. There after Tagore writes, "This produced a sense of serene exaltation in me, the daily meditation upon the infinite being which unites in one stream of creation my mind and the outer world."[21]

This ideal of a permeating process through the realisation of *Jivandevata* in different stages of life inspired Tagore to establish his religion of Man, which is beyond all limitations and contradictions of human life and world, and where man through the development of humanity in him, becomes non-different from all human beings of the world. It is the realisation of completeness in man as the development of a comprehensive outlook that establishes all to a transcendent basis with an experiential possibility.

This comprehensive view of man, developed through Tagore's religion of Man, is sustained by his novel notion of the creative power of *Jivandevata.* He explains, "Its touch comes to me through the same unseen and trackless channel as does the inspiration of my songs. My religious life has followed the same mysterious line of growth as has my poetical life."[22] The touch of this inner power or the realisation of the creative spirit in the poet inspired him to develop the ideal of universal oneness or non-difference between individual existences. This is the realisation of Tagore's innerself, in which he feels the unity with all men and the world. In *Philosophy of Rabindranath Tagore,* Dr Radhakrishnan observes, "He combines in himself spirit and nature. He is earth's child but heaven's heir." This non-difference between the infinite and finite is the final freedom of human being where life becomes free from finiteness or limitations and enjoys infinite pleasure or perfect bliss. Regarding the development of this ideal in his life, Tagore writes, "Thus, my mind was brought up in an atmosphere of freedom, freedom from the dominance of any creed that had its sanction in the definite authority of some scripture or in the teaching of some organised body of worshippers."

So the final freedom from finiteness through the realisation of the creative spirit or *Jivandevata* in different stages makes Tagore's life complete. In '*Navajataka*', Tagore explains, 'My play in this world house comes to an end and now comes the time when the door of the house shall be closed. In the innermost spirit of my life! come now by my side. Give me the peace of your company at the end of my journey.' In this way, Tagore, at the end of the journey of his creative life realises the universal form of *Jivandevata* in his individual existence where the Lord of Tagore's life appears either as personal deity or as Infinite, and thus finally a non-difference between the individual and the Universal or Absolute Self, is established.

In the development of the idea of *Jivandevata,* we find an evolutionary progress of this ideal in different stages of Tagore's life. In '*Sonar Tari',* we get only some hints, and in the poems *'Niruddes-yatra'* and *'Manasa Sundari'* we find a rise towards a vision of this idea, which in '*Chitra*' '*Antaryami*', it becomes conspicuous. And through *Jivandevata, 'The Religion of Man', 'Atmaparichaya', 'Santiniketan', 'Jivan Smriti'* and '*Personality',* and other works we find the progress of this idea of Deity. Thus, through these manifestations in different stages in different forms the idea of *Jivandevata* finally appears as *Visvadevata,* where both the personal aspect and impersonal or universal aspect of the Deity are fused into a transcendent oneness or non-difference. So in the final stage of '*Gitanjali', Jivandevata* appears as *Visvadevata,* and *Visvadevata* as *Jivandevata,* where all apparent distinctions are lost in a comprehensive transcendent vision.

Surveying broadly the contention of some eminent scholars of India, whether the nature of *Jivandevata* is a personal or Universal Deity, P.C. Mahalanobis and others say as below: Mahalanobis interprets *Jivandevata* as personal deity which is recognised by Kshudiram Das as the power of poet's own self.[23]

This power is explained by Tagore as 'creative personality', which inspires a man to realise the infinity in finite existence. For this

S. Dasgupta observes, 'He is a particular form of reflection of *Visvadevata* in the centre of individual life.'[24] But if the universal nature of *Jivandevata* is properly explained, it is found that Tagore does not like to confine this power within the limitations of his own life. Through the development of this power, the non-difference of individual with nature, world and God can also be realised. For this, Subodh Chandra Sengupta points out that the *Jivandevata* is the *Visvadevata* in disguise.[25] The existence of this creative power in man develops the ideal of love that establishes an intimate relation with all other human beings and thus the finiteness or limitations of human life can be removed and oneness of the individual with the transcendent can be instituted. This idea of Tagore is insightfully interpreted by Nihar Ranjan Ray as the infinite ideal of intimate relation of Tagore's *Jivandevata* with his idea of Universalism. In *Manasi,* we find that this transcendent reality is manifested in the form of infinite love, before the poet's life as wife, friend, husband or the beloved.[26] Hiranmaya Bandyopadhyay rightly points out that *Jivandevata* and *Visvadevata* are one and the same[27] in full agreement with this writer's contention in this work. So, in this connection it may be said that this one or infinite personality is operative in human life in a human form through love or bliss, when man becomes divine through the realisation of infinite love, and Universal Deity or God in turn becomes human through His eternal manifestation in human life.

'The humanity of God', through His manifestation in human life in the form of transcendent or absolute value of love makes the development of the idea of *Jivandevata* complete. Thompson also speaks of "a deep and intimate communion with God into which the Jeevan-Devata feeling merged."[28] With reference to the idea of God, it may be said that God of Tagore is neither personal or *sakara,* nor impersonal or *nirakara,* as he does not accept the ideals of mere duality or no-duality, propounded by different thinkers. All these assertions of differences among these Tagore-scholars, Indian and foreign, can be resolved by this writer's renderings of Tagore in the context of India's transcendent reality as stemming out from the *Vedas* to his time. This ideal of transcendent God as the highest value of love, inspires man to realise its existence, and this creative power again, in man as a confronted reality, develops an *infinity* in his being by removing all limitations and contradictions. In this way this highest value becomes manifest in human life and through these manifestations this ideal becomes more and more effective as a concrete process in dedicated individual beings. Dasgupta rightly points out here about this God as a transcendent power thus: 'God is a creative power for all times, who is manifesting His eternal possibilities through these creations.'[29] So the manifestation of this infinite ideal makes the development of all eternal possibilities in finite beings complete.

This development as expressed in the advancement of mind and heart will destroy the narrow ego or poor self and will help operation of the Universal Self or Absolute Idea or the process of transcendent God in human life. So the confronted Absolute is not the achievement of something in finite life but a matter of becoming Infinite. Tagore explains that this realisation of God is 'not to receive but only to become.'[30]

To become is to be a perfect or complete man through the development of infinite personality and the realisation of God in the form of Absolute-love makes this development possible. In this way there will be a death of the poor self as narrow limitations or contradictions of life, and Infinite or Universal Man will come out from the death of this finiteness in finite existence. So death, according to Tagore, is the death of all limitations, and fusion of life in a creative personality through the development of Infiniteness in finite existence.

To become the infinite and Infinite itself are different matters. Infinite or God is the absolute value which is manifested in human life and man becomes infinite through the realisation of the condition of absolute value in one's life. The realisation of concrete Absolute condition is effected through love and service to others. This is the inauguration of humanity, which, in the opinion of Tagore, is the 'meditation on humanity' as the realisation of Universal Man in the finite life, or to become Infinite.

So finally it may be said that Tagore's ideal of *Jivandevata* appears before human being in different stages in different forms and thus

God in the form of *Jivandevata* is realised by man in this world and life. In this way when God is confronted as the absolute or infinite value, the form of *Visvadevata* is realised, and with it, the finiteness or limitation of man is removed and infinite personality emerges to develop Godness in him. In *The Religion of Man,* Tagore points out that the fundamental end of man is to become God. So realisation of God in the form of *Jivandevata* is not the experience of God in the popular or the ordinary sense of religion, but it is the realisation of a transcendent Godness as creative principle of supreme value of truth, beauty and goodness in togetherness in different stages of life through which man himself becomes God or Universal Man, overcoming all limitations.

The development of infinite personality through the realisation of absolute ideal of love or humanity is the fundamental end of Tagore's religion of man. The realisation of the absolute value meditatively makes the life of a man complete when the non-difference between individuality and universality is established. This is explained by Tagore as the meditation on the 'humanity of God', where God becomes human through the perfect realisation of this ideal in human life and thus man also becomes God, which, according to Tagore, is the development of the ideal of *Manava brahma* or the realisation of absolute or infinite spirit in man.

Thus, from Tagore's transcendent-experiential process Man is potentially divine, proceeding towards the realisation of the idea of *So'ham* or 'I am He' when man becomes divine and God also becomes human by His manifestation in human life. This manifestation of transcendent God in human life in the form of Universal Man or the absolute ideal of humanity, establishes the fundamental ideal of the 'humanity of God'.

It may be noted in this connection that God or *Jivandevata* of Rabindranath needs the human life most, as He is manifested through this life where an intimate relation of love between the two is established. So human life is real like God or *Jivandevata,* as both are very intimate and one exists or manifests through the other. This ideal of manifestation of God or *Jivandevata* is human or personal. In this connection the arguments of theists may be referred to.

They accept God as the substratum of infinite values, e.g., truth, beauty and goodness, and these values are realised by man through the establishment of personal relation with God. But Monists or Absolutists do not accept this personal relation of God with man, as this idea of personal relation makes God finite. But how this impersonal God is manifested through the personal life, is not satisfactorily explained by the monistic thinker like Samkara, the Indian monist, recognises the manifestation of Absolute in human life where Absolute becomes God or *Isvara* under the condition of *Maya,* but this stage of God is not ultimately real. Sri Aurobindo, the great contemporary Indian thinker, introduces the integral method for the solution of this problem and accepts Absolute as both personal and impersonal. If Tagore's transcendent-experiential principle is understood in the context of the non-dualist Vedantist Samkara of the eighth century, and Sri Aurobindo, of the present century, his is an alternative programme, conferring more reality to individual's activity, and as such is a process towards Sri Aurobindo's novel gnostic personalities in a transcendent Divine Milieu.

Tagore explains the personality of God in his own way, as he observes that God as the infinite ideal is manifested through the human life in different stages in different human forms. In *The Religion of Man* Rabindranath observes, "Whatever character our theology may ascribe to him (Eternal person), in reality, he is the infinite ideal of Man towards whom men move in their collective growth, with whom they seek their union of love as individuals, in whom they find their ideal of father, friend and beloved". So Tagore, like Hegel, S. Alexander, writer of *Space Time and Deity,* takes finite or human beings as a process towards the realisation of an ideal emergent quality of Deity in the offing. Hegel points out that the Infinite as a whole exists in and through the parts or finites, where a true organic relation can be established. The nisus for Deity is Tagore's love of human beings of a God in descent in human situation or *Jivandevata* in the form of *Visvadevata,* not realised concretely by Alexander, appears in human life through eternal love. In *Gitanjali,* Tagore explains this unity in love between the Infinite and finite when he expresses as follows: "O, thou Lord of all Heavens, where would be thy love if I were not" ?[31] Here Tagore focuses the transcendent-experiential God to concrete human situation.

In this way it may be observed that in and through the analysis of the idea of *Jivandevata* in different transitory stages of human life, Tagore explains his idea of God and its realisation in human existence as the development of godness or divinity. Tagore does it in his own unique manner. In the context of this God-realisation as man's self-realisation, Tagore's idea of God-as *Jivandevata* appears to be a transient one which has been differently treated by different critics and thinkers as transient or permanent, transcendent or immanent, finite or infinite. But this writer has already suggested his solvent process, answering the differing statements of the above mentioned Tagore-scholars.

But in a proper analysis of Tagore's idea of the religion of Man, evaluating his novel outlook of man's emergent creative spirit is to be realised through the creative personality of man in love in his different states of existence. This idea of God in descent in concrete human situation leads god to a complete self-manifestation of Man as Divine or Universal Being.

Thus, this process of the meeting of God in human situation as the realisation of godness or divinity in man, makes God *human* through His gradual manifestation in different states of human existence in different degrees. So, in this context, it may be pointed out that God, as the transcendental value or ideal of universality as *Visvadevata,* gradually becomes real to man through a realisation in different states of existence in different degrees of manifestation of divinity *(Jivandevata),* in experiential process this being a creative or guiding spirit of developing the oneness of God and man meditatively, and prospectively.

Notes

1. Rabindranath Tagore, *Manuser Dharma.*
2. Sachindranath Gangopadhyay and others, *Rabindra Darshan,* p. 127.
3. *Devatare priya kari priyere Devata...*
4. *Srimadbhagavatam,* 11.2.44.
5. Dr D. M. Dutta, *The Chief Currents of Contemporary Philosophy,* p. 574.

6. Dr R. S. Srivastava, *Contemporary Indian Philosophy,* p. 88.
7. *Chhandogya, 3/14/1.*
8. P.T. Raju, *The Idealistic Thought of India,* p. 324.
9. *Dasya Sakhya Vatsalya Sringara charirasa chari bhaber Bhakta yata Krishna tari basa.*
10. Rabindranath Tagore, 'Santiniketan', *Rabindrarachanavali,* (Cent Edn) Vol. XII, p. 270.
11. 'Bhaya and Ananda', *Santiniketan.*
12. *Ibid. Rabindrarachanavali,* Vol. XII, (Cent Edn), pp. 275-76.
13. 'Dwidha', *Santiniketan, Ibid.* p. 355.
14. 'Atmabodh',' Santiniketan', *Rabindrarachanavali,* Vol. XII, (Cent Edn), p. 399.
15. Rabindranath Tagore, *The Religion of Man,* p. 60.
16. *Ibid.*
17. In the following poem (English Translation of 'Jivandevata', *The Religion of Man,* p. 60), the poet illustrated the Idea as explained above. "Thou who are the innermost Spirit of my being, art thou pleased, Lord of my Life ? For I gave to thee my cup filled with all the pain and delight that the crushed grapes of my heart and surrendered, I wove with the rhythm of colours and songs the cover for thy bed, and with the molten gold of my desires I fashioned playthings for thy passing hours. I know not why thou chosest me for thy partner, Lord of my Life! Didst thou store my days and nights, my deeds and dreams for the alchemy of thy art, and string in the chain of thy music my songs of autumn and spring and gather the flowers from my mature moments for thy crown ? I see thine eyes gazing at the dark of my heart, Lord of my Life, I wonder of my failures and wrongs are forgiven. For many were my days without service and nights of forgetfulness; futile were the flowers that faded in the shade not offered to thee. Often the tired strings of my lute slackened at the strain of thy tunes. And often at the ruin of wasted hours my desolate evenings were filled with tears. But have my days come to their end at last, Lord of my Life While my arms round thee grow limp, my kisses losing their truth ? Then break up the meeting of this languid day. Renew the old in me in fresh forms of delight; and let the wedding come once again in a new ceremony of life".
18. Rabindranath Tagore, *The Religion of Man,* p. 58.
19. Rabindranath Tagore, *Atmaparichay,* p. 12. *cf. This outlook of Tagore, according to some commentators, represents the idea of Pantheism. Pantheism points out that God is wholly immanent in human life and material world. *Pan* is all and *Theos* is God, so God is all and all is God. But Tagore's idea of *Jivandevata,* being a creative spirit, is immanent in man and world, but also has the power of transcending the limitations and contradictions of life and society. So this idea of Tagore is both immanent in and

transcendent of this world and human existence as immanent-experiential process permeating the universe and its confronted creatures.

20. Rabindranath Tagore, *The Religion of Man,* p. 12.
21. *Ibid*, p. 58.
22. *Ibid.*
23. Dr K. Das, *Rabindra Pratibhar Parichaya,* p. 105.
24. Dr S. Dasgupta, *Rabindra Manas,* p. 119.
25. Dr S. Sengupta, *Rabindranath,*
26. Dr N. R. Ray, Kaviparichiti.
27. Dr Hiranmaya Bandyopadhyay, *Thakur Parivarer Katha.*
28. Thompson, *Rabindranath Tagore, Poet and Dramatist,* p. 113.
29. Dr S. Dasgupta, *Upanishader Patabhumikay Rabindranath,* p. 89.
30. Rabindranath Tagore, 'Haoa', *Santiniketan.*
31. Rabindranath Tagore, English *Gitanjali,* poem 56.

Chapter - 4

God and Man: An Examination of Godness as the Universality of Man and Humanity of God

In developing the ideas of 'the divinity of man' and 'the humanity of God', Tagore, like a true Philosopher, tries to evaluate the proper relation between man and God. God as the absolute ideal, is manifested through the human life in a perfect form and becomes human, and man, through the realisation of this absolute ideal in life, becomes divine, and thus relation between man and God is finally established. Tagore explains the nature of this relationship 'as the union of the infinite with the finite in finiteness'.[1] The union of the finite life with the Infinite, expresses the complete view about the relation between the finite individual with God.

Regarding the nature of this relation between God and man there is a controversy among the thinkers and some accept this relation as personal and recognises Tagore as Theist. According to them, the personal aspect of God is greater than the impersonal aspect. As many Indian thinkers take God as empirical and the finite aspect of Absolute, they explain the idea of the manifestation of God in human life as the expression of finite aspect of Absolute and the relation of God and man as purely personal.

But others put an emphasis on the impersonal aspect of God as Absolute and interpret Tagore from a transcendental perspective. According to these thinkers, the impersonal aspect of God or Absolute is greater than the personal aspect and the realisation of this absolute value makes human life complete. As they put an emphasis on *Absolutism*, so they recognise Tagore as absolutistic thinker. Sometimes this *Absolutism* of Rabindranath is compared to the absolutistic or non-dual concept of *Samkara*, an Advaita Vedantin, which disregards the claims of finite individuals. *Samkara* emphasises the impersonal, negative, indescribable aspects of Absolute or *Nirguna Brahman* and regards this *Brahman* or Absolute, as the transcendental reality, is the only reality, and this world and human existences are unreal, as these products are not finally real, hence *Maya*. But in this connection it should be pointed out that Tagore opposes the empty Absolute or void or abstract Reality of *Samkara*. For Tagore as already noted, this world and human life, are real as manifestations of God and the impulse for human beings towards perfection. In his collective essays, *Santiniketan* Tagore points out that there is no *Maya* in the confronted world-situation. The manifestation of God in human life is pure bliss or *Anandam;* hence human existence is not an illusion. He explains the proper significance of love or bliss in life: "Coming to the theatre of life we foolishly sit with our back to the stage. We see the gilded pillars and decorations, we watch the coming and going of the crowd; and when the light is put out at the end, we ask ourselves in bewilderment, what is the meaning of it all? If we paid attention to the inner stage, we could witness the eternal love-drama of the soul and be assured that it has pauses, but no end, and that the gorgeous world-preparations are not a magnificent delirium of things".[2]

Again Tagore accepts the manifestation of absolute ideal in human life as real and there are some who try to compare his *Absolutism* with the theory of *Vishistadvaitavada* or qualified non-dualism of Ramanuja who accepts the organic relation between the individual and the Absolute. Regarding the nature of this relation in Ramanuja's system, Hiriyana points out, "Whatever is, is thus the body of God and He is the soul not only of inorganic nature but also of souls or *Jivas.* It is in this connection that Ramanuja formulates the relation so important in his system, of *Aprithak Siddhi* or inseparability which obtains between substance and attribute and may be found between one substance and another".[3] So human beings are the important or vital parts of the whole or Absolute, which is *Vishista* and for this

Ramanuja's system is *Vishistadvaitavada.* As this qualified Monism or *Vishistadvaita vada* is compared with the concrete *Absolutism* of Tagore, these critics recognise Tagore as a concrete idealist of the Ramanuja School, and a follower of Vaisnavism. The concrete *Absolutism* of Tagore, as interpreted by this writer in this work, is the manifestation of divinity in human situation. So in turn it is realising a divinity beyond itself, but both are operative in a transcendent milieu, where the relation between the two as confronted orders are found together as functional. So this process is not the relation between the transcendent subject-Substance relational whole with parts, as in Ramanuja.

However, if the meaning and significance of Tagore's religion of Man is properly examined, it will be found that in the relation of the individual and the Absolute Tagore organises both the personal and impersonal aspects of Absolute and thus he, like all other contemporary Indian thinkers, relates *Theism* and *Absolutism* finally.

In the development of Tagore's idea of *Jivandevata,* it is already seen that God appears both as *Jivandevata* (or personal God) or as *Visvadevata* or impersonal Absolute in concrete human situation. Man, through the realisation of this infinite ideal in life becomes divine or infinite and the Absolute, through His manifestation in life of the finite individual becomes human. The realisation and the manifestation of this absolute ideal is possible in an absolute way, where He is conceived by Tagore as a Supreme Person, absolutely perfect and complete in and through His powers and qualities.

God, as the Supreme Person, manifests in His personal aspect, in human situation and human being in his pursuit for self-perfection moves towards the Supreme Personality. The individual man through his disinterested works surrenders in the form of love and service for others and thereby manifests the potential divinity in him and realises the Infinite Man in him, and finally becomes the Man as Infinite. This stage of manifestation of the Absolute, expresses His humanist nature in a very concrete form, and establishes an organic relation in and through the human beings and the finite world. This idea of the organic relation between the manifest God in the individual, and the adventure of the individual towards the Absolute in a concrete form reconciles Tagore's concrete and dual processes in confronted human situation, where the reality is fully manifest with possibilities.

Tagore's idea of concrete expression and possibility as already mentioned is not the concrete *Monism* of Hegel, who points to a conceptual Absolute unlike Tagore's which is a transcendent-experiential process in concretion. In the objective idealism of Hegel in contrast to Western subjective Idealism it is found that Absolute spirit is immanent in the world and in the finite mind is dialectically operative as the Absolute Idea. The Absolute Idea as the universal reason is manifest more and more in Nature, in the orders of matter, life and human mind. It is consciously manifest in the human, subjective mind in the individual, and in objectively in the Nature or cosmic situation of Society. According to Hegel's conceptual rationalist *Absolutism*, "That only is real which is rational", and "That only is rational which is real". It is a conceptual tautology. Natural world is the externalisation or experiential process of the human mind in its prospect for reaching the order of Universal Reason or Absolute and both are therefore rational and real which as only conceptual, falls short of the concrete that Tagore realises in India's Vedic-Upanishadic-Vedantic prospective universe.

Like Hegel, Tagore also takes the Absolute as universal reason or infinite mind, who, as the creator, represents the finite mind. Tagore argues that one's mind has an intimate relation with other's mind and for this one can understand the nature of other's mind. So one's mind is universal and is related with everything, and thus the universal reason which is in one, represents this natural world and other finite individuals also. To evaluate the nature of this concrete universal phenomenon, from India's transcendent-experiential perspective as mentioned, Tagore explains the significance of Indian *Gayatri Mantra: Om Bhurbhuvahsvah tatsaviturvarenyam bhargo devasya dhimahi dhiyo yo nah prachodayat,* and writes, "Let me contemplate the adorable splendour of Him who created the earth, the air and the starry spheres and sends the power of comprehension within our mind".[4] Tagore's realist attitude in the transcendent frame of reference is always experiential in the form of the manifestation of the reals in fullness and prospect.

This ideal of universal mind is properly explained by Tagore in the transcendent-experiential process of 'Creative personality' stemming from the *Vedas* to the twentieth century developments. Personality is a finite concept, but if Absolute is endowed with infinite will and self-consciousness and determination, then He has also a personality. This infinite personality is the constitution of infinite bliss and goodness. Here Tagore observes that God as infinite personality comprehends all finite personalities. So personality is interpreted by Tagore as the transcendental unity of all finite beings. Individual beings have imperfect personalities in experiential form and God has perfect personality, and Tagore, like Lotze, points out that God as perfect personality is manifested in finite personalities and thus finite becomes Infinite or Divine.

Regarding the manifestation of universal reason in and through the nature and finite minds, Hegel points out that there is a dialectic movement of universal reason in and through the finite existences and this movement is the evolutionary progress of universal ideal, manifested in the different stages of life and existences through the process of thesis, antithesis and synthesis. For example, D is thesis, Non-D is antithesis and both are reconciled in a synthesis F, which again becomes thesis. From the lower to the higher stage these categories move dialectically till the highest and comprehensive category of absolute self-consciousness is reached. So, the movement of this universal reality can be explained thus, "The reality is the universal, which goes out of itself, particularises itself, opposes itself, that it may reach the deepest and most comprehensive unity with itself". Self-consciousness is related to and distinguished from not-self or nature or material objects and reconciles them in a higher unity. The Absolute as the highest unity of self-consciousness is manifested in and through the distinction of self and not-self or finite existences or material objects and in their final unity or harmony. So Hegel's Absolute as the unity of highest self-consciousness contains the whole logico-dialectical process that reveals the life and world in the objective order where contradiction is taken at the root of all existences and everything opposes each other and is reconciled in the higher unity. Similarly the thought of an individual contradicts the other and proceeds dialectically towards the highest Unity through absolute thought. Tagore, accepts that the human reason is the manifestation of divine reason, but human life is not free from contradictions. The opposition between self and not-self or material necessities exists at the root of human existences. Tagore says, "Ever and anon have I spoken of the contradiction of opposites-life and death, power and love, egoism and universal Good". But Tagore maintains that man also has a potential power to overcome these contradictions which will be finally reconciled in a harmony or divine union. This can be possible through the development of religious consciousness. Tagore writes, '...the contradiction is resolved in man's religious consciousness. With the dawning of religious consciousness we realise that the harmony of the whole lies in accepting and transcending the contradiction of opposites'.[5] So Tagore, like Hegel, accepts the manifestation of divinity in human life, through which all contradictions of life and existences will be reconciled. But it should be mentioned here that for the reconciliation of contradictions, Tagore does not adopt any rational law or dialectical process as he points out that rational law is not sufficient to explain the mysterious development and manifestation of divinity in and through the human life.

It should be noted in this connection that Tagore's idea of the development of universality is not a conceptual abstract idealism of Hegel or of the absolutist stands of the post-Hegelians unless they presuppose the transcendental process as basic confronting all manifest orders as illuminated processes towards infinite possibilities, outmoding Western conceptual abstract idealist process of Hegel and post-Hegelian Absolutists, and touching the concrete realist-evolutionist modes beginning with Bergson and going beyond Bergsonian limitations. He, like Bergson, puts an emphasis on the intuitive faculty and observes that man has an intuitive power to realise the perfection or divine union, but unlike Bergson, he proceeds further beyond Bergson's mere vital urges (Elan Vital) to psychic and post-psychic prospects.

According to Tagore, the realisation of this perfection on the establishment of the divine union is possible through the development of the intimate relation between the confronted processes: human and Divine, in a transcendent experiential milieu, individual and the Absolute. Tagore, like Hegel, thinks that Absolute as a whole expresses Himself in and through the parts or finite individuals and the finite individuals become divine through the manifestation of absolute ideal in human life. This, Tagore says, can be possible through a concrete form of organic relation between the individual and the Absolute. A post-Hegelian, Pringle Pattison also points out that this form of relation is an organic one. He observes, "From the side of the Absolute the meaning of the finite process must lie in the creation of a world of individual spirits; for to such alone can He reveal Himself, and from them receive the answering tribute of love and adoration".[6] Similarly Tagore explains the nature of organic relation in the form of love that is a concrete confronted phenomenon in day-to-day human situation, where the finite individuals are the loved objects of the Absolute and the Absolute in turn is perfectly manifested in human life in the experiential form of love, as their eternal guide and possibility.

If the nature of this relation is carefully examined from Tagore's contexts of advanced Indian thought, it will be found that it is expressed in human life in different forms in different stages. In the life of Rabindranath we find the manifestation of love as absolute ideal in different forms in the true spirit of *Vaisnavite* process with the *Vedic-Upanishadic* insight, and through the expression of this ideal the relation with the Infinite becomes more and more intimate in and through the different stages of life.

In the first stage of this relation, the finite individuals, the nature and this world are taken as the objects of love and these are the lovers of the beloved who plays a game of love with them. In this stage the transcendent experience appears before Tagore's life as personal Lord or *Jivandevata* in the form of nature, and different human beings, different natural or material objects. To discuss the intimate relation with *Jivandevata* in the form of nature in manifestation through days and seasons Tagore says, "During the discussion of my own religious experience, I express my belief that the first stage of my realisation was through my feeling of intimacy with nature".[7] In this stage the idea of *Jivandevata* remains distinct from the nature and man, as these are taken as objects of love for His manifestation.

But this relation of love gradually becomes more intimate and the distinctness of God from the nature and man is removed and man, nature and God are intimately related with each other when *Jivandevata* appears as *Visvadevata.* Regarding this realisation Tagore speaks of, "...the daily meditation upon the infinite being which unites in one stream of creation my mind and the outer world".[8] The development of infinite ideal through the establishment of a more intimate relation of love, which is to be recognised as the second stage of organic relation between the individual and the transcendent. In this stage, the human life cannot be taken as distinct and unreal, it is identical with the confronted ever-changing reality where the transcendent exists in and through the other.

Through the evolution of finite nature of the individual person and the confronted nature in different forms, the transcendent infinite nature of man in its aspiration to realise the transcendent eternal human value in the form of the infinite ideal of unity in love, is developed. Man, in this stage, realises *So'ham* or 'I shall become *Brahman* for I am He'. So Tagore, like Green and Bosanquet emphasises the finite-infinite nature of the individuals in a different cultural context. Regarding the development of infinite nature of the individual, Green points out that man has a potential urge "to make himself what he has the possibility of becoming, but actually is not, and hence not merely, like the plant or animal, undergoes a process of development, but seeks to, and does develop himself". Regarding the development of this infinite nature, potential in the individual, Tagore similarly says in the background of advanced Indian cultural process that it is to become Infinite in the sense indicated above. He observes, "yes, we must become *Brahman.* We must not shrink from avowing this. Our existence is meaningless if we never can expect to realise the highest perfection that there is".[9] His, however, with his poetic songs in *Baul* and *Vaisnavite* spirit is a leap forward beyond mere transcendent *Brahman* to practical human situation and relationship.

This 'highest perfection' in concrete human situation is the final stage of development of transcendent consciousness in love, which according to Tagore, is the divine-union in the human orders and social process. Man, through the realisation of eternal human value of love, feels the existence of Universal Man in him, and Absolute as the highest ideal of Universal Man manifests Himself completely in the life of the individual and thus the eternal unity of the Absolute with the individual is finally established, which is Tagore's idea of 'at-homeness' in all or *Sarvanubhuti.* In this stage, there will be no distinctness, no separateness and differences, there will be only *One* and Tagore, like the *Vaisnava* thinkers also points out, 'There is One and the One says, 'I shall become many'...The One wanted to appreciate its unity in diversity,...'[10] This is the final stage of Tagore's idea of the religion of Man; where man, through the development of the relation of love with the Infinite in the different stages of life and society, finally establishes the relation of reciprocity, and becomes Infinite himself as *Manava Brahma.* Here, Tagore ultimately proves that God is eternal, man is eternal in concrete human situation, and the relation of love also is eternal, which is a perfect organic relation in a concrete form in social relations, that proves the idea of 'One in many'. Tagore moved with his select social process as if guiding the people by the insight of a *Rishi.*

Regarding the development of the final stage of advanced human relationship, it may be said that there is an evolutionary progress of the eternal ideal of love in human life, that, through the establishment of the relation of the individual through the transcendent-experiential process of love in the different stages of human life, finally makes a man infinite and founds the eternal relation through love. God or Reality also as love or bliss manifests Himself in and through the human life and finite world in different forms in different stages. So in this connection it may be said that God is a dynamic reality, who is manifested in and through the finite life and world. In *Balaka,* Tagore explains the dynamic aspect of Reality, where he observes, 'you move on, move on, move in speed'. Reality, through its manifestations in different stages of life in different forms and life-processes, through the development of eternal ideal in different stages, refers to the changing aspect of Reality, which has a similarity with the ideas of changing reality of the Heraclitians of ancient Greece, and changing Elan Vital of Bergson, a French, and the ever-growing mysterious religious experience of James, a continuer of Bergsonian Spirit in America, in the present century.

But it should be noted here that Tagore's idea of the dynamic aspect of reality is not final and ultimate in the static idealist-absolutist sense. Reality itself is manifested in and through the finite life and world in an evolutionary or dynamic process for the purpose of establishing the many-sidedness of reality from a transcedent unitive spirit, as of Plotinus of old in post-Aristotelian period. So Reality or God is not the change as it is, but He is in change, who finally is an integral process in varied aspects. In *Balaka,* Tagore says again, *Satya sei chirantan ek* or the eternal ideal of One, is Truth, or Integrality.

This Truth, according to Tagore, is eternally present as non-dual, complete and perfect. If we explain the proper nature of this eternal principle we find that this highest ideal becomes more and more real through its manifestation in and through the human life and the finite world. Again, if the proper significance of life and world is explained, it is found that they try to realise this highest ideal in different stages till the final end of highest integrality is established. So from the point of view of Truth it is found that there is a degree of manifestation of Reality, and from the context of the finite life, we find a degree of realisation of this ideal.

Thus, in this explanation, it is seen that this world and all laws that guide this world are evolved from the divine aspect of Truth or Reality. In *Santiniketan,* Tagore explains the different aspects of Truth in *Upanishadic* ways that are *Sivam, Sundaram, Anandam* and *Santam.* The Eternal presence is *Anandam* or Bliss or *Rasa-Raso vai sah.* All manifest objects of this world originate from this aspect of the Eternal possibility-*Anandaddhyeva Khalvimani bhutani jayante.* This perennial possibility is good or *Sivam* and beautiful or *Sundaram* as these characters are expressed in Bliss or *Anandam.* He is also quiet or *Santam* as He realises order or harmony among the different disorders or contradictions of life like happiness and sorrows, pleasure and pain, life and death, etc. Finally He effectualises a perfect harmony among all the differences and diversities. This ultimate spirit of harmony *exists* in 'the world outside' and in 'the world within', that is interpreted by Tagore, "We learn to perceive the Unity held together by the one Eternal Spirit, whose power creates the Earth, the Sky, and the Stars, and at the same time irradiates our minds with the light of a consciousness that moves and exists in unbroken continuity with the outer world".[11]

Thus, it is observed that God or the Eternal is manifest in and through this finite life in the finite world in different degrees. So it may be said that everything of this finite world comes out of the eternal and infinite nature of God which is explained by Radhakrishnan thus : "While the whole universe is regarded by Rabindranath as the expression of God still different things express God in different degrees. He thus admits the conception of degrees of reality."[12] But ultimately the Infinite Truth or Reality is perfectly manifested in the life of man. In *Sadhana* Tagore explains, "The revèalment of the infinite in the finite, which is the motive of all creation is not seen in its perfection in the starry heavens, in the beauty of the flowers. It is in the soul of man."

So the expression of potential infiniteness in the finite, is the fundamental end of creation or evolution, through which the idea of Truth as Infinite, is manifested in life and in the world in different degrees. The degree of manifestations of Truth is explained by Tagore as an evolutionary progress of the realisation of Truth in human life in different stages in this finite world. In *Manuser Dharma,* Tagore points out, 'In the vast evolution of the world we come across the first meaning in life particles, then in animals and finally in man'. This realisation of meaning means the revelation of Truth that is fully revealed or relished not in external not in external space or time, but in the inner region of human being. Tagore observes, "We must know that the evolution process of the world has made its progress towards the revelation of its truth-that is to say, some inner value which is not in the extension in space and duration in time".[13]

The realisation of these inner values in the inner spirit of man, is the manifestation of different humanistic ideals, which, in the opinion of Tagore, is also eternal. This process of realisation makes the expression of eternality in life possible and also makes the union of finite with the Infinite significant. In *Manuser Dharma,* Tagore explains the significance of this process, 'The outer doors begin to open one after the other, till we come to the innermost region of man. Here we find the finite soaked in the infinite'. This is the infinite nature of man that transcends the limits of physical world and organism and makes him immortal. This immortality is beyond the spatial and temporal differences and diversities. Tagore interprets, "What is it in man that asserts its immortality in spite of the obvious fact of death? It is not his physical body or his mental organisation. It is that deeper unity, that ultimate mystery in him, which from the centre of his world, radiates towards its circumference; which is in the body, yet transcends his body...It is the personality of man, conscious of its inexhaustible abundance".[14] This personality of man inspires him to proceed towards the deeper unity that is the realisation of the highest perfection in life. In *Sadhana,* Tagore points out, "Our existence is meaningless if we never can expect to realise the highest perfection that there is". This highest perfection, according to Tagore, is a perfect union between finite and Infinite. This is explained by Tagore thus: 'I cannot think of any other idea but this. I will definitely say-I shall become the Infinite...'[15] This eternal or divine union manifests a complete view of man's life that produces a harmony or unity among all contradictions or diversities. In *Atmaparichaya,* Tagore explains, 'with the dawning of religious consciousness we realise that the harmony of the whole lies in accepting and transcending the contradiction of opposites'.

Tagore, like all other Indian thinkers of his time, points out that God as the eternal value is manifested in all the objects of the world, but he emphasises also that the highest value of integral experience is finally manifested in the inner spirit or heart of man as the development of universality in love and service for others. In '*Dharma*', elaborating the character of human personality, Tagore writes, 'the exchange of our heart is not possible with water, land, planets and stars as our good deeds have no relation with them'. The intimate relation through human quality as love and service for others, can only develop the universality in the personality of man. So a man, in the opinion of Tagore, can realise his universal existence as the manifestation of eternal value of divine unity in knowledge, love and action. In '*Dharma*' Tagore presents this observation with proper insight thus: 'We can only have man completely in knowledge, love and action. For this, the perfect realisation of the Absolute is possible for man within man alone'. In this observation of Tagore, it is found that man is the proper medium through which God as the eternal or universal value of unity is perfectly manifested.

Thus, it may be said that the essential nature of man is to develop this integrality or universality in his own existence. This, Tagore points out, is the fundamental process of human life as the religion of Man that expresses the universal character of man through the establishment of unity of individuality and universality in love. This, according to Tagore, is the meditation on humanity or *Manusyatver Tapasya.* The significance of this process of life has been interpreted again by Tagore in his *Manuser Dharma* in contrasting ways, thus: 'the animal says, 'enjoy in the way of the natural religion'. Man says, 'meditate in the way of the religion of Man'.' So the religion of Man, as has been developed in this discourse, is the proper expression of human nature, which is the meditation or the realisation of universality through love. Introduction of love in life is to realise the divinity or Godness in man as the development of his universal personality, that is the final, which, finally is the accomplishment of eternal value as Truth, Beauty and Goodness. The realisation of this highest value in life and existence is the inauguration of God in man that finally leads to the introduction of harmony in individual and social existence through the elimination of poor contradictions of disharmonies as evils of this world.

Notes

1. Rabindranath Tagore, *Jivansmriti* (1st edn.), p. 249.
2. C.F. Andrews (ed.), *Thoughts from Tagore,* p. 29.
3. M. Hiriyana, *Outlines of Indian Philosophy,* p. 399.
4. Rabindranath Tagore, *The Religion of Man,* p. 93.
5. Rabindranath Tagore, 'Amar Dharma', *Atmaparichaya.*
6. P. Pattison, *The Idea of God* (2nd edn.), p. 295.
7. Rabindranath Tagore, *The Religion of Man,* p. 12.
8. *Ibid.*, p. 58.
9. Rabindranath Tagore, *Sadhana,* p. 155.
10. Rabindranath Tagore, 'Sahitya Tattva', *Prabasi.*

11. Rabindranath Tagore, *Sadhana,* p. 9.
12. Dr S. Radhakrishnan, *The Philosophy of Rabindranath Tagore,* p. 33.
13. Rabindranath Tagore, *The Religion of Man,* p. 18.
14. Rabindranath Tagore, *Personality,* p. 38.
15. Rabindranath Tagore, *Santiniketan,* Vol. II, p. 336.

CHAPTER - 5

Good and Evil: Social Contradictions and Reconciliation in Unity

Ultimate Reality, as interpreted so far in Tagore's religion of Man, is one and is the substratum of the supreme values like Truth, Beauty, Goodness and Bliss as *Satyam, Sundaram, Sivam* and *Anandam* and is the final harmony of all these values. So in Tagore's thought we see that Truth is One-Eternal which is a complete goodness and beauty and perfect bliss.

In Tagore's religion of Man we get a view about the supreme values or ideals in the background of the controversial problem regarding the subjectivity and objectivity of values. In the history of Philosophy we find an endless discussion about the nature and existence of values. Some people are of opinion that values are related to human circumstances and are subjectively real. Lotze observes, "What we mean by value in the world lies wholly in the feeling of satisfaction or pleasure which we experience from it". Satisfaction or pleasure is the state of feeling in mind, so value is purely subjective. Some thinkers hold that truth, goodness and beauty are the expressions of repressed desires and feelings. Freud's doctrine of value is related to the play theory and the voluntaristic theory. Freud recognises both play and art as imaginative expressions and fulfillment of wish. Values according to him, are akin to day dreaming and are the expressions of repressed and unfulfilled sex-feeling and spite-wishes due to their being thwarted.[1] Values, in the opinion of these thinkers, are the expressions of desires or feelings. Spinoza points out "men think they desire things because they are good; but in truth things are good because men desire them". Again Perry, a neo-Realist, accepts value as an object of interest. Pragmatic theory, Logical Positivism make values subjective, relative and mind-dependent.

But these views are philosophically unsound. Feeling of satisfaction and mental interests or desires may be the index of value, but is not value as such. Rabindranath also points out that valueing is not the matter of feeling, it expresses the nature of the object. Artistic creation of man may express his feeling or mental attitude, but is not the mere product of imagination. There must be some qualities or elements in the object that determine our feeling or attitude towards it. In '*Sahityer Pran*', Tagore writes, 'Literature is not merely the photography of Nature but an expression of objective Nature through our emotions'.[2]

So it may be pointed out that values are not mere expressions of feeling or desire. Some thinkers hold that value judgement is universal as it deals with an objective fact. Moore and Hartmann support the objectivity of value. But the objective value property, according to these thinkers, cannot be compared to the empirical property of the object. Like the empirical property, value property is not observed and verified in the mere objective form; so it cannot be explained in a simple manner. For this, Moore in his '*Principia Ethica*' explains the nature of value as indefinable concept. He says, "Good is simple, unanalysable, indefinable".[3] To define value property in relation to empirical property is to commit the 'naturalistic fallacy'. This type of non-empirical, non-natural, objective property, according to Moore, can be realised by direct insight or intuition. Nicolai Hartmann takes values as 'essences', distinguished from 'existents' and 'qualities'. Objects express values which are essences and real, but are not existents. They cannot be known in the same way as ordinary qualities are, but can be known directly through 'the sense of value'. Values, according to Kant, are not ordinary qualities, but are similar to the *a priori* forms of experience. Hartmann's idea of value is similar to the idea of Plato, and these values are not 'existents', but 'subsistent', real and unchanging.[4] Hartmann takes value as independent both of existence and of mind. He points out "Values have actually an existence in themselves, independent of all imagination and longing".[5] According to these views, values are independent of human mind and are purely objective. Then comes Alexander, a modern Realist, who maintains that values are both subjective and objective and points out that value is a subjectively conditioned objective quality. Regarding values he says, "They imply amalgamation of the object with the human appreciation of it".

So Tagore's idea as evident from the above discourse is not comparable with the psychological ideas of Freud or philosophical notions of Western thinkers from Spinoza to the logical positivists. Value, in the observation of Tagore, is not merely subjective but also is the expression of objective Nature. By objective Nature, Tagore means, Nature in developments in human personality through the values as developed above, from the transcendent-experiential perspective. Tagore's interpretation of values as manifests in human personalist - situation is not comparable in the Western frame of reference from Plato to Kant or from Kant to Hartmann and Moore. For the values in prospects of Truth, Beauty, Goodness and Bliss, as developed above by Tagore, is not other worldly as Plato held, nor is it *a priori* process as Kant held, nor again it is Hartmann's repetition of Platonism, interpreting his other worldly notion of ideas of values, as subsistents merely, due to the phenomenological trends of his time; not finally the values are creations of immediate intuition. Rather Tagore's interpretation of values can be related to British Alexander's view of the qualitative features as values, as emergent qualitative processes of appreciation in interpersonal situations. The Matrix of which is the relativity between space and time as continuum. But Tagore will differ from Alexander's evolutionary concept in Spatio-Tamporal Matrix, for Tagore's transcendent-experiential base is not merely a specific Matrix, but it is a continuum of many dimensional integral processes with prospects as transcendent value with experiential expansion.

So all these thoughts from Plato to Alexander of the West present the view that values are understood always in varied senses of objective reality, but Rabindranath Tagore's position by contrast is that values, as empirical emergences in human personality situations, have to be construed in transcendent-experiential possibilities, as elevating integral processes. He, like Hartmann, observes in an aspect that man is not the creator of values, but entertains them in an other worldly sense in their prospective contexts, elevating man towards Divinity. Truth is coherence and harmony among the values which are revealed to us as ideals in the human minds. Taylor rightly points out, "The Absolute contains all finite existence, and contains it as a perfectly harmonious system. And, therefore, all finite aspirations must somehow be realised in the structure of the Absolute whole, though not necessarily in the way in which we, as beings of limited knowledge and goodness, actually wish it to be realised. The Absolute whole is thus the concrete individual reality in which our ideals have actual existence. As all our ideas themselves are but so many expressions of our place in the system of our relation to the rest of it, so the system itself is their concrete harmonious embodiment".[6] It should be noted in this connection that the values are not separative ideals but integral processes. So to compare values even in Taylor's somewhat comprehensive idea is to lower Tagore to an empirical mode of deliberation without the comprehensive integral attitude of Tagore's personality process.

Again objective reality or truth of Rabindranath can be divided into factual truth or 'tathya', which is restricted or limited, partial and many, and unrestricted or integral Truth as Absolute which is one, complete and perfect. This unrestricted or integral Truth as the final substratum of values, is manifested through the facts or limited truths. In this way absolute ideals or supreme values are also expressed in the life of human beings, as they possess an infinite power to realise the infinite ideals. In *Personality* Tagore explains, "In our life we have one side which is finite, where we exhaust ourselves at every step, and we have another side, where our aspiration, enjoyment and sacrifice are infinite. This infinite side of man must have its revealments in some symbols which have the elements of immortality. There it naturally seeks perfection".[7] Values or ideals in Absolute, an eternal embodiment of truth, beauty and goodness, inspire the infinite power of man to acquire the higher order for the fulfillment of his religious aspiration. Pringle Pattison truly observes, "Truth, Beauty,

Goodness have no reality as self-existent abstractions; they have no meaning apart from conscious experience. They carry us, therefore, to a primal Mind in whose experience they are eternally realised. God himself is at once the supreme Reality and the supreme value. And the highest conception we can form of perfect personality is Love, -the self-giving Love which expands itself for others, and lives in all their joys and sorrows. Such love is the ultimate value of which the universe is the manifestation. The inmost being of God is not solely the realisation of eternal Truth and the enjoyment of perfect Beauty, but pre-eminently the exercise and fruition of his nature as love".[8] Rabindranath from his transcendent-experiential perspective, like Pringle Pattison's Cosmic-Theistic aspects, finds the expression of truth and joy in all parts of life and world. He says, "Truth is everywhere, therefore, everything is the object of our knowledge. Beauty is omnipresent, therefore, everything is capable of giving us joy".[9]

Man realises the perfection, joy or truth not through an empirical way, they are placed in transcendent-experiential process when he intuitively realises the intrinsic values of Reality. Ross, Ewing and others also recognise the form of intuition. Man's intuitive realisation of supreme value means realisation of his infinite personality which is intimately related with the infinite quality. This is an 'Innermost beauty nearer to man'.[10] This, according to Tagore, is goodness or *Mangala.* As goodness is 'innermost beauty' of man, so it exists in the power of *surplus* of human beings. This eternal power of *surplus* in man is expressed through his creative activities. So the realisation of goodness through man's creative activity is the proper way for the realisation of his infinite self. Eudemonists, like Hegel, also regard self-realisation as the highest good, that is possible through self-sacrifice. In this connection we may refer to Hegel's dictum 'Die to live'. The more we can rise above our poor, individual and private self and can identify ourselves with wider and social life, the more we realise higher, social and universal self. From his transcendent-experiential perspective, Tagore also points out that there is a harmony in the individual self and through the creative activity by means of self-sacrifice, we can realise unity or harmony in us. Goodness is a spiritual truth, which is expressed in human life. Tagore uses 'goodness' and 'religion' in the same way as he thinks that the realisation of goodness in life is the fundamental end of the religion of Man.

Tagore considers, Truth, beauty, goodness and other supreme values from an integral transcendent perspective. But this integral approach, according to Tagore, is not static identity, but it is a dynamic experiential process of manifestation through diversities. In this connection we may refer to Bosanquet's view about the concrete universal, where he points out, "The universal in the form of a world refers to diversity of content within every member, as the universal in the form of a class neglects it. Such a diversity recognised as a unity; a macrocosm constituted by microcosm, is the type of the concrete universal".[11]

In *The Religion of Man,* Tagore interpretes the integral process of truth, beauty and goodness, in the life of man through the establishment of relation of one with the other. This truth-beauty identity was realised by others as well. We may refer to the idea of an English poet in this context. Keats points out that beauty is truth, truth is beauty. Herbert relates good with beauty and Wollaston relates good with truth. Truth is the harmony of ideas and judgments, beauty is the harmony of form with matter, and good is the harmony of reason with the sensibility. So Truth creates an order among the sensual desires. In our ordinary life we are guided by the personal desire or self-interest that creates badness or contradiction in life and society. Goodness, as the inner beauty of a man, stands against any type of badness or evil through the establishment of selflessness in life and action that relates a man with all human beings. So selfless or disinterested action of man can form a beauty in his life that refers to Kant's idea in which it is observed, "entirely disinterested satisfaction is called beautiful".[12] The establishment of goodness, through the selfless activities, forms an interrelation among men in the world, both of the West and East in general. This Idea of goodness is similar to the idea of *Maitri* of Buddha who "preached *Maitri*-the relationship of harmony-not only with human beings but with all creation..."[13]

Harmony, according to Tagore, exists in man's inner power of *surplus* which is his idea of beauty as related to that of goodness. When man overcomes his poor ego and feels the existence of universal unity or harmony in him, he can realise the goodness which is the realisation of universal self. This realisation is possible through love, as love is the substratum of goodness. Love is the spiritual truth which is explained by Tagore, 'Love is a relation of oneself with the other, which is intimate, and truest of all'.[14] This ideal of love exists in the very nature of man that inspires him to love others and to sacrifice for other man. So the realisation of goodness through love helps a man to realise a higher or greater self in him. Tagore explains, 'To live the life of goodness is to live the life of all'.[15] In this way, goodness in thought, activity and life, rouses the feeling of a comprehensive consciousness or *sarvanubhuti,* as the feeling of at hominess in one. Finally goodness with love establishes a unity of man with the Universal Man that is the realisation of infinite personality in him, Tagore explains, "And this consciousness of the Infinite, in the personal man, ever strives to make its expressions immortal and to make the whole world its own. In art the person in us is sending its answer to the Supreme Person, who reveals Himself to us in a world of endless beauty across the lightless world of facts".[16] So the realisation of infinite personality crossing all the limitation of confronted facts and contradictions or differences of life, is the realisation of complete humanity where a perfect unity among all men is established. This, according to Tagore, is the final establishment of supreme goodness in human life.

But the limited outlook on life giving rise to the contradictions and differences, produces evil in life. The transcendent integrality which sustains one with all, is goodness; and the difference, which creates many limitations and separates one from the other due to loss of transcendent outlook, is evil. So evil in life and society due to the lack of transcendent vision creates hindrances on the way towards the foundation of integral vision of infiniteness in finite life. But, in *The Religion of Man* Tagore interprets the ideal of humanity as an integral experience from an inner power of transcendent-experiential process. The differences that exist in the inner nature of man are resolved, and man proceeds towards perfection or completeness in life. Tagore says, "Religion means humanity-fireness is the nature of fire, animality is the nature of animal, completeness of man is also the proper nature of man". If Tagore explains the nature of man in this way, then evil has no place in the experience of the religion of Man. For this, some commentators charge against him about 'His notion about evil is not relevant....'[17] But if we follow his transcendent-experiential process as sustaining the core of the religion of Man and importance of evil in human situation, only reflects a lack of transcendental insight.

In the interpretation of the religion of Man Tagore shows that the problem of good and evil exists in the very nature of man. Man is born with two necessities of life, one is for his ordinary needs of life, e.g., want for bread, clothes, shelter, etc., and other is the vital need of elevating himself through religious experience as has been developed in this discourse. Tagore observes, "Religion has its genesis in man's desire to be released from the limitation of what it is. The crudest magical rites, however, weird or meaningless they may appear, have in some vague manner this freedom for their object. Man is the only creature who is a born rebel, never reconciled to the conditions of the existence. In the depth of his nature he carries an instinctive faith in the paradox that the completeness of reality consists in the endless contradiction of what does exist and what should exist".[18]

But so long as man exists in his narrow limitation of life, he follows the claims of poor ego and satisfies his ordinary needs or *Jivadharma.* This procedure of his life makes him alone, separate and selfish. Selfishness and narrowness of heart are the main causes of the evils of human life and society. The activities guided by selfishness create disunity or disharmony among men, which are responsible for producing different types of evils. Too much personal demands, self-interests, individual necessities, etc., increase ordinary desires of man that drive him to proceed towards the fulfillment of gross happiness and poor enjoyments. Aristotle also points out that to seek mere happiness is to create evil. Thus, mere satisfaction of interest and fulfillment of narrow selfishness make a man ego-centric, which is the root cause of the evil in individual's life. In this connection Huxley's opinion may also be referred to. He says, "...the Fall...is due exclusively to ego-centric use of the free will,...".[19] But one should bear in mind that Tagore's consideration of social evils as stemming out of man's lack of transcendent-experiential attitude should not be considered either from intellectual perspective or in any ordinary sense. Interpreting the nature of evil caused by man's selfishness or ego-centric use of his will, Tagore classifies it into moral and social evil. Sins committed by men voluntarily are moral evils. These evils are created by man for his own individual or personal interest. These are arson, murders, adultery, rape, cruelty, theft, etc. These evils can touch the interest of a man or few men on the personal level.

But when evils touch the general interest of men on the social level, they may be called social evils. These evils due to man's narrow interests, create different limitations or differences among men. In India we find different types of racial and communal differences. Due to religious fanaticism, orthodoxy or other selfish views we find clashes between the Hindus, Muslims, etc. Another social evil in India is the evil of untouchability, which exists in the Hindu society where higher caste Hindus impose many limitations on the life of lower caste Hindus. In different writings, Tagore criticises these sectional views of men and in *Gitanjali, Gora,* he writes on the transcendental integrality of Man's Nature. In the Bengali article '*Bharatvarsher Itihaser Dhara*', he writes, 'the truth of all the races of the world can be truly realised only through the truth of one's own'.[20]

Another social evil is due to the industrial development through the influence of modern science. The development of big industry and machine is creating a mechanical relation among men that kills the eternal spirit in man and increases narrow outlook or power of enjoyment. In this connection Tagore points out that man is using science and machine in a destructive sense, that is, for the fulfillment of his own personal interest. But it should be used for general good, that is, for the development of life of the people in general and in truly creative sense. In his plays *Muktadhara, Raktakaravi,* etc., Tagore establishes the victory of life over machine. In *The Religion of Man* he points out, "Let us know that the Machine is good when it helps, but not so when it exploits life; that science is great when it destroys evil, but not when the two enter into unholy alliance."[21]

This 'unholy alliance' between science and machine increases the power of different nations of the world and develops a violent *nationalism*. This nationalism is nothing but a social evil as it whets the greed of a nation or state for the fulfillment of its own interest. This will lead to war which is nothing but the destruction of mankind. In different writings, Tagore criticises this global evil that affects the different nations in their chase for a super power. In *Prayaschitya, Char Adhyay,* etc., he establishes the ideal of non-violence or *ahimsa* against the political weapon of violence. In this connection Tagore points out that modern nations are politically free; but political freedom is not freedom in the true sense of the term as it develops the narrow political craving for power of domination over others. Proper meaning of freedom is the freedom of mind which cultivates the disinterested feeling of love for others and through this selfless love an intimate relation among men can be possible. This is the highest social ideal which is to be practiced by all nations. Regarding this Tagore points out, "The ideals that strive to take form in social institutions have two objects. One is to regulate our passions and appetites for the harmonious development of man, and the other is to help him to cultivate disinterested love for his fellow-creatures. Therefore, society is the expression of those moral and spiritual aspirations of man which belong to his higher nature".[22] If man is able to realise his higher nature, he will learn to regard the ideal of other nation and through this procedure the higher ideal of *internationalism* among men of different nations will be established.

We find that the narrowness of heart, selfish attitude and misuse of the freedom of will are the proper causes of moral and social evils. Besides these moral and social evils, there are physical or natural calamities, e.g., floods, cyclones, earthquakes, famines, etc. These are natural disasters leading to general sufferings, over which man has no control. These events are due to the violations of laws of nature. But imperfections of man are the causes of evils and these can be removed by the proper realisation of the perfection of human nature. Man is endowed with the freedom of will, hence he is free to accept good through the realisation of perfection or unity, or evil through narrow and selfish activities in the world. Tagore always draws attention to the transcendent-experiential process which man can realise in the depth of his freedom and achieve his objective for the good of humanity both as an individual and as a nation. Martineau truly points out from a theistic perspective, "It is because He is Holy and cannot be content with an immoral world where all the perfection is given and none is earned, that He refuses to render guilt impossible and inward harmony mechanical".[23] But Spinoza, a pantheist, denies human freedom and points out that evils are nothing but illusory appearances. He says "As for the terms good and bad they indicate nothing positive considered in themselves ...For one and the same thing can at the same time be good, bad and indifferent".[24] But we cannot deny evil by calling it an illusion. As illusion also requires an explanation, so the existence of evil cannot be denied. Rabindranath also does not explain evil as an illusion. Evils like sorrows and sufferings of human life are not unreal. These, according to Tagore, are created due to imperfections in the worldly life of man which will lead to an incomplete realisation of truth. Tagore's attitude from his transcendent-experiential perspective is neither theistic like Martineau, nor pantheistic like Spinoza. He has broad attitude towards the confronted experience.

In this connection theists point out that everything in this world is finite. Finite means limitation which produces imperfection as the cause of evil. So evil is an inevitable result of finitude. Rabindranath from his transcendent attitude rightly points out that evils of finite beings exist in this material world. Evil and finiteness are inter-related and only for finiteness and limitation evil is created in human situation. It is mostly man-made in his failure to accept the transcendent ideals.

But it may also be mentioned that evil has a good purpose as it offers a scope for the realisation of good through the moral training of man. In the world there are the existences of both good and evil. Through the evil of life man can also learn how to overcome it. So evil will lead to good in life. Leibnitz observes, "Afflictions are for the time being evil, but in effect good, since they are shortcuts to a greater perfection".[25] Tagore's transcendental ideals as developed here, is not an adherence to a conceptualist like Western Leibnitz, who has a self-created argument of his own.

So, in Tagore's philosophy, we find that no evil is permanent or absolute, as it influences a man to remove all his imperfection through the realisation of his perfect nature. From Tagore's transcendental attitude "Evil cannot altogether arrest the course of life on the highway and rob it of its possessions. For the evil has to pass on, it has to grow into good, it cannot stand and give battle to all".[26]

Now in this context the idea of *pantheism* may also be referred to, which accepts the relativity of evil and points out that evil is a necessary step or a means to the good. Evil is neither the denial of goodness, nor an illusion, nor absolutely necessary. Evil, appears as an absolute evil due to imperfect realisation of truth. Evil and fighting for freedom from evil are real as the later procedure of life inspires man to realise higher freedom as harmony. Hegel rightly points out that life is for an achievement of higher unity in diversity. Tagore also observes that the feeling of evil is not absolute, for feeling of Absolute is the feeling of Truth which is unity or harmony. This higher feeling of life does not give us pain, as feeling of Truth is Absolute Bliss or *Ananda.*

Evils of life, according to Tagore, appear as evil due to incomplete outlook of human life or human nature. But infinite personality of man transforms all the evils of his life into goodness. Through different selfless activities; man tries to realise infiniteness that produces a harmony between good and evil. In this way the evil turns into good through the establishment of harmony in life and activities of man. Rabindranath does not deny the existence of evil as illusion; on the other hand, he has explained its nature and existence in the light of Truth or Absolute Goodness that transforms evil into goodness. In this connection Tagore explains the importance of evil in human life as he thinks that through pains and sufferings, man tries to overcome all his limitations and contradictions and thus finally realises the perfection in him. Tagore observes, "It is pain which is our true wealth of imperfect beings, and has made us great and worthy to take our seat with the perfect".[27] Now it may be said that Tagore does not question the reality of this world and worldly sufferings. Through these worldly sufferings man gradually learns to be free from all pains and sufferings in which he may be helplessly placed by forces, over which he has no control. Through his transcendental-experiential attitude, expressed through the disinterested feeling and selfless activities, man can realise the highest Truth in life, which is perfect harmony or *Advaitam* or Absolute Goodness or *Sivam.* So the infinite personality of man which is intimately related *with* all men as Universal Man is free from all evils. Evils come from the finiteness or limitedness of human life which is responsible for the creation of contradictions and paradoxes. But to conquer all these contradictions or evils of human life is to develop infinite personality through the cultivation of goodness. Tagore says, "...when a man begins to have an extended vision of his true self, when he realises that he is much more than at present he seems to be, he begins to get conscious of his moral nature".[28] Thus, through the proper realisation of his own *nature* man can understand the true significance of the religion of Man that influences him to overcome all the conflicts of life and to proceed towards a perfect condition which is realisable. For this reason Tagore expresses the *Upanishadic* Visions, in his own ways, "...man who affords to pay thus-'lead me on from unreality to the realm of the Real, from darkness and desolation to the safety-zone of Light supernal', the verb 'to lead' imports, for aught we know, to cause to go straight across a pathway and not to go round about it or avoid it".[29]

The end of Tagore's religion of Man is to conquer or to overcome the evil, but not to avoid it; nor to reject its existence. The conflict of self and not self, or selfishness or unselfishness, which is the proper cause of evil, can be solved through the expansion of heart or mind through selfless activities. Selflessness or disinterested attitude towards life finally lead to ultimate freedom from all sufferings through the cultivation of moral, perfect and infinite nature of Man as Truth in him. From this transcendent-experiential attitude, expressed in *Dharma,* Tagore explains the eternal craving of man, 'O, the mighty'.

"One, you are leading mankind from untruth to Truth, darkness to light and mortality to immortality but the path of salvation lies through pains, evils and sufferings."[30]

Pains, evils and sufferings can be conquered and salvation of man from all evils can be achieved, when man can remove all his limitations or finiteness and can realise Infinite or Universal Man in him through the establishment of goodness or perfect harmony in life. This can be possible through love and work for all, as Tagore observes, "To live the life of goodness is to live the life of all".[31] It should be mentioned that Tagore's transcendent-experiential attitude is not necessarily philosophic, religious, moral or social, it utilises the best of the ideals of these processes.

Notes

1. Holt, *A Modern Book of Aesthetics,* pp. 132-7.
2. Rabindranath Tagore, 'Sahityer Pran', *Sahitya,* (3rd edn.).
3. G.E. Moore, *Principia Ethica,* p. 37.
4. N. Hartmann, *Ethics,* Vol. 1.
5. *Ibid.*, p. 93.
6. Taylor, *Elements of Metaphysics,* p. 394.
7. Rabindranath Tagore, *Personality,* p. 30.
8. Pringle pattison, *The Idea of Immortality,* p. 190.
9. Rabindranath Tagore, *Sadhana,* p. 138.
10. Rabindranath Tagore, 'Sahitya' *Rabindrarachanavali* (Cent. Edn.), Cent. Vol. XIII, p. 756.
11. Bosanquet, *The Principle of Individuality and Value,* p. 38.
12. Kant, *The Critique of Judgement.*
13. C.F. Andrews (ed.), *Thoughts from Tagore,* p. 105.
14. Rabindranath Tagore, *Manuser Dharma.*
15. Rabindranath Tagore, *"Sadhana,* pp. 56-57.
16. Rabindranath Tagore, *Personality,* p. 38.
17. Subodh Chandra Sengupta, 'Introduction', *Rabindra Darshan* by Hiranmay Bandyopadhyay.
18. C.F. Andrews (ed.), *Thoughts from Tagore,* p. 207.
19. A.Huxley, *Tue Perennial Philosophy,* p. 209.
20. Charu Chandra Banerjee, *Rabi Rashmi,* Vol. II, p. 329.
21. Rabindranath Tagore, *The Religion of Man,* p. 164.

22. Rabindranath Tagore, *Nationalism,* p. 120.
23. Martineau, *The Study of Religion.*
24. G.E. Moore, *Ethics,* IV.
25. Leibnitz, *Philosophical Writings,* p. 41.
26. Rabindranath Tagore, *Sadhana,* p. 52.
27. *Ibid.*, pp. 64-65.
28. *Ibid.,* p. 54.
29. Dr S.K. Das, *Tagore and the Perennial Problems of Philosophy,* p. 56.
30. Rabindranath Tagore, *Dharma,* p. 107.
31. Rabindranath Tagore, *Sadhana,* pp. 56-57.

Chapter - 6

Freedom in Unity: Humanistic Processes of Realising Universality

In the religion of Man, Tagore explains the nature of Reality and evaluates the nature of man against the background of Reality in manifestation in cosmic and human situations. The life of man, Tagore observes, stands on the realistic admission of man's helplessness, being subject to cosmic and social forces. But man himself with social and internationalist cooperative attitude can overcome the obstructive processes and can rise to a tolerably perfect social and internationalist frame of reference, with the elements of love, cooperation and mutual appreciation.

Two fundamental points in this connection are to be considered: (a) the importance of ways for the realisation of Reality and (b) the proper nature of Reality at the final state of life which is the salvation from evils and sufferings. These two important objectives of any intellectual discourse from Myth to Philosophy, Religions and Sciences are realisable through human prospects. Important views or humanistic ideals are to be discussed in this connection and are also to be compared with Tagore's thought which are to be critically evaluated in the background of his religion of Man, developing his idea of salvation or freedom which Tagore has developed comprehensively.

The term 'Salvation' in Indian philosophy is *Mukti* or freedom, but Tagore has given an extended meaning to this process from his transcendent-experiential attitude explained in this discourse.

Mukti, according to Panini, is originated from *Much* which is *Mokshana.* The meaning of *Moksha* or *Mukti,* is the salvation from sorrows and suffering and attainment of ultimate peace and pleasure. All thinkers, except Indian Materialists or Charvakas, recognise it as the highest goal or summum bonum of human life. But Charvakas and other Western materialists also recognise that hedone or enjoyment of material pleasure in this world should be the fundamental end of human life. The problem of salvation or freedom as *Mukti* according to them, does not arise at all, as death is the end of life.

But the idea of salvation or freedom occupies an important place in Indian philosophy and religion. This material world has creation and destruction, and individual life also has birth, rebirth and death. To stop this process of life is to be liberated from all limitations and contradictions and the final state of salvation or freedom is to be reached. In this state, an essential and intimate relation of oneness of the individual with the Absolute or Ultimate Reality can be established, when the individual or *Jiva* will be totally free from the bondage of non-eternal worldly happiness and sufferings. In the *Upanishads* the liberated condition is *Anitya samsara-sukha-duhkha-vishaya-samasta- kshetra-mamata bandhaksayo mokshah.* According to the *Vedas* and the *Upanishads,* salvation or freedom means the attainment of *Amritatva,* where the individual self enters into the ocean of Absolute like a river meeting the Sea and thus an individual self being reduced to the Universal Self or Absolute.[1]

Vaisnava Philosophy, in further developments in consequent realist processes in India's social developments through the centuries, admits three types of *Jivas* or individuals: (a) *Nitya-siddha Jiva.* who is always free, (b) *Sadhansiddha Jiva* who becomes free through meditation and (c) *Baddhya Jiva* who lives in the bondage of this material world. Matter or this material world is the cause of bondage that creates ignorance or *avidya* and thus through the influence of *avidya,* man takes everything of this world as real and so cannot realise the proper nature of reality. Jaina thinkers also point out that the influence of matter or *pudgala* is the cause of sufferings of human life. Ignorance of reality and affection through four passions, *krodha* or anger, *lobha* or greed, *mana* or pride and *maya* or delusion, called

Kashaya attract the flow of karmic matter that unites the soul with the body or the bondage of the material world. *Samyak Darshana* or Right Faith, *Jnana* or Knowledge and *Charitra* or Conduct are the *tri-ratna* or three jewels of Jainism, which are the only ways for the attainment of perfection in life. So, according to these thinkers, freedom from the attachment of matter or material world and attainment of the perfect state of life, is salvation. This is differently realised by Buddha in a state of *Nirvana* which is the highest and the indestructible state-*nibbanam padam achyutam,*[2] fearless *goal—nibbanam akutobhayam*[3], a state of highest bliss-*nibbanam paramam sukham.*[4] This ideal state, according to Buddha, can supply happiness here and hereafter–*iha nandati peccha nandati.*[5] In this state of perfection there will be a right knowledge and complete realisation of ultimate reality, that can be possible through *Ashtangika-marga,* or eightfold path containing eight steps: (a) *samyag drishti* or right faith, (b) *sankalpa* or right resolve, (c) *vak* or right speech, (d) *Karmanta* or right action, (e) *ajiva* or right living, (f) *vyayama* or right effort, (g) *smriti* or right thought, (h) *samadhi* or right concentration.

Indian Realism, i.e., *Nyaya, Vaishesika* observes, that the individual self is a substance with material body and mind without the knowledge of reality. In the state of liberation the self exists as a pure substance which is free from material body, worldly suffering and pleasure, having no consciousness of anything at all.[6] It is a supreme state of freedom, which is presented in the scriptures as *abhayam* or freedom from fear, *ajaram* or freedom from decay and change, *amrityupadam* or freedom from death etc.[7] According to these thinkers, to attain salvation is to acquire the state of perfect bliss through a perfect knowledge [8] of reality, which can be possible through *shravana* or hearing of scriptural instructions about reality, *manana* or reasoning about reality, that self is not body and *nididhyasana* or *yoga* on reality.

Mimamsakas also think that salvation or freedom is the highest good beyond the bondage of body-mind, which is an unconscious state where self exists in its own nature free from pleasure and pain.[9] *Sankhya* and *Yoga* also put an emphasis on the idea that the intrinsic nature of self is pure consciousness free from material body and material pleasure. But relation of *Prakriti* or matter with self creates bondage and freedom from the attachment of matter is salvation or *purusartha; Yadva tadva taducchittih purusarthastaducchittih purusarthah.*[10] In this connection *Sankhya* accepts both *Jivanmukti* and *Videhamukti.* The time when pure knowledge of self dawns, an individual becomes free though he is embodied due to *Prarabdha Karma.*[11] As there is self realisation here and now, the individual in this state is unaffected by the vicissitudes of the worldly body and mind. 'Just as the dancing girl ceases to dance after having entertained the spectators, so Prakrti ceases to act and evolve the world after manifesting her nature to the self'.[12] In this stage of *Jivanmukti* the individual self can realise itself and so can enjoy freedom in this life and world. After the death of its body when a total detachment of *Purusa* or self from *prakriti* or matter or the complete disembodied isolation can be possible, then an absolute emancipation or *videhamukti* automatically results.[13]

Both *Sankhya* and *Yoga* accept that the state of salvation or freedom can be acquired through the spiritual insight or *prajna* into the reality of the self as pure and eternal, distinct from material body and mind. To stop the material influence of *chitta* or mind is called *yoga-Yogashchittavrittinirodhah.*[14] *Yoga* and *Samadhi* are the same and in the stage of *nirvikalpa samadhi,* activities of mind or *chitta* are totally stopped and spiritual insight about the intrinsic nature of self is developed through the purification of *chitta.* For the enlightenment and purification of *chitta* or mind, yoga prescribes (a) *Yama* or restraint, (b) *niyama* or culture, (c) *asana* or posture, (d) *pranayama* or breath-control, (e) *pratyahara* or withdrawal of the senses, (f) *dharana* or attention, (g) *dhyana* or meditation and (h) *samadhi* or concentration.

Indian idealism of *Vedanta* philosophy as 'the end of the *Vedas',* and developed through the *Upanishads,* primarily admits 'All is *Brahman'-Sarvam Khalvidam Brahma.* Matter and mind have no independent existences as they are grounded in *Brahman.* Samkara, the *Advaita Vedantin,* also accepts that the individual self is non-different from *Brahman* which is the only reality and this embodied soul or ego as the creation of material world is ultimately false;-

Brahma satyam Jaganmithya Jivo Brahmaiva naparah. Under the influence of *Maya* or *avidya* or ignorance, an individual takes ego as self which is bondage. So salvation or freedom is the removal of ignorance by knowledge-*mokshapratibandhanivrittimatram eva atmajnanasya phalam.*[15] Thus, the distinction between self and *Brahman* is removed and so bondage also disappears and the blessed individual realises the ultimate Reality 'I am *Brahman*' in this life and world.[16] This, according to *Samkara* is *Jivanmukti.* In the stage of *Videhamukti,* after the death of this body, the individual soul finally merges into the Absolute.

But Ramanuja, *vishistadvaita* thinker, points out that liberation is not the merging of the individual self into the Ultimate Reality or Absolute, but it is the intuitive realisation of God. The liberated self is similar to the Absolute or *Brahmaprakara* and so cannot be identical with the Absolute. So long as a man lives in this world, he cannot be liberated as he is related with body, his *karmas* persist and thus he cannot acquire the final purity of self. When *Karmas* in this world are destroyed, there will be the dawning of the Divine Grace and thus the real *Bhakti* or *Jnana* is matured and that is the immediate intuitive realisation of God.

Considering the views of liberation in Indian philosophy in different ways, it is to be noted that *Buddha, Jaina, Sankhya* and *Advaita Vedanta* Schools of Philosophy recognise the idea of *Jivanmukti,* but Ramanuja and others do not accept it. It is further to be pointed out that all thinkers deny the existence of matter and material world in the state of liberation and they think this material world is the cause of all sufferings of individuals. Liberation, according to them, is the final freedom from all sorrows and sufferings, pain and pleasure. So, how a man will be liberated and free, and what are the fundamental ways through which a man can acquire final freedom are the ultimate quests of Indian philosophy. Regarding this matter, different thinkers have advanced different views and means; some put an emphasis on 'religious experience' some others emphasise on 'knowledge', a few others speak about *Karma,* and still some others think *Prema* or *Bhakti* should be the only way to acquire salvation or freedom as in the *Vaisnava* and other theistic Vedantic processes.

Evaluating these views, Rabindranath tries to probe deep into important values of different ideals from his transcendent-experiential perspective as has been developed in this discourse which is a comprehensive attitude in perfecting man to a possibility. It is not the negation of human life or rejection of material and socio-cultural processes of the wood. But it is a programme of overcoming the sorrows and sufferings of all human situations by a broad optimistic ideal coming out of the contradictions or limitations of this life and world, raising them towards a creative possibility in broad humanist directions.

The establishment of this intercultural and international prospect for mankind as a whole, according to Tagore, can be acquired in this life and world. In different writings,[17] Tagore says that salvation is the freedom of man in this world which is not the 'life beyond' but is a life in and through this world linked up internationally and interculturally with a prospective objective. Firstly, man is born in this world where he learns the significance of life in nature and also learns the meaning of freedom with his relation with nature and the life of other individuals.[18] It is a life with continuous extension of outlooks and possibilities with thrills and urges.

But mere propensity for meeting material necessities of life creates the limited conditions for selfish existence and life as 'ego' or *chota ami.* But in the later stage of life, a man learns to overcome different limitations of his selfish existence and thus destroys his 'ego' which, in the opinion of Tagore, is 'death'. So a man has to transcend such a restricted mode with restricted interests and prepares himself for confronting all odds with a courage to be. This type of suggestion is also introduced in contemporary Western-American thought.

In this way, he finally achieves the 'Life Eternal' or *Amrita* which is not merely Indian but international. Regarding these three stages of the development of life, Tagore says, "reference may be made to the three phased development of religious consciousness-first, life according to nature, next death, suppression or supersession of this life, and finally participation in the life eternal."[19]

'Participation in the life eternal' means the existence of the individual in international and intercultural contexts with an openness of mind or attitudes of the universal human life, above limitations or individualities. The reality of this existence becomes true through the development of the greatness of human life. In *Manuser Dharma* Tagore points out, 'Man is great, man will have to prove that he is great, then it will be proved that he is a man.' To become great is to be God, when he will realise a great unity or *So 'ham.* This, according to Tagore, is the realisation of great 'I' or *Manava Brahma,* when the individual man becomes Universal or International Man through the development of universal human outlook. The embodiment of this universal ideal in human life is, according to Tagore, 'the meditation on humanity' or *Manusyatver Tapasya,* through the suppression of any kind of restricted attitude as animality or *Jivabhava.* In *Manuser Dharma* Tagore again observes, the animal says, 'enjoy on the way of the natural religion.' Man says, 'meditate on the way of the religion of Man',[20] and rise to comprehensive humanist consciousness by overcoming all restricted visions from myths to the sciences and technologies.

Regarding the meditation or the ways of the realisation of the highest state of life or the optimum humanist conditions, different thinkers furnish different methods. Among these methods, (a) *Karmamarga* (b) *Jnanamarga* and (c) *Bhaktimarga* are supreme. But these individualised prospects of Indian thought have to be reinforced by the novel ideas of Western politics, economics and ecologies that are emerging in intercultural social processes. Tagore tries to evaluate all these methods of realisation and then presents his different appreciative ways represented as values, derived from these methods for the establishment of a comprehensive humanist process as evident from his transcendent-experiential process as reflected in his religion of Man.

(a) *Karmamarga:* In the development of Indian philosophy, the *Vedas* occupy an important place which have four divisions- *Samhita, Brahman, Aranyak* and *Upanishad: Samhita* and *Brahman* form

Karmakanda and *Aranyak* and *Upanishad* form *Jnanakanda.* The philosophical systems like *Jaiminisutra* or *Purva-Mimamsa* deal with the earlier portion of the *Vedas* and put an emphasis on *Karmakanda,* and so is called *Karma-Mimamsa.* According to these philosophical pursuits, *Karma* or action and *Upasana* or meditation are essential paths towards salvation or freedom as an optimum condition or possibility. *Mimamsakas* divide *Karma* into three classes (i) *Nitya Karma,* that can be done everyday, e.g., prayers in the evening and morning, (ii) *Naimittika Karma,* that is to be done occasionally, e.g., particular work at the time of ceremony, (iii) *Kamya Karma,* i.e., work that will be done for happiness in heaven, e.g., Vedic sacrifice.

Jaimini, Shabarasvamin and *Prabhakara* do not speak about liberation or *Moksha,* but Kumarila, Salikanatha and their followers point out that attainment of salvation or *Moksha* through the destruction of results of past activities as the cause of reincarnation, is the fundamental end of human life. For this the *Gita* also puts an emphasis on *Nishkama Karma*[21] or activity without any desire, that is 'Vedic sacrifice' for the freedom from bondage.[22] Whatever may be these objectives of the Indians, they remain ego-centric till the end, if not extended to socio-cultural processes as Tagore's consequent modification introduced by his, religion of Man as developed here.

According to *Karmamarga,* Vedic sacrifice, ceremonies, rites, etc., are the only religion that will lead us to heaven. These types of ceremonial activities, rites, ete., are extended further with new insights in successive Indian traditions in Buddhism's eight-fold path, and in other ways in Jainism, Vaisnavism, Islam, Christianity etc., in philosophic and Yogic-Tantric ways.

But too much importance on rites and ceremonies, or similar such thing in later *Tantras* emerging from different religions and philosophies of India Form the *Vedas* to the Islam and Christianity later-ignore the real significance of religion and philosophy, that is the realisation of further advanced ideas to the stages of truth in life of Indian savants of this and nineteenth century from Rammohan, Vidyasagar, Vivekananda to Tagore and others. According to Tagore, specially different rites in religion create a false attitude leading man away from truth, and plunging one to darkness instead of light, and illusion instead of religion.

Religion, according to Tagore, is the realisation of the conditions as mentioned, of the inner essence of man, through the closest contact with nature, man and society, where Truth in the sense as developed is manifested in different degrees. So Truth cannot be limited to a particular religious procedure, adopted by a particular type of religion.[23] This limited procedure directs a man to follow its importance, instead of the realisation of Infinite, beyond its limitation.[24] Thus, different limited and narrow outlooks are introduced in society which create limitations and contradictions, e.g., different superstitions, orthodoxies, caste-systems, etc. Rabindranath wants to establish his religion of Man above all these limitations. He says, "For it is evident that my religion is poet's religion, and neither that of an orthodox man of piety, nor that of a theologian."[25]

In *Visarjan, Achalayatan* and other writings, Tagore criticised the narrowness of rites or vedic sacrifices and finally established 'religion of love' above all contradictions as it founds man in religion and relates all men through the development of an essential bond in love. This procedure through love removes all limitations and contradictions and finally inspires man to acquire the highest state of life, the freedom or interpersonal affinity in love. In *The Religion of Man,* Tagore observes repeatedly the need for "...an atmosphere of Freedom–freedom from the dominance of any creed that had its sanction the definite authority of some scripture, or the teaching of some organised body of worshippers." It is as suggested in this discourse so far from an over-all transcendent-ecperiential attitude from the ancient *Vedas* to the present century developments in the direction of sciences and technologies.

Love in the highest state of freedom, establishes broad human feeling or sociality which is a basis for a new spiritual life of man, where the existences of man, society and world of any type with broad ideals are not ignored. Tagore puts an emphasis on the development of the humanist aspects as the optimum conditions for man to follow.

For this, Rabindranath criticises *Sannyasmarga,* the ascetic, asocial ideal of the past in any form, his is an inspiration for a broad-based socio-political life with no exclusive preference for any kind of aloofness in a mountain-cave, forest etc., rejecting the society of man and world by any abstractive process of the past and present modes of exclusive materialist linguistic ideas. But the real significance of Tagore's religion of Man points out that religion is the realisation of the general truths in this life and world from deeper perspective in love or appreciation of other's qualities or achievements in any aspect of one's specialties. It is for this reason he expresses him in his Santiniketan (abode of peace) a University for World culture from Arts to Sciences. In different poems of *'Sonar Tari, Naivedya, Chaitali* etc., and in different, essays like '*Dharmer Saral Adarsha*', '*Parashratan*', '*Atmasamarpan*', etc., and in different dramas like '*Prakritir Pratishodh*', '*Chirakumar Sabha*', '*Banshari*' etc., Tagore established the varied realist projects for developing his 'religion of love' or *Premadharma* through a detachment from any type of abstractive process of *Sannyas-dharma.* The ideal of love develops the infiniteness in the finite, integrality in the diversities and differences of the world. The realisation of Infinite, according to Tagore, is not possible through the rejection of the life and world. On the other hand, it is to be realised in and through life-process in this very life and world through love. It inspires a finite individual to work and to live or to enjoy in a disinterested *manner-Tena tyaktena bhunjitha* and thus he tries to become free from the restrictedness or contradictions of the material world and finally overcomes all finiteness through the development of the spirit of renunciation. In this connection Tagore explains, "It is only when a man truly realises what his possessions are that he has no more illusions about them, he knows his soul as far above these things and he becomes free from their bondage. Thus, man truly realises his soul by outraging his possessions and man's progress in the path of eternal life is through a series of renunciations".[26] In this way man rises to a true perspectives of advanced phenomenology and existentialist attitude of authentic life-process, or lived reality. In and through this process, a feeling for others is developed in man and thus he tries to sacrifice his poor interest for the cause of others and in this way he finally establishes an integrality of love in all, which is the highest state of perfection in human existence. In this state of perfection, a *Sannyasin* or *Yogin,* who is disinterested in this life and world, and an ordinary individual man who has an interest about the worldly things, will understand the significance of life by way of contrast when the difference between the two views about life will be removed and both these ideas will be entertained in togetherness with a liberality and understanding through the development of the sense of oneness in all.

The human life, where a highest state of integrality or affinity is possible, may refer to the *Karmamarga* or the realisation of this state through *Karma* or works. Again he has *mananashakti* or power of reason, through which he can know the true nature of reality. He has also an inner heart as a seat of love, through which he relates himself with all. So more importance on *Karmamarga* is to put an emphasis on the one procedure of human life that withdraws him from other procedures of life and thus the realisation of the final state of integrality is arrived at.

(b) *Jnanamarga* is the knowledge of One or Infinite.

In Vedic religion, importance is attached to two methods, *Karma* or *Pravrittimarga* and *Jnana* or *Nivrittimarga.* According to *Jnanvadi* or followers of *Jnanayoga,* final objective or *Moksha* is possible only *through Jnana* in a transcendent-experiential sense that is the true knowledge of Ultimate Reality as a process and possibility which is different from the world of bondage due to *karma* or activities under the influence of any restricted concept. All activities or *karmas,* good or bad, create the bondage of life and liberation is knowledge of reality as unrestricted. For this *Mahabharata,* the great Indian epic, points out *Karma na badhyate janturvidyaya tu pramuchyate, Tasmat karma na kurvanti yatayah paradarsinah.* So *karma,* according to this point of view, is responsible for producing evil for the embodied state of this life and knowledge of self as different from body or *anatma* can only lead to salvation or freedom. So any restricted *karma* or activity process is suicidal; which has to be replaced by detached activity-process.

The six systems of Indian philosophy or *Astika Darshana,* except *Mimamsa,* which is mainly ritualistic, accept *Jnanamarga,* persuits towards progressive knowledge addressing one self to the transcendent-experiential self, which according to *Samkara*, an *Advaita Vedantin,* is non-different from Absolute and bondage in this worldly life, is due to restricted *karma* under *avidya* or the darkening power or *tamasa pratyaya* that hides the real: *avaranatmakatvadavidya.* The knowledge of Reality or self or unrestricted activity-process, on the other hand, removes this darkness or *avidya* and destroys *Karma* or bondage by a final detached attitude as developed in his *Aparakshanuvute,* the salvation or freedom is attained. To acquire the knowledge of reality, three steps of *shravana, manana* and *nididhyasana* are to be practised, selectively and continuously. *Sharvana* is the hearing about the true nature of *reality, manana* is the rational enquiry of this nature and *nididhyasana* is the meditation on reality through which ultimate knowledge of reality or *Prajna* is realised. Tagore's religion of Man is such a process of religion in the making an unrestricted ways.

Sankhya also emphasises on the knowledge of reality in its own way leading to an ultimate condition. But reality, according to *Sankhya,* is not one, but there are two realities: (i) *Purusa* or self as pure consciousness and (ii) *Prakriti* or world-cause, consisting of three material *elements-Sattva, Rajas* and *Tamas.* Worldly bondage is due to *karma* or actions as the functions of *gunas* under the influence of ignorance or *avidya* which is the non-discrimination of *Purusa* or self from *Prakriti* or not-self. This ignorance can only be removed by right knowledge, when the final state of salvation through the realisation of *Jiva* as pure *Purusa* can be attained. *Yoga* philosophy or *Dhyanayoga* or *Rajayoga* or *Patanjalayoga* stand on *Prakriti-Purusatattva* of *Sankhya* system which is a practice of an ultimate detached condition. Patanjali observes that the knowledge of the difference of self from not-self will lead to salvation or freedom.

Nyaya philosophy also points out that the non-discrimination of self from body, mind and senses, is ignorance or bondage, and through *shravana, manana* and *nididhyasana,* a metaphysical knowledge of reality or self can be acquired.

Non-Vedic Philosophers, like Buddha and Mahavira, also point out that knowledge of reality will effect removal of ignorance in their respective senses, to a perfect condition, which leads to Salvation or freedom. For *Nirvana* or freedom or salvation, Buddha emphasises on the 'eight fold path' or *Astangikamarga,* which is divided into *Prajna, Sila* and *Samadhi. Prajna* or complete knowledge of reality inspires man to work in a disinterested manner that brings a state of equilibrium or *Nirvana* in his life. For the conquest of all passions or *jina,* Jaina philosophy also observes that the realisation of intrinsic nature of self as eternal knowledge, power and pleasure leads to salvation or freedom that can be possible through *Yogasadhana* or meditation, which is the synthesis of knowledge, reverence and character. In the words of *Umasvamin, Samyagdarshana Jnanacharitrani mokshamargah,* it is a triadic discipline of one's insight, knowledge and character should be mentioned here that both Buddha and Jaina do not put importance on *Jnanamarga* only, but they emphasise on the disciplined ways of life as lived or *karma* in a disciplined sense, to be detached from one's passion, intellectuality or *Karma-matters.*

Jnanavadi or the followers of *Jnanamarga,* point out that light and darkness, *Jnana* and *Ajnana* do not coexist, so there cannot be a relation of *Jnana* and *Karma,* which is due to *Ajnana* or *Maya.* But there should be a close relation of *Jnana* with *Karma. Jnana* supplies the essential characters of reality and man can apply these characters in life through *karma.* So the true knowledge of reality is to be experimented and to be applied in life through *karma* and thus a true nature of reality is to be realised in life.

In *The Religion of Man,* Tagore rising to a further advanced transcendent-experiential attitude, points out that through knowledge or *Jnana* as he has developed, man can know certain characters of reality, which are nothing but the appearances of reality. Reality in itself is something different from the usual somewhat restricted notions of reality, where the reality was separated from individual's life-interests, and a social nature. In this connection the opinion of Kant, a great German idealist, may be referred to. He points out that we can know the phenomenon or appearance only, but Noumenon or reality in itself can never be known by human knowledge. So in the context of the analysis of reality as closely related with human life and existence, Tagore had this worldly internationalist perspective. It is an aspect close to Kant's development of peace by eliminating war with a difference that this world as confronted is not an appearance but Noumenon itself.

Tagore thinks that man can realise the reality as it is with a knowledge and possibility. Knowledge, according to him, derives certain characters of reality that will lead mankind to an unrestricted process of social activity with a progressive detachment and mutual appreciation of human achievements as of one cosmic family.

For this Bradley also observes that thought or knowledge can never do justice to reality. Tagore thinks, *'Brahman* cannot be known by debates. He is to be known only through *Anandam'*,[27] which is a concrete this-worldly attitude. So Ultimate Reality or One, according to Tagore, is to be realised in and through an integral feeling and affinity, a closeness that is broadly humanist process through unity of *Juana* and *Karma* in *prema* or love. Tagore observes, "... He can be known by joy, by love. For Joy is concrete knowledge in its completeness, it is knowing by our whole being."[28]

(c) *Bkaktimarga* is the realisation of God through the inner feeling of heart. *Karmayoga* of *Mimamsakas, Jnanayoga* of *Advaita Vedanta* and *Rajayoga* of *Patanjali* have no relation with *Bhakti* as these systems of Indian philosophy put emphasis, on *Karma, Jnana* and *Dhyana* for the realisation of reality. All these general statements of thoughts are to become obsolete if one pursues Tagore's transcendent-experiential process as has been developed in this work.

Bhaktimarga points out that common man can realise the presence of the Ultimate in his heart when he tries to establish a personal relation with the Ultimate as personal God or *Saguna Brahma* through *Bhakti.* Thus, the final reality of Philosophy appears as God in religion. The *Upanishads* also describe the Absolute or *Brahma* as *Nirguna* or indeterminate and *Saguna* or determinate.

The followers of *Bhaktimarga* refer to the personal God or *Saguna Brahma,* who is *Sat-Chit-Ananda,* Existence, Consciousness and Bliss. God is the appearance of the Absolute in and through this world and human life, who, according to Ramanuja, a follower of

Vishistadvaitavada, is an organic unity or identity in diversity, a concrete whole *(Vishista)* consisting of interdependent subordinate elements or *Vishesanas;* and the immanent guiding spirit as *Vishesya.* Unity is the realisation of being, a vital member of the organic whole; *Vishistantarbhava eva aikyam.* So God is Absolute or Whole, who is *Brahman to Jnani, Chitadmasvarupa* to *Yogi* and *Sacchidanandavigraha* to *Bhakta.* Through *Bhakti,* the intrinsic power or *Svarupa Shakti* is manifested in and through the life of individuals. So *Bhakti* is a divine feeling in individual through which a man can realise the eternal nature of Ultimate Reality in him.

Bhaktishastra refers to nine types of *Bhakti sadhana* or methods of realisation- (i) *Shravana,* (ii) *Kirtana,* (iii) *Smarana,* (iv) *Padaseva,* (v) *Archana,* (vi) *Vandana,* (vii) *Dasya,* (viii) *Sakhya,* (ix) *Atmanivedana.* Among these methods, the self surrender to God or *Atmasamarpana* is the important method in *Bhaktimarga.* Through this method of realisation, a highest state of realisation or *premabhakti* is developed, when a man realises God as 'you are mine' in pure love. To love God as 'mine' is greater than the mere knowledge of God, as in love a unity between God and man is realised. So to *Bhaktivadi* love is the only *purusartha* through which an essential and intimate relation can be established between the individual and the Absolute. Tagore does not develop this process as an academician. One may again review Ramanuja's theistic position as below just to extend some notions of devotional attitude.

Ramanuja, a follower of *vishistadvaitavada,* accepts *Bhakti* as the only way to salvation or freedom through which the knowledge, meditation and realisation of God become identified and thus through this process the metaphysical Reality or Absolute and God of religion will appear as one and the same. Madhvacharya, the champion of unqualified dualism *(dvaita),* introduces the duality between the individual and God and he, like Ramanuja, observes that only *Bhakti* can lead to the salvation or freedom. Acharya Nimbarka, whose philosophy is known as *Dvaitadvaita* or *Bhedabheda,* points out that God manifests himself in and through the human life and world; so the world of *Jivas* is equally true and real like God, and he maintains that there is duality and non-duality between the individual and the

Absolute. God or Absolute is something more than the individual, whose essential and intrinsic nature of unity is to be realised through *Bhakti,* when in the highest state of salvation or freedom he is totally manifested in human life. Acharya Vallabha, whose view is called *Suddhadvaita* or pure non-dualism unconditioned by *Maya,*[29] points out that God, as substratum of all qualities of unity and plurality, is to be fully realised by man in the state of salvation or freedom through *Bhaktimarga.* Mahaprabhu Chaitanya, the founder of *Achintyabhedabheda* or 'Identity-in-difference', finally introduces pure *Bhaktimarga* devoid of *Jnana* and *Karma* as the only way to salvation or freedom. Liberation, according to him, is the eternal enjoyment of blissful love of God.

So *Bhaktimarga,* according to these thinkers, is the proper way to salvation or freedom, reconciling knowledge and action, in varied senses. Finally, the *Gita* also points to the synthesis of *Jnana, Karma* and *Bhakti* that leads to salvation or freedom. This can be possible through love or *prema* as the highest state of *Bhaktimarga.*

Rabindranath's religious position in contrast to these exclusive positions, fosters a general transcendent-experiential attitude with an operative principle of practice of love in international and progressive social and educational contexts. So that life becomes possible in a social and humanist atmosphere, somewhat aloof from confrontations and solitariness as Whitehead of the contemporary West conceives of Tagore that he makes it practical in his Santiniketan through a dynamic educational programme in his University of the World where all can meet and exchange ideas.

Tagore thinks that mere knowledge of reality may be possible, but it cannot be completely realised by knowledge only. In *Sadhana,* Tagore explains, "Intellectual knowledge is partial because our intellect is an instrument, it is only a part of us, it can give us information about things which can be divided and analysed and whose properties can be classified part by part. But *Brahmam* is perfect and knowledge which is partial can never be a knowledge of Him". In this connection it may be mentioned that Bradley, the Western idealist also says that in knowledge or in intellectual judgment, the subject and predicate, i.e., 'that' and 'what' are always to be distinguished and separated. But reality or life is harmony or unity where these attributes are inseparable. So abstract non-relational knowledge cannot explain the reality or life completely. In the same way, mere action or reverence also cannot explain the total view of life or reality as these are blind or without reasoning. These blind methods may establish a futile ritualism or asceticism in the life of man. But these, according to Tagore, express the negative view of life devoid of human outlook. For this, Tagore explains that the relation of mere knowledge or emotion or action increases attachment or egoism, greed and selfishness.[30] These methods of religions denounce the human qualities and try to find religion on something that rejects humanity and human beings. In *Naivedya*[31], Tagore expresses this view and in his *Manuser Dharma* he raises a question, 'If the liberation of individual is possible by destroying the human beings, then why I become a man?' So any ideal, without the natural process of human life as has been developed in this dissertation can be a mere abstraction, but can be rendered into a dynamic process for eliminating all restrictions, preparing man for the elevated consciousness of true freedom and fellowship.

Thus, it is found that Tagore's idea of human liberate condition is a cry for a humanist view which is to establish *humanism* as a form of an objective possibility with concrete methods to its credit for knowledge, love and action. Tagore observes the significance of this continuum of processes in the development of the idea of human freedom, because he thinks that an emphasis on a particular method or the way of life can destroy the universal spirit in the process of a harmonious development of human life. Evaluating this comprehensive outlook of Tagore in his religion of Man, Sen[32], in his '*Rabindranather Dharmachinta*', criticises the reference to a particular method or one-sided procedure of life, as it fails to explain the many-sided development of human life. In the background of this idea he examines different thoughts and observes that Upanishadic Sages may have the vision of the highest truth, but are incapable of formulating any religion of Man that can inspire human beings. Thus, Upanishadic religion becomes lifeless and leads to inactionism as it is lacking in love. The ideals of cooperation and kindness in Buddhism and Christianity conquered the whole world but the weakness of knowledge made these religions fruitless and futile. *Bhakti* occupies a supreme place in Vaisnavism but the weakness of knowledge limits it to abstract speculation and pleasure. But the final end of Tagore by a contrast is to found a universal religion on the basis of a prospective attitude of different ideals supplied by the different religions of the world. Hiranmoy Banerjee interprets this comprehensive outlook of Tagore thus: 'The religious practice that supplies a proper place to apply the power of knowledge, action and love completely is an ideal religion.'[33] Man can know his total existence by the harmonious combination of knowledge, action and love, that can help him to realise the supreme ideal of *Santam, Sivam* and *Advaitam* in him. Rabindranath feels, '...we can achieve peace or *Shanti* by our total knowledge in continuum or possibility, we can see *Siva* by our total and progressive action, we can realise *Advaita* by our total love'.[34]

This is 'the introduction of the idea of an integral experience in possibility, which alone can be *Santam, Sivam* and *Advaitam* in a transcendent-experiential sense with dynamic elements of knowledge, action and love. In the highest ideal of possibility by progressive contrast Tagore also suggests the highest method of realisation, which, according to him, is the method of love that makes for continuous reservoir of knowledge and action in prospects. All methods or ways of life, according to Tagore, are incomplete without the dynamism of love and so the ideal of love finally introduces the elements of inspiring spirit of unity that makes all in ideals and methods.

The significance of reality in life can be known or understood through knowledge, but its perfect manifestation in life can be possible through its realisation in love that makes the salvation or freedom of individual complete. Tagore observes: "...he can be known by joy, by love. For joy is knowledge in its completeness, it is knowing by our whole being".[35] The realisation of our whole being means the realisation of perfect' pleasure in us that is finally identified with the infinite or absolute pleasure. This can be explained by Tagore in *The Religion of Man:* "It is not the magnitude of extension but an intense quality or harmony which evokes in us the positive sense of time infinite in our joy, in our love, for *advaitam* is *anandam;* the infinite One is infinite Love". Thus, Tagore observes the existence of an integral consciousness is love which is the manifestation of absolute value as *Anandam* in life, which, according to him, is nothing but the expression of *Advaitam* or non-dual integrality in love.

This realisation of a comprehensive integral value is the inauguration of non-duality, that, in the traditional sense and yet in an advanced sense of Tagore, can be recognised as the realisation of God in life. So the realisation of God, according to Tagore, is the accomplishment of a new divinity in man. Thus, to worship God in a temple, church, mosque or in a mountain cave, according to Tagore, is an erroneous procedure of realising Him. The *Baul* in him, asks for a non-restrictive process of search possibility. Tagore thinks, God can only be realised by love that exists in the heart of a man. In *Manuser Dharma,* Rabindranath explains, 'At least, my mind admits the meditation which says there is a place for realising the great Person in one's own self without renouncing lower self. He is the self of the Universal Man. If anybody seeks to reach non-human or superhuman truth by ignoring Him totally, I am unable to understand their contention. For my intelligence is human intelligence, my heart is human heart, my imagination is human imagination...What we call science, is understood by man's intelligence, what we can *Brahmananda* or Absolute pleasure, is also a pleasure apperceived by man and that floods human consciousness. He who is realised in this intelligence, in this pleasure, is *Bhuma,* but it is *Manavik Bhuma.*'[36] So Tagore realises the existence of God with proper qualifications in progressive humanist way. Individual self becomes united with the Universal Self of Man through the establishment of an integral interrelational possibility where the participants are all the human beings of the world. The realisation of love or pleasure that is present in all individuals, makes this integral relation a possibility. Tagore says, 'The relation of one self with the other, deepest of all, truest of all, can be recognised as love'.[37] That is why Tagore observes that a perfect harmony or synthesis in the whole universe can be revealed to a man through the complete realisation of love or pleasure in him that inspires him to go beyond the limitation of sensible material world. For this Tagore points out, 'Our material acquaintance with the physical world is through sensual knowledge, our real acquaintance with the spiritual world is through love'.[38]

This love in human life is eternal and ultimate, that relates the individual with the Universal Man and thus establishes a unity with the Infinite Self or the Absolute. In *Gitanjali*[39] or in other writings, Tagore expresses this view which is evaluated by Nandi: 'In the stage, prior to the attainment of the company of God, the poet tells us about the relation with all men. This relation only supplies us the opportunity to see the happiness - sorrow, pleasure, pain of other individuals as our own'.[40] Thus, it is observed that the divine relation, according to Tagore, is *human* as it is expressed through the *human* feelings that finally develop the intimate and eternal relation of integrality with others. This feeling of integrality in non-duality in the opinion of Tagore, is expressed through the feeling of love which is not blind and inactive but it, on the other hand, develops the rational and active spirit in man for the development of his universal nature through love and service for mankind. This process of life creates the disinterested feeling for others that urges him to work for all and thus he becomes *Visvakarma* which is the inauguration of the spirit of non-duality in his highest existence as 'world-worker'. In *The Religion of Man,* Tagore points out, "Our Union with a Being whose activity is world-wide and who dwells in the heart of humanity cannot be a passive one. In order to be united with Him we have to divest our work of selfishness and become *Visvakarma,* 'the world-worker', we must work for all". The self-less love and service for people remove the narrow interest or poor ego of man and inspire him to proceed towards the development of unity in him. In *Manuser Dharma,* Tagore observes, ' "I" in man is greater than self-centered ego and has a unity with all ; His work is work for all.' This disinterested and selfless service for all in love makes a man free from his poor interest or 'ego', which is explained by Tagore: "Work for individual self *(Ekla Ami)* is bondage and work for all selves *(Sakal Ami)* is freedom".[41] Man, therefore, becomes free from all his bondages of life when he works freely in love for all. In *Sadhana,* Tagore examines this ideal: "We find in perfect love the freedom of our self. That only which is done for love is done freely, however much pain it may cause. Therefore, working for love is freedom in action". So 'love', that exists in the heart of human beings is expressed through the development of the intimate relation of unity in love and service to others. Thus, the end of life, according to Tagore, is to attain the perfect state of love as the freedom in unity, through the method of love in this worldly process of developing an eternal relation with others in a disinterested manner.

Thus, it may be observed that the fundamental object of Tagore is to attain freedom in this world through the human method of love which is a humanist approach to freedom for it does not deny the human existence in this world and also recognises the humanist process of love and service for men for the development of the ideal of freedom in unity. So the freedom of man in society through realisation of social value of love as very pragmatic is the final object of Tagore's religion of Man, which, it may be said, stands on the religion of love. This procedure of Tagore in love, in a broad humanist sense as developed, is the core of human order and existence. But in the development of the highest ideal of human freedom in the religion of Man, Tagore does not take this body and world as the medium for the fulfillment of narrow, poor and individual interest. This restricted interest for enjoyment of material world and body, supplies a material pleasure or attachment that confines us in the narrow limitations of a lower self or ego. This ego creates social tensions, conflicts and clashes fostering disunity in the life of human beings. This, according to Tagore, is an obstacle to man's realisation of final freedom or objective. In the elimination of these obstacles on the way to prospects, Tagore points out, man will have to transcend this narrow limitation of life by love that supplies him perfect Bliss of *Anandam* which is to be attained in this life overcoming all the poor interests for pleasure. So through the realisation of love or bliss or *Anandam* in life, man, on the one hand, transcends all the limitations, disharmonies, caused by the narrow self interest due to material ego and, on the other hand, establishes a perfect non-duality of his highest existence as Universal or Infinite Self with the material existence as 'ego'. The transcendence of this narrow limitation due to ego does not mean the denial of its existence but to overcome it through the realisation of a broader ideal in love or bliss. In *Atmaparichaya*,[42] Tagore explains: 'Man has, by virtue of his birth-right, acquired the right of entry into the Life Eternal, because of all creatures man alone, on the sharp-edged way to the realisation of his spiritual well-being, has welcomed sorrows and even embraced death...and, for this very reason it is only man who can afford to pray thus–'Lead me on from unreality to the realm of the Real, from darkness and desolation to the safety-zone of light supernal'. The verb 'to lead', imports, for ought we know, to cause to go straight across a pathway and not to go round about it or avoid it. In this process of life, Tagore's object is not to avoid but to overcome through the harmonious development of the completeness or perfection in life as the development of non-duality. The development of this human existence or human personality is explained by Tagore in *The Religion of Man*: "The animal in the savage has been transformed into higher stages in the civilised man–in other words has attained a truer consonance with Man the divine, not through any elimination of the original materials, but through a magical grouping of them, through the severe discipline of art, the discipline of curbing and stressing proper places, establishing a balance of lights and shadows in the background and foreground, and thus imparting a unique value to our personality in all completeness". In this explanation of human personality, Tagore emphasises the well-disciplined or harmonious development of human existence for the realisation of human freedom. But it should be noted here that this realisation is not negation or rejection; because freedom from contradictions in love is not negative in character. This positive of realisation is evaluated by Andrews: "This emancipation cannot be negative in character for love can never lead to negation".[43] The realisation of love in this way helps a man not to negate but to conquer all the contradictions or disunities and thus finally establishes eternal unity among these disharmonies of life. This is the last or final stage of human life, which is explained by Tagore in *Atmaparichaya:* '... The end is love, pleasure, where there is a confluence of *Ganga* and *Yamuna* of happiness and sorrow, enjoyment and sacrifice, life and death. There lies the *Advaitam.*' The entire human life is an evolutionary progress towards this final state of existence, which according to Tagore, is a human or religious procedure towards the final realisation of eternal life or the stage of non-duality, after crossing the different stages of limitations. In *Atmaparichaya,* Tagore states, '...reference may be made to the three phased development of religious consciousness- first, life according to nature, next death, suppression or supersession of this life, and finally participation in the Life Eternal'. The development of this 'Eternality' in life is not an accidental or unnatural or supernatural factor, but Tagore observes that it is an essential or natural progress of human life that makes a man, Man, the Universal, through the suppression of limitations or contradictions of his life in love. The ideal of love, potential in man, helps to suppress and to overcome the contradictions that are created in his social and worldly life. These contradictions, according to Tagore, are due to poor individual interests which are created by poor self or ego of man. The suppression of this poor self and its contradictions can be recognised by Tagore as death ; but this death is not annihilation or destruction but this is for another higher form of life which is the final salvation or freedom of individual and where a divine union between individual self and Infinite self or Absolute will be completely established through love. This is the fundamental object or end of Tagore's religion of Man, which is explained by him: "If in and through my literary contributions there runs a philosophy of religion, then it is precisely this; religious consciousness is the intuitive realisation of that harmonious relation of perfect love between the individual and the supreme soul, that love which embraces, on the one hand, all duality and on the other, unbroken unity, on the one hand, division and discord, and on the other, union and concord; finally, on the one hand, bondage and on the other, freedom or redemption".[44] This explanation of Tagore perfectly brings out his integral consciousness of a detachment from diversities, once admitting them as basic currents that are to be confronted. The realisation of this prospective freedom by a detachment from confronted diversity is Tagore's *Sharvanubhuti* or 'all-consciousness". It can be interpreted as 'the feeling of at-homeness in the whole'. In spiritual union Tagore tries to explain this state when he compares it with the idea of *Brahmavihara* of Buddha that is 'living in the infinite'. In *The Religion* of *Man,* Tagore explains this state completely: "To be dwelling in such contemplation while standing, walking, sitting or lying down until sleep overcomes thee, is called living in *Brahma"*. This process of the 'living in *Brahma'* is not the superhuman or inhuman process, but it, according to Tagore, is purely a humanist procedure that leads to the development of the highest existence of unity in love. This finally establishes an integrality between the processes of the finite and infinite in man, and thus makes him a medium of manifestation of perfection of truth. In *The Religion of Man,* Tagore expresses this feeling: "The poet sings of the central bond of union between the infinite and the finite soul, from which there can be no *mukti,* because love is ultimate, because it is an interrelation which makes truth complete".

In the development of this completeness as freedom in unity, a man always tries to establish an interrelation in his knowledge and activities that eliminates his isolation or alienation in life and society. This process of life develops a feeling of dependence which is purely human and social as it creates a synthetic outlook in man for a synthetic and harmonious development of life towards his highest existence as unity in love. In *Santiniketan*[45] Tagore evalutes thus: 'Man is, after all, craving for dependence upon one–a dependence which knows no bounds or limits. From the depth of his being rises forever the prayer 'O, my peerless beloved, thou art subservient to me, when shall I be subservient to thee as well?' When, pray, will this dependence of mine fully harmonise with that dependence of thine?' Thus, this feeling of dependence urges him to depend upon his beloved as the fulfillment of the social relation in love that finally develops his divinity as the realisation of divine union in love.

The harmonious development of human life as the divine union in love makes a man divine, as it makes the manifestation of Godness or Divinity in human life complete. This, according to Tagore, is nothing but the expression of the humanity as the final expression of human freedom in unity in love. In this humanistic approach to freedom, we may observe the development of the interdependence of different stages of human life that transcends the limitations or contradictions of life due to finite existence or poor self and thus a unity of non-duality between man's finite self and his infinite self is established in the final state of freedom. This, according to Tagore, is the manifestation of truth in man as *Advaitam.* This, in the observation of Tagore, is the final self-revelation or self-realisation of man. Self-realisation means the realisation of truth or perfect freedom that is a complete unity in love and can be realised in this human life in the humanist process of love, because the ideal of love exists in man's intrinsic nature. In *The Religion of Man,* Tagore observes, "... *mukti* is in the truth that dwells in the ideal man". Self-revelation also means the revelation of Infinite Truth or Reality in love completely, for Ultimate Reality or God as Love or Bliss does not only transcend the contradictions or disharmonies of life and world but also manifest Himself in this life and world through and experiential process in a perfect state of unity and harmony. So to love God is to love man as God as perfect Unity or Bliss,-or this God likeness exists in human nature and can be manifested in the human life through the selfless service and the disinterested love for men: "For the God in man depends upon men's service and men's love for his own love's fulfillment".[46] The ideal of love or bliss or *Anandam* is manifested in human life and the world or universe and can establish a perfect unity between the finite and the Infinite which is the final end of the theme of Tagore's religion of Man. In '*Jivansmriti*' Tagore explains, 'So far I have furnished an introduction to all my poetical works. Speaking for myself, this I consider to be the one theme of all my compositions. The theme may be given the name of effecting the much-prised union with the Infinite within, in and through the limits of the finite'.* In this 'much-prised union' the essential nature of man is completely manifest as in this state of unity a perfect realisation of love in man is complete as it finally introduces unity in the finite and the infinite existence of man.

Thus, it may be observed that the inauguration of this unity in human life is very much significant in Tagore's religion of Man, which may be treated as the final salvation or freedom of man as it reconciles all the contradictions of human life. But its significance lies not in the rejection of contradictions or 'the limits of the finite', but in the introduction of unity in contradictions, which, according to Tagore, is the essential progress of human existence in this material world. In this observation of Tagore, unity exists in the Universal or Infinite nature of Man, that is naturally manifested in and through the harmonious development of human personality, which, according to Tagore, is the expression of divinity in man and this manifestation becomes complete through the final reconciliation of contradictions in unity in love which may be recognised as purely a humanistic approach to the idea of freedom through unity. This type of humanistic approach of Tagore in a transcendent-experiential sense of developing the state of freedom means the cultivation of different human values in a transcendent sense. This is nothing that the cultivation of socio-cultural values in different stages of life and existence in different degrees, developing the spirit of detachment in an experiential form that is the establishment of socio-cultural relation of unity among men of this world.

Notes

1. *Yatha nadyah syandamanah samudre hastam, gacchanti namarupe vihaya. Tatha vidvan namarupadvimuktah parat-param purusamupaiti divyam-Mundaka 3/2/8.*
2. *Suttanipata Vijnanasutta.*
3. *Itivuttaka,* 112.
4. *Dhammapada,* 203.
5. *Ibid.,* 18.
6. *Na yatra duhkham na sukham na chinta na dvesaragau na cha kachi diecha.*
7. *Vide Bhashya,* 1.1.22. cf. *Prashna Upanishad,* 5.7.
8. *Mithyajnanottarottarapaye tadanantarapayad apavargah.*
9. *Vide Shastra—Dipika,* pp. 125-31.
10. *Sankhya Pravachana Sutra,* 6/70.
11. *Samyag jnanadhigamaddharmadinam karanatapraptau. Tishthati smskaravashaccakra bhramivat dhritashrirah-Sankhyakarika,* 67.
12. Cf. *Karika* and *Kaumudi.* 59, 65-66.
13. *Prapte sharirabhede charitarthatvat pradhanavinivritteh aikantikamatyantikamubhayam kaivalyamapnoti-Sankhyakanika,* 68.
14. *Yogasutra, samadhipada,* 2.
15. *Sharirakabhasya,* I.1.4.
16. *Ibid.*, III, 2.21.
17. For references: (a) Essays: 'Niyama O Mukti', 'Samajer Mukti', 'Jagater Mukti', 'Muktir Diksha", 'Muktir Path', etc.
18. *Prane mane purna kari gathiteche krome, Durlava. Jivan, pale pale nava ash,* 'Bandhan', *Sonar Tari.* This idea of Tagore is presented in the poems 'Vairagya of *Chaitali* ', 'Anuraga and Vairagya' of *Kanika,* 'Bandhan' and 'Mukti' of *Sonar Tari,* 'Mukti' of *Puravi, Parishesa* and *'Punaseha'* of *Vithika,* No. 119 poetry of *Gitanjali,* No. 37, 49 poetries of *Gitali,* No. 30 of *Naivedya,* No. 6 of *Prantika,* No. 32 of *Arogya,* No. 15 of *Patraputa,* No. 15, 46 of *Sesh Saptak,* etc.

19. Dr S.K. Das, *Tagore and the Perennial Problems of Philosophy,* p. 56.
20. Rabindranath Tagore, *Manuser Dharma,* p. 27.
21. *Karmanyevadhikaraste ma phaleshu kadachana... Srimadbhagavadgita,* ch. II, 47 *shloka.*
22. *Yajnarthat Karmano'nyatra Lako'yam Karmmabandhanah.... Gita,* III, 9 *shloka.*
23. *Bhajan pujan sadhan aradhana samasta thak pare...,* No. 119 of *Gitanjali.*
24. *Tomar pujar chhale tomay bhulei thaki ... ,* No. 132, *'Puja', Gitabitan.*
25. Rabindranath Tagore, *The Religion of Man,* p. 58.
26. Rabindranath Tagore, *Sadhana.*
27. Rabindranath Tagore, *Santiniketan.* Vol. II, p. 342.
28. Rabindranath T. agore, *Sadhana,* p. 159.
29. *mayasambandharahitam shuddham ityuchyate budhaih, Shuddadvaita-martanda.*
30. Rabindranath Tagore, *Manuser Dharma,* p. 53.
31. Rabindranath Tagore, *Naivedya-'Manusyatve tuccha Kari Jara saravela, Tomare laiya kare shudhu puja khela'.*
32. Prabodh Chandra Sen: 'Rabindranather Dharmachinta', *Visva-Bharaii Patrika.*
33. Hiranmaya Banerjee, *Rabindra Darshan,* p. 88.
34. Rabindranath Tagore, 'Santam-Sivamadvaitam'.
35. Rabindranath, Tagose, *Sadhana,* p.159.
36. Rabindranath Tagore, *Manuser Dharma,* pp. 97-98.
37. *Ibid.* pp. 43.
38. *Ibid.* pp. 43.
39. Rabindranath Tagore, *Gitanjali,* poem No. 94-'*Visvasathe yoge Jethay viharo, Seikhane Jog tomar sathe amaro*'.
40. Dr Sudhir Kr. Nandi, *Rabindradarshan Anuvikshan,* p. 76.
41. Rabindranath Tagore, *Manuser Dharma,* p. 65.
42. Dr S.K. Das, *Tagore and the Perennial Problems of Philosophy,* p. 56.
43. C.F. Andrews (ed.), *Thoughts from Tagore,* p. 105.
44. Rabindranath Tagore, 'Atrnaparichayaya', translated by Dr S. K. Das, *Tagore and the Perennial Problems of Philosophy,* p. 56.
45. Dr S. K. Das, *Tagore and the Perennial Problems of Philosophy,* p. 57.
46. Rabindranath Tagore, *The Religion of Man,* p. 44.

* ' ...*amar samasta kavyarachanar ihao ekti bhumika / Amar to mane hay, amar kavyarachanar ei ektimatra pala / Se palar nam deoya jaite pare, simar madhyei asimer sahit milansadhaner pala'* Rabindranath Tagore, *Jivansmrti.* translated by Dr S. K. Das, *Tagore and the Perennial Problems of Philosophy,* p. 58.

Chapter - 7

An Evaluation: A Socio-Cultural Exploration of Universal Humanism

Rabindranath Tagore, a contemporary Indian thinker, occupies an important position in contemporary Indian philosophy for his integral human outlook of the religion of Man. In the development of this idea he deals with the humanists approach to the traditional problems of philosophy and religion through a process of love.

A careful examination or a proper evaluation of the total character of the religion of Man, in the background of a comparative study of different views of great thinkers, proves that the final object of the religion of Man is to found religion on life as it is not separated from life, which is a harmonious development for the introduction of truth as unity in man and society.

In the background of this idea of unity, Tagore explains the nature of religion as nothing but the harmonious development of the nature of man towards the highest unity that also exists in the very root of human existence. The expression of this unity as truth is the reconciliation of different problems or contradictions in life. In *The Religion of Man* Tagore observes, "… at this point, comes his religion, whereby he realises himself in the perspective of the infinite".

This is the inauguration of universal humanity in the life of a man that is the unity with Universal Man, which means the realisation of unity with all men of the world in one individual being. It can be recognised as the synthetic explanation of life and if the life and the world can be explained from this comprehensive point of view there cannot be any contradiction or disunity. The comprehensive outlook, that is, unity between individuality and universality can lead to the development of the idea of Absolute or Universal Person who exists in all the individuals- *Sada Jananam hridaye sannivishtah,* - and who can be recognised as *Visvakarma* the world worker and can be worshipped by different men of different religions in different ways. But the fundamental object of this method of worshipping God or Absolute is to establish personal relation with Him, which, according to Tagore, is nothing but the realisation of non-duality between the individual and the Absolute as the inauguration of Universal Man in man. In this connection it should also be mentioned that the different methods of worshipping God, introduced by different religions, create differences in the outlook among the followers of different faiths. Hindus worship the personal Gods or Goddesses like Krishna, Siva, Kali, etc., the Christians adore the trinitarian concept of God, the Mohammedans offer their prayers to Allah, and the Buddhists and the Jainas, through avoiding reference to God, prescribe a rigid code of conduct as the highest religious method, but Tagore follows none of these methods. Again it must also be mentioned that the term 'worship' implies a partial difference between the worshipper and worshipped and if they are one or identical, the question of 'worship' does not arise. So to remove these differences Tagore used the term 'realisation' that means the realisation of Truth or Reality that is One and non-dual and is present, in all men. This has been explained by some commentators thus: 'For this, the harmonious human existence can be recognised by Rabindranath as 'Perfect Truth', 'Peace', 'One', 'Pleasure' and particularly 'Universal Man'.[1] For the realisation of truth or reality as peace and pleasure in man, the idea of universality arises in thinking, feeling and willing of individuals for the explanation of the universal nature of truth existing in the universal nature of human beings. Inauguration of universality is the establishment of the relation of unity between man, the individual and God, the universal. And thus the universality in man is the establishment of the highest state of non-duality or *Advaitam.*

To develop this humanist-universalist process from India's transcendent-experiential process on a broad realist-social process,

Tagore, like Swami Vivekananda, Gandhiji and Sri Aurobindo, established an educational centre at Santiniketan, which he called *Ashrama.* The aim of this *Ashrama* is neither to found any particular sect of religion, nor to follow any obligatory rule of particular religion; but it is to establish a unity or harmony of purpose among men and women, that, according to him, is the perfect realisation of truth. He writes, "... the mind of man is studied in its realisation of different aspects of truth from diverse points of view",[2] and that can be possible through love and service to human beings, which, according to Tagore, requires "good fellowship and co-operation between the thinkers and scholars of both Eastern and Western countries free from all antagonism of race...".[3] His aim was to develop one's inner personality through cooperative activity between men and women in a socio-cultural milieu, to bring out from each personality, his creative special attitude in some artistic, philosophic or literary activities.

This universal outlook through one's choice for a study for a subject forms the nucleus of Tagore's idea of the religion of Man, which expresses the inner spirit of the other contemporary Indian thinkers as mentioned earlier, who in their own special ways emphasise on the universality in man, and its development lies, according to each, in one form of social process. Going into details of Tagore and Vivekananda, another great contemporary Indian thinker, we can see in both a common theme that man is 'potentially divine'. He also, like Tagore, founded *Ashrama,* that is Ramakrishna Math and Mission. Though its aim is to establish Vedantic religion or Vedic culture, still like Tagore, Vivekananda also tried to link up the East with the West spiritually through this Mission. For this he preached the ideal of Universalism or a spiritual brotherhood through love and service. In this connection the idea of Gandhiji may also be referred to. Like Rabindranath, Gandhiji also thinks of the Ultimate Reality as truth and love which can be practiced "by disinterested service to humanity".[4] So the greatest merit that we find in these three greats of their times, Rabindranath, Vivekananda and Gandhiji, alternative programmes of religious ideals of love for humanity and serving it without any partiality. It should be noted here that the fundamental object of Tagore's religion of Man is to develop the proper meaning of religion as the expression of the universal nature and existence of man and for this development, he establishes religion on love and service to humanity in a human and social process of education in a natural environment as far as possible. So the charge against Tagore, that his idea of the religion of Man is different from the traditional sense of religion, is based on the narrow explanation of the term religion, and after the examination of the thought of Tagore, it is observed that the universal and humanist approach to Tagore's religion of Man in natural milieu expresses the proper meaning and significance of religion as the religion of Man.

It may also be pointed out that for realising universality and manifestation of the infinity in nature and man in integrality with beauty Tagore discerns a continuous relationship of love and service to humanity in times of a cosmic play or display each other's secrets and mystic vibrations, not revealed in manmade artificial situations. But the conflict between individual and collective interests and the solutions of those conflicts are purely on humanist level within a sphere of nature in change through days and seasons. Tagore sets up a process of religious expressions of man without disconnecting himself from nature in its varied expressions and panoramic changes.

Ideal of love that inspires man and nature in togetherness, elevates man with an eternity- the infinity that is mysteriously hidden in him. Man has to discover his inner spirit in being with nature through all seasons, and from dawn to night, luminous and non-luminous by heavenly messengers, moon and stars at night and sun during the day, bright and sunny, stormy or rainy. So the realisation of love in man and dancing nature, on the one hand, unites him with nature and in that process with all other men of the world and on the other hand, it produces a disinterested feeling that inspires him to work for all. This process as bodied forth in his idea of the religion under naturalist condition where man loves man and woman and nature as common participant. Suggesting a universal ideal for humanity as symbolically directing both to an order of perfection as already referred to a generalised religious process for the realisation of Universal Self or Truth in man. Tagore says it is love for nature that inspires man towards an ideal of knowledge and action for the highest realisation of truth as unity. Because, Tagore thinks that mere organised knowledge and action can produce a blind attachment or egoism that creates contradiction or disharmony in human life, but man's naturalist basis in knowledge and action through love of nature and its expressions in man can lead us to the realisation of truth as unity or harmony.

Again a particular method of knowledge or action can develop the particular aspect of human life, but the comprehensive method of love develops the total nature of man that helps him to realise the completeness of reality or truth in union with nature. Thus, a man, through this procedure, develops his heart, intellect and will in a natural way that is the expression of total human nature towards perfection or completeness. This process of human life with nature is the evolutionary progress from the duality to non-duality or unity. In the advancement of Tagore's life and thought this type of naturalist evolution of humanity in closeness with nature is the discernment of his idea of God or *Jivandevata* in different stages towards a perfect realisation of the spirit of non-duality of individuality and universality. In *Prabhat Sangit,* the poet sings, "My heart has opened and the entire universe flows into it".* For this naturalist attachment Tagore starts with the realisation of duality in love as expressed through his *Manasi, Sonar Tari, Chitra, Kshanika, Naivedya* etc. But the final end of this realisation with and within nature is the perfect reconciliation of the duality and the non-duality, finiteness and infiniteness in the unity of the humanity and divinity in love of man for man in a naturalist context as manifested through his *Gitanjali, Gitimalya, Gitali* and other writings. In all these works address to nature is basic and man is inspired by nature, his basic teacher and guide.

So in this process of life and thought in human situation from the stage of duality to the final stage of non-duality in naturalist milieu. Tagore finally introduces the ultimate ideal of unity in and through the method of unity in love with nature. Tagore develops this ideal of unity in *Santiniketan,* through the application of the term *Samanjasya* or harmony as the end, that is non-duality or *Advaita* and as means, that is the synthesis of knowledge and action in love with a naturalist atmosphere. 'For this the union of self with Supreme Self in the vast realm of nature and its panoramic presentation is the union in knowledge, love and action. This union is the union of pleasure. To be united with the completeness, is possible through completeness-then all that we possess in human situation will be fulfilled'.[5]

By the realisation of unity or completeness through a synthesis between nature and man, or man and his companions in love, man expresses his proper nature or existence, that according to Tagore, is his religious expressions. In life, activities and writings, Tagore expresses this naturalist outlook of his religion, that is the humanist ways where he observes that realisation of truth as unity or completeness is primarily from nature or nature in manifestations. This can be possible in human life only through a complete process of knowledge, love and action by a continuous extension of one's sphere of knowledge in association with vast nature. Tagore says, 'In knowledge, love, action, we can have man completely. For this, the complete realisation of Absolute in man, can be possible for man'.[6] Tagore thus puts an emphasis on the realisation of Truth or Absolute in man through a cosmic naturalist process, which can be compared with the synthetic outlook of the French philosopher Comte, if his ideas are transferred to social frames of reference of knowledge, feeling, etc, for the proper understanding of truth. He observes, "And whilst reason is admitted to its due share of influence on human life, imagination also strengthened and called into constant exercise. Henceforth it will assume its proper function, the idealisation of Truth".[7] This truth, according to Comte, is the idea of humanity and for the realisation of this idea, a unity of methods of feeling, reason and activity is required. He says, "There would be a central point in this system, towards which feeling, reason and activity alike converge. Such a centre we find in the great conception of Humanity..."[8]

In *The Religion of Man,* Tagore emphasises the development of Universal Man in the individual and Comte also in his religion of humanity, puts an importance on the social man. For the development of social nature of man and for the realisation of the religion of humanity, Comte writes "Our thoughts will be devoted to the knowledge of Humanity, our affections to her love, our actions to her service". So both Tagore and Comte, from two different perspectives, give importance to a process where knowledge, love and action are operative together for the development of the disinterested feeling in man, that helps him to love and work for others. This selfless attitude of man towards life and society can solve different contradictions of moral and social life. For this, Comte, like Tagore, emphasises on the unity of love, knowledge and action, and observes, "such is the moral standard which positivism puts forward for individuals and for society".

Now it may be mentioned that this comprehensive method, introduced by Tagore and Comte in the religion of Man and in the religion of humanity respectively, is an ideal and important method, that on the one hand, solves the different religious problems and on the other hand, solves the ethical and moral problems of human life. It has already been discussed that the contradictions between the individual self or ego and the Universal or Infinite Self, according to Tagore, are at the root of the human existence. But through love, man can overcome this poor self or ego through the realisation of highest unity of ego with the Infinite Self. In this connection we may refer to the fact that the contradictions between individual interest and the social or general interest are also the main problems of moral life of man. As a man is conscious of his own individuality, he prefers his own individual interest to the interest of others, and this ordinary procedure of human life produces a contradiction between the individual life and the moral or social life of a man. But the ideal methods prescribed by Tagore as love and work for human beings can solve these contradictions, because this procedure can develop a selfless or disinterested spirit in a man that helps him to overcome all his poor individual interests for the cause of his greater being or universal social life. For this universal cause, man should work for all human beings. Tagore in *Manuser Dharma* indicates a social attitude, 'Work for-individual cause (*Ekla Ami)* which is bondage, but work for all individuals *(Sakal Ami),* which is freedom'. So freedom means freedom in action, that is to be free from the narrow individual interest and to be united with universal interest of all human beings, which, according to Tagore, is the sacrifice of the narrow interest or ego for the cause of greater life which is love of human beings or the welfare of the people. This idea of freedom puts an emphasis on the moral approach to life that stands selfless actions for others. This is a proper humanist outlook as it leads to the development of social freedom in unity through the disinterested service for human beings in a practical and social form. In the evaluation of this type of practical or social approach to human freedom or liberation, a noted modern philosopher rightly observes, "...The problem of liberation must not only be genuine but practical in import, having to do, not with human knowledge, but with human conduct. That being so, those academic disciplines that are concerned with knowledge in abstraction from action can have little to do with the problem of liberation".[9]

In the light of this evaluation it may be said that the moral and social approach to life, developed in Tagore's idea, is nature oriented experientially and transcendentally along the *Vedic-Upanishadic* lines and applied to socio-cultural process of the time with insight. As Tagore's religious consciousness developed above is nature oriented in a transcendent mystic-experiential sense, Ray's criticism of Tagore that "Religion of Man has no clear-cut boundaries, sometimes it passes on into ethics and sometimes into philosophy,"[10] is not relevant.

As mentioned earlier Tagore's religious experience of *Isho-panishad-Tena tyaktena Bhunjitha ma gridhah kasyasiddhanam,* helps a man to know how the Universe has to be confronted with the realisation of truth through the selfless or disinterested actions. Lord Buddha also preached the ideal of peace and love from a disciplined perspective in experiential ways in contrast to the Upanishadic meditative ways and insightfully applied to social-process of his time in eight-fold disciplines, *Astangika-marga,* rising to a condition of brotherhood or *Maitri,* happiness in everything or *Mudita,* indifference or *Upeksha* and sympathy or *Karuna.* This psychological disciplined process prescribed for men and women in general is a discipline for detachment, and Rabindranath, like Buddha, but from his poetic vision of nature in operation, realises the same sort of detached attitude towards worldly materials and immediate interests.

It may be observed in this context that Tagore, like Buddha, emphasises the realisation of the highest state of pleasure in this life and world and thus differs from *Advaita Vedanta* and Vaisnavism, as these schools of thought put an emphasis on the final realisation of absolute pleasure in the transcendental world, beyond this worldly illusion. But the existence of man in this material world is not illusion or unreal to Tagore, but unreality lies in its contradictions which are to be reconciled through the manifestation of unity as absolute pleasure, potential in the infinite existence of Man in love and service for mankind. So the *Upanishad,* Buddha and Tagore put an emphasis on the sacrificial spirit in love and service for the welfare of the people that leads to the humanistic approach to unity in religion and morality. Hiranmay Bandyopadhyay in his *Rabindra Darshan,* observes that the ideal of *Visvakarma* in Rabindra Philosophy of religion is similar to the ideal of 'sympathy mingled with love' in Bauddha Philosophy. Again the ideal inspiration of Upanishadic morality has a similarity with the idea of *Brahmavihara* introduced by Buddha. But all these comparisons with the *Upanishads,* Buddhism and the *Vedanta* as mentioned above have to be understood from Tagore's broad nature oriented process.

Now, we may also observe some points of similarity between Rabindranath and other contemporary Indian thinkers which may help us to emphasise on the ethical point of view of Tagore's religion. Like Rabindranath, Vivekananda also thinks of the establishment of universal brotherhood through love and service of humanity. He recognises the divinity of man, as God exists in man as love or bliss. So to love man is to love God.[11] But unlike Tagore, Vivekananda explains this ideal of love as love with power, which can be developed in a spiritual manner, and the realisation of Reality, according to Swamjji, is possible through the development of power or a control of human nature by *Yogas-Jnana, Bhakti* and *Karma.* This idea of power or *Shakti* has been explained by Sri Aurobindo in another way. Though Sri Aurobindo, like Tagore, accepts Reality as *Anandam,* still he thinks of the primal Reality as *Shakti* or Dynamic Divine, which, according to him, has two forms Transcendent Divine and Cosmic Divine. The Cosmic Divine is always adjusting with the present circumstances, but its adjustment of work is for the realisation of the Transcendent Divine: "...the cosmic will is working towards the eventual realisation of the will of the Transcendent Divine".[12] So man tries to realise *Shakti* of the realisation of the Transcendent Divine and in this way through a spiritual procedure or *Yoga* he becomes a

Superman, that is a complete surrender to the Divine. Similarly, bearing in mind Tagore's special approach from nature in transcendent-experiential process and possibility, if one compares Tagore's religious experience and social process from Vivekananda to Gandhiji and Sri Aurobindo, one has to develop Tagore's position as another alternative way of life and society, running parallel with them, though not similar to them. Where as, Vivekananda's experience and way of life in religious aspect follows from a Yogic insight, Sri Aurobindo, from his understanding of the *Upanishads* in a post vedantic perspective, beyond *Samkara*, discovers an operation of a transcendent-experiential power beyond the mental and over mental processes to a transcendent power of Supermind. Thus, it may be observed that both Sri Aurobindo and Vivekananda are religious in traditional senses with some differences. Tagore, unlike both these thinkers of his time, realises a new transcendent divinity in and through nature manifesting itself both in cosmic and social situations to develop a transcendent personality in social process through a service of a different sort, which is deeply poetic and beauteous and also exalting. On account of the importance of the spiritual outlook in Vivekananda and Sri Aurobindo, they recognise the spiritual development of man and try to relate or link up men spiritually in the name of spiritual brotherhood under One Eternal Reality. But Reality, according to Tagore, is pure bliss and can be completely realised through pure love without any such power as condition. The realisation of this love or bliss from the nature oriented process creates a disinterested feeling in him that inspires a man to work for human beings in a selfless manner. Through this procedure of love and service of humanity as inspired from nature's infinity and beauty, a man can realise the Universal Man as Ultimate Reality, which is Tagore's idea of becoming *Visvakarma* or 'the world worker', in a naturalist sense with a depth. Now it is to be mentioned here that for the realisation of the Universality, Tagore does not prescribe any spiritual procedure or *Yoga,* but prefers a new moral procedure of life through a disinterested service of humanity. In this connection, the idea of Gandhiji may be referred to. He in *Young India,* writes, "...to me God is Truth and Love", and recognises the ideals of love and non-violence *(Ahimsa)* as the moral inspiration for the disinterested service of humanity. But here also there is a difference between Gandhiji and Tagore, and others. For the religious development of human mind or for the establishment of Humanism, Vivekananda and Sri Aurobindo emphasise on the spiritual procedure of human life, that according to Vivekananda, is a supra-moral that is principally Vedanta in development, and according to Sri Aurobindo is a supra-mental process of life that also is a process beyond *Vedanta* to create a condition for him; and on the other hand, Gandhiji emphasises on the moral procedure of religion as the moral development of life where he follows the suggestions of *Bhagbata* and *Gita.* But Tagore puts much importance on the socio-cultural development of human life that includes the development of the different elements of human existence in a integral form in transcendent-experiential sense. For this Tagore's religion of man is 'all-too-human', where he tries to establish an eternal relation of love among men culturally but not spiritually, as he thinks "the mind of Man is to be studied in its realisation of different aspects of truth from diverse points of view".[13]

So the humanistic thoughts of each of these contemporaries, about reality and love in man, and social situation are differently inspired. They are all alternative types of dedicated personalities- they can not be smashed with the same mould. Hence they are giants in their own ways.

The humanistic approach of Tagore to truth, existing in man, is to be realised through human process of love, that finally expresses its completeness in the highest state of life in non-duality or *Advaitam.* For the final recognition of this ideal, Tagore like a philosopher, firstly evaluates rationally the ideals and methods of different religions and thoughts of the world. It is already observed that due to the evaluation of different ideals at the different stages of Tagore's life, there is an evolutionary progress for the synthetic development of these ideals in the highest form of unity. Again it is also discussed that Tagore tries to evaluate all the methods or ways of life like knowledge, work and reverence in a synthetic manner for the realisation of reality as unity. In this connection it must be mentioned here that Tagore does not confine himself to mere examination of ideas but he evaluates everything for the elimination of dogmatic assertions and for the establishment of the highest unity through the synthesis of different ideals and different methods of life. This proves the special outlook of Tagore's religion of Man. It may be said in this context that through this process of analysis and synthesis, he finally unites his new religion with his new philosophy as he thinks that his new philosophy is an evaluation and synthesis of the experiences of life and existence. Thus, it may be noted that the charge against Tagore, that he confuses the idea of religion with philosophy, does not arise as he avoids the traditional dogmatic view of religion and places it above the limitations of the particular nation and country where all human beings are to be united under a bond of love in a transcendent-naturalist-experiential process. Through this idea of perfect union between individual man and all the human beings within the naturalist milieu, where the nature is divine, Tagore tries to liberate religion from its narrow limitations or dogmatic outlook. He throws a new light on philosophy or a wider view of the ideal of a new *Universal Humanism* with a claim to serve mankind by his mystic poetic vision which brings the entire humanity to one cosmic-psychic process. All analysis of religious experience and development of social process and service from ordinary scriptural perspectives is not appropriate to Tagore. So for a proper explanation of the religion of Man according to Tagore, one has to understand Tagore in a new setting.

Regarding the philosophical analysis of thy religion of Man as the inauguration of *Universal Humanism* in its comprehensive development in love, it may be pointed out that there may arise some confusions in the development of this ideal of *Humanism* as the expression of the ideas of 'the divinity of man' and 'the humanity of God'. Because in this analysis, some commentators observe, Tagore in some places puts an emphasis on the personal God and in other places he emphasises on the impersonal God or Absolute. So in the analysis of the religion of Man, as Tagore puts an importance on both *Theism* and *Absolutism*, so he does not introduce any clear-cut system of thought.

For a sound evaluation of the religion of Man as the *Universal Humanism* in the background of its comparison with the thoughts of different philosophers, its proper meaning as the unity of the dualistic and non-dualistic approaches to the human life and society, has to be examined. The object of this examination is to establish its significance and natural basis of life that is not to be confused with any unnatural process of thought. In order to develop this natural idea of the *Universal Humanism,* exists in the development of universality in man as Universal Man, Tagore starts with a critical and comparative study of this idea. In this connection it may be pointed out that his idea of the Universal Man is not that of a Superman or of any unnatural and supernatural idea of religious consciousness given by Nietzche and Sri Aurobindo. Nietzche's idea of Superman is that of an universal demoniac power that is unnatural. It may also be mentioned here that Sri Aurobindo's Superman is a divine power, that is supernatural. Tagore's idea of Universal Man is the highest form of realisation of human nature or existence, that is not extra-human or super-human. In order to understand this highest form of human nature we should know the comprehensive idea of human existence in a transcendent-experiential sense. This, as Tagore observes, is due to the expression of the intrinsic power or *surplus* in man, and through the development of this power in this life, a man gradually realises the truth or highest form of unity or non-duality as the final salvation of human life. The idea of harmony which is beyond all the limitations and contradictions of human life is naturalistically oriented. Again Tagore observes that the ideal of unity in love, which potentially exists in the human nature, is also responsible for the development of this idea of harmony as it helps a man to overcome the poor limitations or contradictions and establishes a final unity or identity. Through love, man firstly can realise his own existence, then in the second stage he relates him with other men through socio-cultural relations of love, and in this way finally he develops his universality as the Universal Man through the perfect realisation of the universal love as non-duality which is the highest state of human existence as Unity or *Advaitam.* The consciousness in the form of love exists potentially in the human nature or existence that is developed in the human life for the realisation of Ultimate Truth or Reality as unity or harmony in universal love. But this idea of unity is not the one Absolute Consciousness of *Samkara*, the *Advaita Vedantin,* as Tagore thinks Ultimate Reality as the Universal Love or

Bliss manifests Himself in this world as real and the human life in this world, is not also rejected by Tagore as illusion or *Maya,* but on the other hand all the contradictions of the world or the limitations of human life are to be reconciled with the eternal expression of love in man. This, Tagore observes, leads humanity and social process towards the expression of the highest types of personality-service with love for man or humanity as a whole, as a community which has to be served. This type of creative process in society develops unity in several differences. So the significance of this unity is not to avoid this world and human life but to include them under the idea of Oneness, which is the proper meaning of Reality as non-duality or *Advaitam.* Again Tagore concedes that man can have some acquaintance with this Reality in life and existence through the ordinary mode of knowledge but cannot completely realise Him in this way. Our ordinary pattern of knowledge is in the form of predications and it thus implies a partial difference. Hence Tagore prefers mystic intuition to ordinary knowledge. The Reality, which is absolutely non-dual or *Advaita,* can, in his opinion, be intuitively apprehended and realised in love, for Reality itself is perfect Bliss or Love. Human nature as cosmic nature is potentially universal, again finally realises this ultimate state of unity or non-duality in love that is the self-realisation or truth-realisation of man. The truth or reality as the union between individual self and Universal Self, is the unity or identity in differences or diversities, and this, according to Tagore, is the infiniteness in the finite. It may be mentioned here that some commentators find the similarity of Tagore's idea of unity or harmony with the idea of *Pantheism* and *Panentheism* of Hegel, Bradley, and others. But the important difference of Theistic or Pantheistic from the humanistic approach of Tagore lies in the application of Tagore's idea of unity not on God or Absolute beyond human existence, but it exists in man as the realisation of the highest state of harmony between finite and infinite existence of Man. Thus, it may be observed: "This 'harmony' in Rabindra Darshan is not resorted to Absolute, independent of man, this harmony is the manifestation of 'I exist'."[14] So unity, according to Tagore, lies in the human existence which is to be manifested in the highest state of human life. This highest state of life, as Tagore observes, is to be recognised as the human freedom or the salvation through unity. The salvation is not the super-imposition of something on human nature, but it is the natural expression or self-manifestation of human existence in its highest state of unity in contradictions.

For this, the salvation or freedom is self-creating or self-manifesting idea. On the one hand, it manifests the highest state of human life, and on the other hand, it creates in love a state of unity or harmony that does not deny the nature or existence of man and world. The final idea of salvation which is in the form of universal nature, cannot reveal itself in an individual in a particular process, but it is revealed as the eternal or universal union of individual man with all human beings that is a perfect unity with Universal Man or Absolute. This is the absolute freedom of human life where man becomes free from all his bondages due to contradictions of life. Tagore thinks that the poor interests or demands of life can create contradictions as of human life, but a man may be free from these bondages through love that creates a disinterested feeling in him and this feeling inspires a man to work for the human beings in a selfless manner. Thus, from the beginning of life a man proceeds in an evolutionary process towards the final freedom that is the perfect realisation of the universal nature of man in the eternal love. In this universal realisation, man finds his completeness and perfection in life. The realisation of completeness in the highest state of freedom in unity is the natural expression and self-manifestation, which is to be recognised as the proper religion of Man.

This meaning of the religion of Man as the expression of the universal nature of man in his material existence may be called the manifestation of the total man which, is properly required for his freedom in unity. In order to explain this nature and existence of man in freedom, Dr Ganguly observes, "Man today not only has to strive for but also to fight against, in order to learn and use the basic alphabet of 'Self-expression'. Marx correctly called the present stage 'pre-history'. Thus, freedom is both an objective challenge and a subjective state. This subjective state can be regarded as a consciousness of a demand-felt need and its fulfillment in the historical context of envisaged goal. Freedom, therefore, involves the total man".[15]

In the context of this analysis of the total nature and existence of man towards the achievement of his final freedom, Tagore's idea of the religion of Man may be evaluated in the background of Marxian approach to human life. Both these thinkers accept man is the centre of history and also observe that the proper essence of man lies in the expression of his idea of freedom. In the analysis of the human essence, in the context of his historical existence, both Tagore and Marx put an emphasis upon his material existence where his natural demand of life is the fulfillment of the material needs of life. Marx observes, "Hunger is the objective need of a body for an object which exists outside itself and which is essential for its integration and for the expression of its nature".[16] This objective need of body, according to Marx, expresses the essential nature of man that fundamentally determines his existence in history. But Tagore, though like Marx puts a stress on the material existence of man, still he thinks that the essential nature of man lies in transcending the limitations or contradictions, born of his material existence. So the essential nature of man lies in his infinite or universal existence as the expression of the consciousness of unity in freedom that reveals his 'divinity'.

It may be said in this context that Marx takes man and his consciousness as the product of matter. But the development of consciousness in man makes him cautious about freedom from all types of exploitations and engages him in creative activities and thus makes him a free man.[17] So, consciousness, though is coming out of matter, still is an infinite power in man that helps him to fight against all types of social and material exploitations which are responsible for his alienations, as a socio-economic being. Marx observes four types of alienations: (1) alienation from the process that work, (2) alienation from the products of labour, (3) alienation of the worker from himself, (4) alienation of the worker from others.[18] The self-alienation due to these factors, present in the class-structure of the bourgeois society, creates contradictions in the natural life of man. The consciousness of the exploited or alienated people or the proletariat class as the embodiment of universal humanity, urges them to be free from exploitations through the change of society in the introduction of *Communism*. This ideal, according to Marx, is a scientific socialism that makes a man free from all contradictions and exploitations. He observes, "*Communism* as the positive transcendence of private properties as human self-estrangement, and therefore as the real appropriation of the human essence by and for man; *Communism* therefore as the complete return of man to himself as a social (i.e., human) being a return accomplished consciously and embracing the entire wealth of previous development".[19]

Thus, the introduction of *Communism* is to change the society for the social freedom of man as the expression of his essence or true individuality, free from all contradictions. For this, Marx, in *The Holy Family* explains freedom as 'the positive power to assert his true individuality'.

But the true individuality in the state of freedom, as Tagore observes, lies in the natural existence of man which is the self-transcendence of material contradictions through love and self-manifestation of potential universality in the harmonious development of his existence in freedom as unity.

Thus, the development of the highest state of human freedom, in the observation of Tagore, is the manifestation of his universal nature that is potential in his material existence in this world. But man, in the opinion of Tagore, is not a mere material being as it in man expresses false 'ego', that is responsible for producing contradictions in life and society. But the universal or eternal 'I' in man can overcome this contradictions through the development of universality in him. But this development does not mean the change or elimination of contradictions in the society, but it is the reconciliation of contradictions through a harmonious development of human existence as a creative personality that finally leads to inauguration of unity in the highest state of freedom. Ganguly rightly observes, "Man is creative and therefore his primary concern is to overcome constrains towards his goal of freedom".[20]

Thus, in this connection it may be said that Tagore's idea of the human freedom is the essential expression of universal nature of man which is not through the elimination of contradiction but through a reconciliation in unity through a process of love that reveals the totality or completeness of human life. This totality, according to Tagore, is the truth of man, manifested in the different creative spheres of his life. For this, Tagore observes, "to study the mind of Man in its realisation of different aspects of truth from diverse points of view".[21] But the significance of this truth lies in its existence in freedom as unity, which is the harmonious development of man and society. So Tagore, like a true Indian philosopher or like Hegel, points out that freedom of man is the freedom in unity in diversities of life and existing society, they, in the context of modern existential analysis, may be said that freedom of man is the normal and essential expression of human nature without any imposition or restriction. For the evaluation of this idea we may refer to the observation of Banerjee: "So, while for Indian philosophy and for Hegel (in a somewhat different manner though) freedom can be achieved within the existing society as it does not count much, for Marxian philosophy it has to be achieved by changing the material conditions of existence in the bourgeois society. For *Existentialism*, "...freedom in the sense of freedom of choice is unlimited and is there in this society but in the sense of complete authenticity it is never to be achieved."[22] In the light of this observation we, in this context, may refer to the existential approach of man which has a similarity with Tagore's analysis of human existence as the manifestation of universal nature in the highest state of freedom in unity.

In *Existentialism*, we find the universal form of human freedom where the universal nature of the human being is completely revealed. Tagore thinks that through love and selfless service of humanity man reveals his universal nature, and thus he becomes united with all men that is the revelation of the highest state of human nature or existence. J.P. Sartre, a great Existentialist, also expresses the same view when he says that the bondage of human life lies in the contradictions between the life of an individual and the life of others. But when man becomes free from this poor bondage of his life and realises the infiniteness in his finite existence or realises the highest unity between him and all the human beings, can reveal his universal nature which is man's salvation or freedom. In *'The Problem of Method'* Sartre writes, "And in thus willing freedom, we discover that it depends entirely upon the freedom of others and that the freedom of others depends upon our own". This idea of human freedom refers to the social freedom of man, who, as an individual, exists with others in the society, and so his freedom is the expression of his social or universal nature which is intimately related with others and thus is manifested in its highest state of unity in social life. This unity, in the opinion of Tagore, is the highest state of human freedom as the expression of infinite or universal nature of man through disinterested love and service of mankind. This universality in man is not supernatural or superhuman but is a complete manifestation of perfection in the nature and existence of man. For this the idea of Sri Aurobindo's Supermind is regarded by Tagore as the human mind and the realisation of the Life Divine is the accomplishment of human value as love that directs him towards his highest state of life as non-duality or *Advaitam.* This humanist ideal of Rabindranath influences Sri Aurobindo also, who observes in Tagore's idea, "...the greater era of man's living something that seems to be in promise".[23]

Thus, it may be observed that the humanistic approach to Tagore's religion of Man is to deal with the universal nature of man, which, due to the material existence as 'ego', may start with duality or differences, but finally it can remove or overcome the differences through the emergence of unity or non-duality in universal love in man. This is interpreted by Tagore as the final state of human life where a non-duality between the individual man and the Universal Man or Absolute can be established. So in the analysis of the religion of Man, Rabindranath starts with the idea of duality and thus sometimes refers to the idea of personal God, but finally he introduces the idea of non-duality or Absolutism.

The development of Tagore's idea of *Jivandevata,* sometimes may refer to the idea of personal God as the expression of duality, but finally it introduces the idea of *Visvadevata,* or Absolutism that inspires some commentators to observe Tagore's idea of *Jivandevata* as potentially *Visvadevata* or Absolute Oneness, which is to be manifested in human life through the realisation of universal nature, at the highest state of human freedom in unity through love. The realisation of this unity in life, according to Tagore, is the establishment of the idea of non-duality or *Advaitam* as Absolute which is perfect love or bliss. Radhakrishnan rightly observes,

"Ishwara, the highest manifestation of the Absolute, is the personal Lord of the Universe. The distinction of the lover and the loved is kept up till the last point, when in perfect love the two become one. The personal God is then dissolved in the Absolute".[24] Thus, if the thought of Rabindranath is evaluated in this manner, his synthetic approach to duality and non-duality in the development of the idea of the religion of Man can be understood, which reconciles the charge against him that he confuses *Theism* and *Absolutism.* In the analysis of the religion of Man as the explanation of human nature, Tagore may start with the theistic approach of duality in life and society but the significance of this approach lies in the development of non-duality or Absolutism, Thus, it may be observed that the final object of Tagore's religion of Man is to develop the universal nature of man which is to introduce unity or oneness as non-duality or *Advaitam* in his final state of salvation or freedom.

Thus, in the development of final state of salvation or freedom through unity in love, God or Absolute as One is manifested in human life, which appears in the religion of Man as the 'humanity of God'. The expression of this ideal of humanity in man, makes him divine; which, in the observation of Tagore, is the 'divinity of man'. So the expression of the idea of 'the humanity of God' in man makes him divine, that finally makes God or Absolute as human personality. Because Tagore thinks that Absolute as human value of love or bliss is perfectly manifested in human life. This manifestation of divinity in love, introduces unity or non-duality in the individual and the Absolute, which is the complete expression of God in man.

In the light of this evaluation, it may be observed that in the development of the ideals of the religion of Man as 'the divinity of man' and 'the humanity of God', Tagore explains the nature and existence of God or Absolute as the supreme human personality. Thus, Tagore observes that the idea of God is perfectly manifested in the creative life of man and through the perfect realisation of God as the ideal of love in man, a complete unity of man and God is established.

If it be so, then a question may arise: Why is God completely manifested in human life only? As He is not bound to have human form, why will He have the human personality? So what is the meaning of Infinite personality? Again God being the preserver of infinite quality or attribute, He cannot be completely manifested in the finite life. Man also being finite cannot realise Him completely, and therefore, in the state of salvation or freedom, a complete unity between the individual and the Absolute cannot be established. For this some commentators take the philosophical explanation of the religion of Man by Tagore as personal, poetic and subjective. Dr Srivastava observes, "A philosopher who is not free from subjectivism and anthropomorphism fails to give us an adequate, transcendental, non-empirical and realistic account of the nature of the Infinite".[25]

In order to meet this charge against Tagore, the philosophical basis of the religion of Man is to be properly evaluated. In the analysis of the religion of Man, Tagore points out that everything in the world evolves from the eternal and infinite nature of Absolute and He manifests Himself in this finite world. It may be noted that He is manifested in different objects of the world in different degrees but is perfectly manifested in the human life only; as man, according to him, is potentially perfect. The infinite ideal of love or bliss can be perfectly realised in the eternal or inner nature of a man. Through the complete realisation of this infinite ideal, all the imperfections of individual life can be removed, and the ideals of the religion of Man as the 'divinity of man' and the 'humanity of God' can be fully realised through the establishment of unity or identity. This, according to Rabindranath, is the transcendental unity of all finite beings in the supreme human personality as Universal Man, or Absolute. Regarding this explanation it may be observed that Tagore, like Hegal, also thinks that the idea of Absolute as Unity comprehends all the finite beings. Individual man possesses imperfect personality so long he lives under the influence of 'ego' or poor material interest of ordinary life. But God or Absolute as perfect personality manifests Himself in the finite existences, and that Lotze observes, finite personalities are the manifestations of the Divine. Reality of Rabindranath, Narvane points out, "can be regarded as the personality acting upon personalities through incessant manifestations".[26] These manifestations develop the unity between the divinity and the humanity that finally lead to the harmonious development of human personality as the expression of the unity of his individuality and universality, which, according to Tagore, is nothing but the expression of divinity or God in man through the human process of love in man. Thus, through this human process and human method of love, Tagore observes, man as a finite being expresses his infinite personality or universal nature in and through his finite existence, and in this way the highest ideal of divinity as infinite or absolute value also is manifested in the finite life of man. Man, though is finite or limited can overcome his limitation or finiteness through the realisation of absolute value of divinity or infiniteness as love or bliss which potentially exists in man. The individual man, in his life, tries to realise love through different human actions and human relations that produce a selfless or disinterested feeling in him and this selfless attitude of man inspires him to overcome all limitations, contradictions and imperfections of life. Thus, through the influence of the ideal of love, man becomes related with other men and in the perfect realisation of this infinite ideal in the highest state of human freedom, a complete unity between individual man and Universal Man can be established. In this state of salvation or freedom, man becomes free from all his limitations through the perfect and complete realisation of the infinite ideal of love, that creates ultimate unity or identity.

In this way Tagore in his religion of Man supplies an objective analysis of how a man in this objective world reveals his infinite personality through the human love and actions. Thus, God or Absolute also becomes manifested in human life through the perfect realisation of God as infinite ideal of love in man that develops his infinite personality.

It may be pointed out that though some commentators observe some inconsistencies about Tagore's idea of God, self and liberation, still all these inconsistencies are reconciled through the humanistic approach to Tagore's religion of Man, where he relates religion with man: "I have expressedly said that I have concentrated my attention upon the subject of religion which is solely related to man".[27] Religion, according to Tagore, is the expression of human nature that stands on the life of man as the unity of 'ego' and 'I' as a completeness through the realisation of universality. The development of this ideal of completeness in the extent of universalism relates a man with the world of nature and human beings and this union makes him finally free from all individualities and thus the existence and life of man become significant and perfect. Banerjee rightly observes, 'Perfection of man- the joyful freedom is through the love of nature and man. For this perfection or freedom the transcendence of narrow individuality, vileness and mental poverty are necessary; and through an inseparable and intimate relation with men and nature the attainment of this perfection is possible'.[28] This idea of perfection or completeness of man in society as the establishment of human freedom in the human process, in the opinion of Tagore, solves different social and moral problems and finally develops a humanist outlook in religion and in the philosophy of life, that is the introduction of *Humanism* in the religion of Man.

To discuss human nature, transcending contradictions and to establish man in society with an intimate relation with others are the fundamental ends of *Humanism*. It points out that inner essence of man lies in his social nature that finally inspires him to love and to work for humanity. Comte says, "To love Humanity may be truly said to constitute the whole duty of Man".[29]

Comte, in his general view of positive philosophy, explains the evolution of this social nature of man in three different stages- theological, metaphysical and positive through which a man proceeds under the guidance of a necessary law. Comte observes: "This law consists in the fact that each of our principal conceptions, each branch of our knowledge, passes in succession through three different theoretical states. The theological or fictitious state, the metaphysical or abstract state and the scientific or positive state". So the idea of human value or the ideal of *Humanism*, according to this thinker, came at the end of the history of human thought through the development of science and technology.

This scientific outlook of *Humanism* brought a revolutionary change in history, politics, literature, sociology in Europe in the eighteenth century. This change or movement in society, due to the influence of *Humanism*, is called by Russell, 'The Romantic Movement', which according to him, is "a profound revolt, both philosophical and political against traditional systems in thought, in politics and in economics, gave rise to attacks upon many beliefs and institutions that had hitherto been regarded as unassailable. This revolt had two very different forms, one romantic, the other rationalistic".[30]

The result of this revolution puts a great importance on the value of man, who has infinite potentiality, which is explained by Rousseau, 'The father of romantic movement', thus: "man is naturally good, and only by institutions is he made bad...."[31] Man expresses the significance of this goodness when he manifests his infinite potentialities through art, culture, science and philosophy. Thus, his knowledge of God as creator or preserver of truth, beauty and goodness will be realised through his creations in different stages in society. So to know God is not the only object of human life, but his final and fundamental end is to become God through the manifestation of his infinite potentiality, when a man gradually becomes Infinite Man.

This new evaluation of man, in the background of the idea of infinity, brought the *Renaissance* in Bengal through the revolutionary works and thoughts of Rammohan, Vidyasagar, Bankimchandra, Vivekananda and Rabindranath. Rammohan as a great social reformer, emphasises the social, political and moral freedom of man, that according to him, is his proper religion. Man, he says, reaches his absolute freedom, through the knowledge of the highest ideal of humanity in him. The knowledge of humanity, according to Vidyasagar and Bankimchandra, becomes complete through the work or service for mankind. The knowledge and realisation of man through the service of mankind, Vivekananda observes, should be the fundamental end of religion. He says, "Religion is neither word nor doctrine. It is to be and become, not to hear and accept". So this 'man-making' ideal of religion of Vivekananda introduces the ideal of non-duality of *Advaita Vedanta* in man that develops the idea of unity through love and work for mankind.[32] The ideal of unity or universality, according to Vivekananda, is at the root of human existence; which, Rolland observes, is "His universal soul was rooted in its human soul".[33] This potential universality in man can be developed through the disinterested love and selfless' service for human beings. This idea of 'the divinity of man', presented through this new outlook of *Humanism* expresses the ideas of the *Vedas,* the *Upanishads* and other traditional Indian views that express the infiniteness of man over his finite contradictions in this material world. For this Sinha rightly observes, "World is the field of Moral actions of God and men....God is the meaning of human existence. *Humanism* enlightened by Theism is the desideration".[34] This type of the divine outlook of man, presented by the different thinkers of the East and the West, is synthetically evaluated by Tagore through his introduction of a complete view of *Universal Humanism.*

In developing this ideal of *Universal Humanism,* Tagore goes through the controversial meaning of the term *Humanism* and finally tries to find out its proper nature. Different thinkers have explained the significance of the term Humanism from different points of view. According to some the idea of *Humanism* is used against the *Naturalism* and *Absolutism.* Schiller points out, "*Humanism* in philosophy is opposed to naturalism and absolutism".[35]

Naturalism treats man as a natural event and puts a less emphasis on human values. Again *Absolutism* places divine personality over and above everything of the world. Finite beings of the world are nothing but the manifestations of the Absolute. So human life is also determined by the divine spirit. Some thinkers are of the opinion that this idea of God or Absolute, kills the human personality and human freedom as it denies the separate existence of man. Sartre, the Existentialist, concedes that man has existence and this existence is his truth, which is not determined by God. He denies the existence of God. Man is free to solve the different problems of life and to develop the human relation with other men. Comte, a Positivist, also establishes the religion of humanity instead of non-human supernatural God. The existence of man can only be perceived in the world as the preserver of different values or qualities. But the particular individual cannot be worshipped. For this the Ideal of humanity, which is the synthesis of all men and different human values should be worshipped. This ideal of humanity according to Comte, is the 'synthetic idealisation of our existence' and is free from our imperfections. So it must be respected and worshipped by all.

However, through the changes of outlook and thoughts, ideas of old *Naturalism* and *Absolutism* have undergone great changes. Today the *neo-Naturalism* accepts the human value and the personality of man. Again the idea of concrete Universal established by the modern Absolutists, supplies the opportunity for the development of human personality. If we discuss different modern conceptions of *Humanism* we may get two meanings- either anthropocentric or Divine. The former takes man as his own centre and the centre of everything. But special emphasis on individual man increases his 'ego' which is responsible for the dualism of self and not-self or different contradictions and imperfections of life. In *True Humanism,* Maritain points out that this type of *Humanism* is an 'inhuman humanism'.

Rabindranath is aware of this fact and for this he denounced the individual interest and emphasises the collective interest. Work for one's own interest creates 'ego' that creates contradictions in life and society. But work for others through love, Tagore observes, develops a selfless outlook in man, that urges him to be related with all other men intimately and thus he realises universality in him, which, in the final state of life, express unity in life and society.

Regarding the attainment of this final stage of *Universal Humanism* in unity, Tagore puts a great importance on love, that firstly suppresses 'ego', which is due to the influence of the material interest in life. Ordinarily man works under 'ego' and produces different contradictions which appear to be discrete and opposite to each other. But the ideal of love, potential in man, inspires him to suppress this view through the development of the relation of continuity with a continuous process of life of man in society. This, Tagore observes, finally unites man with the universal process of life in the world. So it is a continuous process of developing human life which relates the life of an individual with other individuals in society that makes the expression of universality in human personality. Thus, the life of man, according to Tagore, acquires its significance and meaning through the inauguration of Universal Humanity in this life, when he himself becomes the Universal Man.

This explanation of human life as given by Tagore, is unique, as it differs from the traditional outlook of the 'Divinity of Man' given by Western and Indian Idealism. These thinkers of the East and the West, though put an importance on the divinity of human life, still emphasise the transcendental divinity, which is to be realised in the life beyond. But Tagore explains the significance of the 'Divinity of Man' as the expression of the universality in human personality in man's social and worldly existence. This explanation of Tagore also differs from European Humanists and Socialists as they denounce the ideal of the 'Divinity of Man' and emphasise the development of socio-economic and socio-political values in this life of man. Rabindranath does not deny the importance of these values in human life, but he thinks that the life of a man is something more than these values. He writes, 'To-day, in Europe, everything is to be judged in the context of science. Thus, the explanation is going on, that the human material is only physiological or zoological or psychological or too much extent is sociological. But man is not this reality, he is with all these realities and manifests own self towards the Infinite beyond all these realities ...'[36] Tagore's ideal of humanity is to be operative with man and society to raise both to a process of divinity in activity.

In the manifestation of this infiniteness in man, his life and existence become complete. In this idea of completeness, different explanations of different thinkers are synthesised, as in this explanation of Tagore, we find the unity of the individual, the social and the Universal Man. Regarding the development of this complete spirit in man in this world, Tagore says, 'the consciousness of man with the Universal Man is the greatest spiritual Truth'.[37] This universal consciousness or spirit is fully developed and fulfilled through love and service for man as Universal Man or God.

So the introduction of the idea of *spiritualism* or God in *Humanism*, according to some commentators, makes his idea of *Humanism* as 'God-centric', spiritual and theistic. But inauguration of *spiritualism* in Tagore's idea of *Universal Humanism* is something more than the traditional view of spiritualism or theism as it develops a synthetic outlook of man where both theistic and atheistic values are synthesised, which according to Tagore, is the 'greatest spiritual Truth'.

Atheism stresses the importance on social values that are to be realised in this life and world and Theism emphasises the intrinsic and eternal values which cannot be completely realised in this life and world, but are to be realised in the life beyond through the union with God who is the final substratum of all values. Tagore, on the other hand, interprets man as the synthesis of both these material and spiritual values. Through the development of mere material and social values in life, he expresses 'ego' or finiteness; but infiniteness in him inspires man to cross all limitations due to finiteness and to realise universality in this life.

This development of infiniteness or universality, according to Tagore, is the development of the 'Divinity of Man' and manifestation of universality in human life is the 'humanity of God'. One is the realisation of universality in human life. Through this process of life an individual man becomes free, selfless and complete, which, in Tagore's opinion, is something divine and spiritual. He says, "For free spirit is godly and alone can claim kinship with God".[38]

This 'kinship with God', according to Tagore, is the divine union, when man becomes free from all limitations and thus relates himself with all men, that, he observes, is the realisation of unity in love.

This view of Tagore's *Universal Humanism* in the religion of Man, explains how a man becomes Infinite or Universal Man. In this process of becoming, Tagore accepts both social and spiritual or eternal values. But Tagore observes that man realises all social values not in limited sense, but all these realisations through selfless service for mankind in love are for the realisation of absolute values of truth, goodness and beauty as essential unity in man. This explanation of Tagore is something more than the traditional explanation, as it expresses a comprehensive attitude towards human life, where (a) man becomes divine, through the realisation of absolute values; (b) God is taken as the substratum of absolute values, who is both personal and impersonal, dual and non-dual. The manifestation of God as absolute valve in human life in different stages, expresses Him as personal and dual, but through the development of the ideal of unity, the idea of oneness and non-duality in man is established. (c) Values, which are to be realised in human life and in society, are, in the view of Tagore, man-and-society-conditioned absolute values. With reference to man the value becomes true and with its development in society through its realisation in human life, it becomes real. But the total nature of value is not fully realised by the individual man, so it is infinite or absolute. Man, who is potentially infinite, can realise this absolute value through the development of his infiniteness. So value is neither purely social in limited sense, nor purely transcendental, but in a transcendent-experiential sense, it is both, as it is to be realised in this life and world through the experiential process of developing of unity in different degrees in different stages of human life and society. (d) Love, according to Tagore, is the only ideal that has the essential quality of infiniteness and universality, which establishes the intimate relation in men in different stages in different forms and finally establishes the final stage of unity and identity, Man in love, gradually learns to extend his heart through the establishment of social relations with others, that finally develops a purely selfless feeling for others. The development of this selfless and disinterested feeling in love urges man to be free from limitations and contradictions due to his finiteness or 'ego' and thus there is a gradual inauguration of unity in love for all, which is the development of universality in human personality. This, as Tagore observes, is the 'Divinity of Man'. Through the development of this idea of 'Divinity', a man can lead a good life in society, which is well-balanced, well-conducted and well-regulated social life. This type of well-regulated, good life in love leads to the human unity as suggested by Tagore in the analysis of his religion of Man, as nothing but the inauguration of Infinite or Universal Man in the finite existence of the individual, developing the socio-cultural relation of integrality.

This introduction of the idea of Universal Man in Tagore's religion of Man expresses the idea of the continuous process of developing human life with infiniteness or universality, that is beyond the mere social, economic and political analysis of man. The mere realisation of these finite values in limited sense may exhaust the total potency of man; but the development of the infiniteness or universality in human life speaks of his infinite potency and nature. The development of this nature in different stages through different activities in this world, make a man great when he reaches the perfection or the completeness through the final realisation of 'unity in love' or *So'ham,* which, according to Tagore, is to become *Manava Brahma* or Universal Man.

So the philosophy of *Universal Humanism,* introduced by Tagore, is a philosophy of becoming Universal Man, through disinterested love and service for mankind. This can be recognised as transcendent-experiential process as it introduces a process of transcendence of different limitations and contradictions through the manifestations of potential and transcendent human value of love in different creative socio-cultural activities in experiential process in different degrees, developing the socio-cultural relation of unity in diversities. In the context of this analysis, the *Universal Humanism* of Tagore, can be treated as Socio-Cultural Humanism that inspires man to overcome different types of contradictions, created out of the evils of the modern age of mechanisation, through a creative development of socio-cultural relation of integrality. Regarding this socio-cultural process of developing universality in man, Tagore was an out and out optimist and in his 'Crisis of Civilisation', he expressed emphatically, "As I look around I see the crumbling ruins of proud civilisation strewn like a vast heap of futility. And yet I shall not commit the grievous sin of losing faith in Man.... A day will come when unvanquished Man will retrace his path of conquest, despite all barriers, to win back his lost heritage."

While Tagore is elevating man to a transcendent-divine and experiential human processes, Swami Vivekananda before him has already prepared the ground for the activity of man to the *service* of man, for, in the service of man, man realises the *divinity* in man. This new *Humanism*, as realised by Tagore and Vivekananda, is a process of mutuality of activity, where the gulf between God and Man is completely bridged over with a suggestion for a new society to emerge. Those are alternative social processes with a new dynamism and creativeness on a par with similar social and humanist programmes, as differently devised by Sri Aurobindo, Gandhiji and Radhakrishnan, moulding the dynamic traditions of India from the *Vedas* to the *Upanishads, Bhagvadgita, Brahmasutras, Buddhism* and the *Vedanta* through the historical evolution of Indian thought, transcending the static systems of logic, metaphysics, theology and epistemology of the Western philosophy to the stage of Hegel and rising to the advanced currents of post-Hegelian transcendental phenomenology, existentialism, and evolutionism of Western thinkers from Bergson and Santayana to Dewey and Whitehead, with a stress on their non-discursive integral processes. Indian social *Humanism* in its universalist attitude in varied alternative patterns and senses, is not only an advanced current in all modern senses, but each is revolutionist in spirit with an intercultural prospect, realised in aspects in Western counterparts of such processes.

Notes

1. Sachindranath Gangopadhyay and others, *Rabindra Darshan,* p. 31.
2. Visva-Bharati, *Memorandum of Association.*
3. *Ibid.*
4. M. K. Gandhi, *Ethical Religion,* p. 62.
   **Hriday aji mor kemane gela khuli, Jagat asi setha karichhe kolakuli.*
5. Rabindranath Tagore, 'Samagra Ek', *Santiniketan,* p. 265.
6. 'Dharmaprachar', 'Dharma', *Rabindrarachanavali,* (Cent Edn.), Vol. XII, p. 44.
7. 'The Religion of Humanity', *General View of Positivism,* p. 341.
8. *Ibid.*, pp. 348-9.
9. N. V. Banerjee, *The Concept of Philosophy,* p. 83.
10. B. G. Ray, *The Philosophy of Rabindranath Tagore,* p. 110.
11. *Jive prem kare jei jan sei jan, sebichhe Isvar.*
12. Sri Aurobindo, *The Riddle of This World* (1st impression), p. 73.
13. Visva-Bharati, *Memorandum of Association.*
14. Sachindranath Gangopadhyay and others, *Rabindra Darshan,* p. 40.
15. Dr S. N. Ganguly, 'Rationality versus Reasonableness', (Freedom: A Reinterpretation), Dr J. N. Mahanty and Dr S. P. Banerjee (ed.), *Self, Knowledge and Freedom,* p. 62.
16. K. Marx, *Early Writings,* ed. T. B. Bottomore, p. 207.
17. Karl Marx and Frederick Engels, *The German Ideology,* ed. S. Ryazanskaya, pp. 44-45.
18. Karl Marx. *Economic and Philosophic Manuscripts of 1844,* pp. 64-70.
19. *Ibid.*, p. 90.

20. Dr S. N. Ganguly, 'Rationality versus Reasonableness', *Self, Knowledge and Freedom,* p. 69.
21. Visva-Bharati, *Memorandum of Association.*
22. S. P. Banerjee, 'Alienation and Freedom', *Self, Knowledge and Freedom,* p. 211.
23. 'Sri Aurobindo and Rabindranath Tagore', Sri Aurobindo Ashram, Pondicherry.
24. Dr S. Radhakrishnan, *The Philosophy of Rabindranath Tagore,* p. 55.
25. Dr R.S. Srivastava, *Contemporary Indian Philosophy,* p. 105.
26. V. S. Narvane, *Rabindranath Tagore-A Philosophical Study,* p. 74.
27. Rabindranath Tagore, *The Religion of Man,* p. 119.
28. Dr S. P. Banerjee, 'Bharatiya Darshane Manavatavad' *Desh.*
29. A. Comte., *General View of Positivism,* p. 378.
30. Russell, *History of Western Philosophy,* p. 691.
31. *Ibid.*, p. 663.
32. *Jive prem kare Jei jan Sei jan seviche Isvar.*
33. R. Rolland, *Swami Vivekananda.*
34. Dr J. N. Sinha, 'Preface', *Moral Idealism and Theisin.*
35. F.C.S. Schiller, 'Humanism', Hasting (ed.), *Encyclopedia of Religion and Ethics.*
36. Rabindranath Tagore, *Ghare Baire.*
37. Dr S. B. Dasgupta, *Upanishader Patabhumik ay Rabindra Manas.*
38. Rabindranath Tagore, *The Religion of Man,* p. 33.

Chapter - 8

An Epilogue: Final Observations on the Expansion of the Theory of Creative Man, The Universal

A careful examination of the idea of the religion of Man proves the existence of the ideal of unity, potential in Tagore's analysis, develops a comprehensive outlook, revealed in this harmonious development of philosophy and religion, as a process of expressing non-duality of man and God in society. This development of Tagore's religion of Man, places his idea above the ordinary sense of religion, as the ordinary view of religion takes it as the substratum of supernatural and superhuman values that are finally to be realised beyond this life and world; but Tagore's idea of the religion of Man is the humanistic ideal as the synthesis of transcendental and natural characters of human values in a transcendent-experiential sense, that are to be realised and manifested in life in this world in different stages by degrees.

This idea of the religion of Man explains religion as the nature of man who is potentially perfect that reconciles all the contradictions of human life and society through the harmonious development in perfection. Thus, the proper meaning of religion, in the opinion of Tagore, is the expression of the perfect nature of man in the development of unity in contradictions that is evaluated by Dr Radhakrishnan, in his *Religion and Culture:*

"The need of religion, for a system of thought, for devotion to a cause which will give our fragile and fugitive existence significance and value does not require much elaborate argument. It is an intrinsic element of human nature". All limitations and contradictions in human life and existence are apparent and the intrinsic nature of man in this sense is to reconcile all these contradictions through a comprehensive development of man's perfect existence as the religion of Man.

In the comprehensive development of human existence, Tagore observes a comprehensive process in love that is potential in man and also manifests itself in a harmonious manner towards the expression of universal nature of individual in all his contradictions. The ideal of love in man, thus also helps to apply a method of love as the synthesis of all social processes for its harmonious expression as the reconciliation of all contradictions of human life in the development of universality as love or peace. In the interpretation of the meaning of the religion as the expression of the universal nature of man, Tagore evaluates this procedure: 'that which brings peace among all the dissimilarities and contradictions in this world, which is only the bridge of integration among all the disintegrations, is called religion'.[1]

For this process of developing peace in human life and society and fostering unity in diversity. Tagore introduces a comprehensive method of love that can completely be realised in the inner nature of man as unity. The realisation of this unity in man is his freedom from limitations and contradictions, which, in the opinion of Tagore, is the self-creating and self-manifesting process of human life that can be complete in this world. This, as Tagore observes, is not unnatural or supernatural, as it is purely humanistic process that is different from *Soul-Mysticism*, as the meditation of silent consciousness which exceeds human consciousness and *Nature Mysticism* that speaks of divine truth of the supernatural world.[2]

The religion of Man, as the realisation of universal unity in man as truth, according to Tagore, is purely human; because Tagore recognises it as the natural expression of human life and he also introduces a humanistic method of love for making this expression of universality in man complete. The ideal of love that exists potentially in the intrinsic nature of man, is expressed externally through a method of synthesis in love that creates a feeling of disinterestedness in human life and thus it inspires man to sacrifice his poor 'ego' or narrow demands of life for the greater cause of social service of humanity. These ideas of selfless love and service for mankind, urge a man to suppress his petty demands for the satisfaction of poor 'ego' and also inspire him to love and work for others. In *The Religion of Man,* Tagore aptly observes in this context: "...to divest our work of selfishness and become *Visvakarma,-'The World-worker'*, we must work for all".

In this way Tagore introduces the idea of God as the highest value of unity that is manifest in human life as perfect bliss or *Anandam,* to be realised through disinterested love and service. This idea of Tagore has a similarity with the views of other thinkers. J. Royece, following Hegel, holds that Reality is the conserver and preserver of values. Tagore, like these thinkers takes God as supreme value or ideal of love or bliss which is to be expressed in man through selfless or disinterested love and service for mankind. Thus, this procedure makes the manifestation of God in human life possible and also introduces the idea of non-duality of God and man, as man, through this creative process of love and service, becomes 'world-worker'.

To become 'world-worker' is to love and work for all, that finally solves the moral and the social problems of human life. These problems of life stand on the contradiction between individual interest or 'ego' and social interest. But the methods of love and service to humanity remove these limitations or contradictions, because a man in unconditional love for others sacrifice his poor interests for the welfare of the people in society. This comprehensive method of love and service introduces the moral law as the harmonious development of man's individual and social life, which, to Tagore, is 'the divinity of man' or the expression of God in man. This comprehensive method or the introduction of the law of divinity as the order or harmony of individuality, sociality and spirituality of man, is evaluated by Gandhiji as Law and God are one.

The introduction of this law as harmony leads to the realisation of the highest value of unity in man as the expression of Absolute or Universal Oneness in man, which, in the opinion of Rabindranath, is the introduction of the highest ideal of the religion of Man as 'the humanity of God' where God or Absolute appears as *Manava Brahma.* This human outlook of reality leads to the explanation of its intimate and essential relation with man that requires the explanation of human nature as universal. In support of this explanation, Tagore refers to the traditional Indian outlook, presented in the idea of *Ucchishta* in *Atharva Veda.* The meaning of *Ucchishta,* according to Tagore, is the intrinsic nature of *surplus* that exists in man, above all his limitations or contradictions. Universality, in the form of love, potential in the nature of *surplus* in man, urges him to develop this eternal nature for the introduction of unity between man the individual and Man the Universal. The realisation of this Universal Man in human existence, is explained by Tagore as self-realisation or truth realisation, which becomes complete through the final realisation of the highest stage of unity or non-duality in the perfect state of human freedom.

Here it may be pointed out that this is a social approach to human freedom in love, as in this process, the universal ideal of love, potential in man, urges him to love others unconditionally and in this way a man is related with others through which a social justice, equality in the form of unity can be established as it also introduces a selfless and disinterested way of life in society. The development of this way of life is to introduce unity in individual and social life of man as it expresses the universal nature of man in unity in love. This process of human life, according to Tagore, is a human process that synthesises the material existence of man with his spirituality as the expression of divinity in the form of humanity. This interpretation of human life, it may be said, is not merely material or not merely spiritual or transcendental but it, in the opinion of Tagore, is purely human in transcendent-experiential form as it finally develops the philosophy of *Humanism* in the explanation of the human nature as the religion of Man, which expresses unity in and above all diversities and differences. Dr Radhakrishnan, in his *Religion and Culture,* rightly observes: "It is an age of humanism. Religion which are insensitive to human ills and social crimes do not appeal to the modern man. Religions which make for division, discord and disintegration and do not foster unity, understanding and coherence, play into the hands of the opponents of religion." So the idea of religion which is the imposition of something on man denying of his material or social existence in differences, cannot appeal to Tagore. He, on the other hand, explains religion as the religion of Man, which is the introduction of unity in and through the contradictions in this material world.

This outlook of Tagore's religion of Man, may be said, is the evaluation or the critical examination of the common idea of religion as the imposition of something, but on the other hand, it centres round the human life that introduces the idea of synthesis of philosophy with life and religion as the expression of universal nature of man. This comprehensive view of Tagore finally establishes religion of Man for the foundation of religion on *Humanism*. But it should be noted in this connection, that the idea of *Humanism*, present in the religion of Man as the expression of universality, does not mean the mere development and welfare of individual man; but it, on the other hand, refers to the collective approach of developing universality, present in collective or social life of man. The reference to this development of collective life means the establishment of unity between individual and social life, that, according to Tagore, is purely human; as it expresses the total nature and universal existence of man.

In order to explain this humanistic process of life, Tagore explains the nature of man, and observes that his material existence may create' narrow interests, responsible for producing contradiction between individual and social interests of life. But the universal love, present in the intrinsic nature of *surplus* in man, urges him to overcome this contradiction through the development of his universality in love for the sacrifice of the narrow individual interest in and through love and service to others. This helps a man to sacrifice his individual 'ego' or poor interest through the inauguration of the idea of unity in the love of humanity.

This method of developing the universal unity in love helps a man to manifest his universal or infinite nature in his material existence in this world, which, according to Tagore, is 'the divinity of man' or the expression of divine values like infinite love or bliss in man as the expression of God as the substratum of these universal or eternal values.

Thus, through the evaluation of the different stages of the religion of Man as different states of the realisation of values, expressing the universal nature of man, Tagore finally explains the supreme state of the human existence as the expression of universal unity in love, which, in the opinion of Tagore, is the inauguration of God in man. This, as Tagore observes, is the final development of the universal existence of Man as God. It may be noted here that God as divinity of goodness is taken by Tagore as the highest human value, that is to be realised in different stages in different forms towards the final state of completeness. The realisation of the absolute value in and through love, makes man divine; and manifestation of divinity in human life through love and service for mankind, makes God human. This, according to Tagore, is the fundamental and final development of the religion of Man, as the expression of "The idea of the humanity of our God, or the divinity of Man the Eternal."[3]

The expression of this divinity in man develops his infinite or universal personality through love and work for human beings, that establishes a harmony in the individual, the social and the universal life of man, and thus solves all individual, moral and social problems of life and world. This attitude of human life through a social process establishes a universal humanistic outlook, that is the expression of the Ultimate Reality as the synthesis of the life of the individual, the social and Universal Man. Tagore points out, "Truth is the infinite pursued by metaphysics; fact is the infinite pursued by science, while reality is the definition of the infinite which relates truth to the person. Reality is human, it is what we are conscious of, by which we are affected, that which we express." This perfect state of Reality, developed through the human life in this world, expresses His universal and infinite personality, that according to Tagore, 'is a self-conscious principle of transcendental unity within man which comprehends all the details of facts…' Thus, through the development of personality as unity in love, a man transcends the separateness of facts and synthesises them in a continuous process towards the establishment of the "world of personality".[4] For this reason Tagore says, "we can make truth... by actively modulating its inter-relations."

This humanistic idea of truth as the unity and interrelation of man with others in the universe, developed through a disinterested love and selfless service for mankind in a transcendent-experiential sense, is the fundamental object of expanding religion of Man as the philosophy of *Humanism*. The universal outlook of man, as has already been discussed, expresses his infinite or complete nature that finally helps him to solve all contradictions of morality, religion in society through a proper development of moral and spiritual side of his nature that is explained by Tagore; "The moral side represents training of unselfishness, control of desire, spiritual side represents sympathy and love." This moral or spiritual development of man directs him to lead a good life in society, which is well-balanced, well-conducted and well-regulated social life. Bhattacharya rightly points out, "Good life meant, for most people, performance of well regulated socio-moral duties and carrying on economic and other material pursuits equally well-regulated."[5]

The social and moral development as good life, thus presents the ethics of the universal personality of Man, that expresses the true significance of the religion of Man, where it is taken as the expression of the proper nature of man, that finally is the realisation of his true existence in completeness. Tagore says, "Religion is the truth of our complete being, it is the true centre of gravity of our life".

In the idea of completeness, a total or the infinite existence of man is fully realised and the development of comprehensive attitude or humanistic outlook towards life and society becomes complete. In the process of developing completeness, the meaning of all religions get the true significance and this universal outlook, Tagore thinks, should be the guiding spirit of education, culture and civilisation. Education, according to Tagore, is the manifestation of man's universal or 'complete being', which is affirmed by Whitehead also, as he observes, "Education is the guidance of the individual towards a comprehension of the art of life. Each individual is nothing but an embodiment of this adventure of existence. The art of life is the guidance of this adventure." This 'comprehension of the art of life', in the opinion of Tagore, "is not a peace which is in negation or in some mechanical adjustment, but that which is in truth of perfect Union..."[6] Our culture, according to Tagore, is also the fulfillment of this universal spirit. He thinks, "...any special truth or special culture which is wholly dissociated from the universal is not true at all."

Thus, it may be observed that the comprehensive and universal outlook, as developed through the humanist outlook of education and culture, is also finally established in the human civilisation. In this context, Tagore evaluates the mechanical view of Western civilisation and tries to establish the eternal and infinite spirit of human civilisation through a proper development and fulfillment of the infinite nature of man at the centre of human civilisation. Tagore observes, "I have felt that the civilisation of the West today has its law and order but no personality. It has come to the perfection of a mechanical order, but what is there to humanise it? It is the person who is in the heart of all beings. We have seen, we have known Him within us, in the depth of our consciousness...peace can only be realised in the spiritual revelation of Man who in exhaustible wealth is in his won fulfillment."[7]

'The spiritual revelation of Man' is the manifestation and the development of man's universal personality, through which the idea of 'peace' is manifested through the introduction of a new social system or order of intimate relation of creative unity in love. Thus, the civilisation of man becomes true and significant with reference to the life an existence of man. Regarding this view of Tagore, Radhakrishnan rightly points out, "...there is only one history, the history of man. All national histories are merely chapters in the larger one.... Our national cultures are varied expressions of the one culture which is emerging for the whole of civilised humanity. Only that will survive which is basically consistence with the Universal outlook. We can not be content with anything less than the world order."[8]

Thus, finally it may be said that the inauguration of 'the universal outlook' in Tagore's religion of Man, is the introduction of the *Universal Humanism* through a creative unity in love that develops a new social order. This socio-cultural and humanistic outlook of

Tagore, is evaluated by Dr Radhakrishnan thus: "Tagore is a symbol of the undying spirit of man who lifted the hearts of mankind to the heights we aspire for a new society, a new civilisation."[9] In the light of this evaluation, we may conclude the chapter with a great conviction that Tagore's idea of the religion of Man as the expression of universal nature and existence of human beings, stands on his idea of *Universal Humanism* in a socio-cultural form. It is an eternal process of unity between the individual and the collective or social existence of man in this world. This wider view of *Universalism* should be the fundamental basis of human culture and civilisation and the guiding principle of the history of human life and society. So Tagore's philosophy of *Humanism*, expresses in one hand the inner essence of man as the evaluation of his eternal inspiration and aspiration of life for the dynamic development and expression of his multidimensional nature and existence, beyond any static conception or mere linguistic interpretation and logical enquiry. This creative form as *Socio-Cultural-Humanism* on the other hand develops the philosophy of integration, preparing an international and intercultural programme for realising creative humanistic values and integrates *Jnana, Karma* and *Bhakti* as the disinterested ideals and ways of Indian culture, beyond orthodoxy or dogmatism. It also relates this humanistic process with a creative scientific outlook of the Western culture, beyond mechanical contradictions, alienations, psychoses and other modern evils.

In the context of this analysis of Tagore's novel socio-cultural programme of *Universal Humanism* expressing the eternal optimism of man, we may refer to the utterings of Dr Radhakrishnan, a noted thinker and a statesman of India. With the creative possibility of man and culture, he also refers to an idea of 'International Peace' where he observes, "The way of peace requires that men and nations should recognise their common humanity and use weapons of integrity, reason, patience, understanding and love. There are many forces at work which give us hope and assurance. Even if we fail, we should not give up our efforts. Failure we have with us always, but man possesses, an unconquerable self that through failure and tragedy may rise to higher reaches of spiritual victory by the transcendence of evil."[10]

In the background of this evaluation of Tagore's philosophy of *Universal Humanism* in socio-cultural form, he develops in man a creative awareness. He thinks that if we put an emphasis on finite, egocentric and material philosophy of man then it makes man cautious about his poor self-interest. In this context, if we accept the opinion of Protagoras as man is the measure of all things, then satisfaction of individual '*ego*' and individual interest, Tagore observes, our social existence and social relation will be ignored. Again, in the context of denying the importance of fulfillment of individual interest, if we simply welcome the collective Man upon the expansion of his collective interest only, then there is a possibility of developing narrow *Nationalism* in creating contradictions or evils in social existence of man.

That is why Tagore emphasises the creative expansion of Universal Man and *Universal Humanism* in a socio-cultural form that is to be expanded through a transcendent-experiential process. Tagore believes that there is transcendent power of '*surplus*' in human nature that expounds man's infinite possibilities through a creative experiential process of manifesting universal human value and universal human truth over contradictions or evils due to mere satisfaction of poor self-interests.

This humanistic process, according to Tagore, is a creative transcendent-experiential method of awakening of universality through transcending evils and experiencing creatively the different states of manifesting universal value as *Universal Good* as *Mangala* in deferent degrees.

So finally it is to be noted that Tagore's philosophy of *Humanism* is very much unique and distinct from Western *Humanism*. According to Tagore, man is a creative being and through the creative transcendent-experiential process in expounding universality and infiniteness of man and expanding it in human existence in deferent degrees so that man himself becomes creative universal being like God in manifesting '*the Divinity of Man*' and God as universal human value of goodness or *Mangala*, becomes human in developing '*humanity of God*' so Tagore's *Universal Humanism* examines man as creative being or *sristisheel manav* and thus Tagore accepts man as active, direct and creative, so his philosophy of man is finally stated as The Theory of Creative Man, The Universal as *sristisheel manavbad* distinct from Western *Humanism* or *Manavatabad* as indirect, passive state of realising of some socio-cultural and human qualities.

Notes

1. Rabindranath Tagore, 'Dharma', *Rabindrarachanavali* (Cent. Edn), Vol. XII, p. 41.
2. S. Gangopadhyay and others, *Rabindra Darshan,* p. 137.
3. Rabindranath Tagore, *The Religion of Man,* p. 11.
4. Rabindranath Tagore, *Personality,* p. 57.
5. Dr Kalidas Bhattacharya, 'Spiritualism not anti-Humanistic', *Bulletin of the Ramkrishna Mission Institute of Culture.*
6. Booklet, *A Vision of Indian Culture.*
7. Rabindranath Tagore, Address on 'Education Week'.
8. Dr S. Radhakrishnan, *Religion and Culture,* p. 172.
9. *Ibid.*, p. 176.
10. Dr S. Radhakrishnan, *Religion and Culture,* pp. 88-89.

A Select Bibliography

Works by Tagore

In Bengali:

Atmaparichaya, Visva-Bharati, Calcutta, 1961.

Balaka, Visva-Bharati, Calcutta, 1363 B. S.

Chhinnapatravali, Visva-Bharati, Calcutta, 1367 B. S.

Dharma, Visva-Bharati, Calcutta, 1355 B.S.

Gitanjali, Visva-Bharati, Calcutta, 1965.

Gitavitan, Parts I, II, III, Visva-Bharati, Calcutta, 1363-65 B. S.

Jivansmriti, Visva-Bharati, Calcutta, 1968.

Manuser Dharma, Visva-Bharati, Calcutta, 1972.

Rabindrarachanavali (all Vols.), Visva-Bharati, Calcutta, 1363 B.S.

Rabindrarachanavali, Achalita Samgraha, Parts I and II, Visva-Bharati, Calcutta, 1962.

Rabindrarachanavali, Centenary Edn., Govt. of West Bengal, Calcutta, 1368 B.S.

Samaj, Visva-Bharati, Calcutta, 1344 B. S.

Sanchaya, Visva-Bharati, Calcutta, 1356 B. S.

Santiniketan, Vols. I and II, Visva-Bharati, Calcutta, 1356 B. S.

In English:

Child, Allen & Unwin, London, 1931.

Collected Poems and Plays, Macmillan, London, 1961.

Creative Unity, Macmillan, London, 1959.

Crisis of Civilisation, Visva-Bharati, Calcutta, 1957.

Fruit Gathering, Macmillan, London, 1961.

Gitanjali (Song-Offerings), Macmillan, London, 1962.

Letters from Abroad, Ganesh & Co., Madras, 1924.

Lover's Gift and Crossing, London, 1954.

Man (1st Edn.), Kitabistan, Allahabad.

Nationalism, Macmillan, London, 1918.

One Hundred Poems of Kabir, Macmillan, London, 1918.

Personality, Macmillan, London, 1954.

Religion of Artist, Visva-Bharati, Calcutta, 1953.

Sacrifice and other Plays, Macmillan, London, 1961.

Sadhana, Macmillan, India, 1970.

The Gardener, Macmillan, London, 1961.

The Religion of Man, Unwin Books, London, 1970.

Towards Universal Man, Bombay, 1961.

Works on Tagore

In Bengali:

Banerjee, C., *Rabi Rashmi,* Vols. I and II, A. Mukherjee & Co., Calcutta, 1346 B. S.

Bandyopadhyay, H., *Rabindradradarshan,* Sahitya Samsad, Calcutta,1369 B.S.

Bandyopadhyay, H., *Santiniketaner Bhashanmala,* Pustak Bipani, Calcutta, 1976.

Bandyopadhyay, H., *Rabindra Shilpatattva,* Calcutta, 1377 D.S.

Basu, S., *Rabindranatake Tragedi,* Calcutta, 1377 B.S.

Bisi, P.N., *Madhusudan Theke Rabindranath,* Calcutta, 1381 B.S.

Bhattacharya, J., *Rabindra Kabitashatak-Pratham Dashak,* Calcutta,1974.

Chaudhuri, B., *Kavye Rabindranath* (3rd Edn.), Mitra O Ghosh, Calcutta.

Chaudhuri, P.J., *Rabindranather Saundarya Darshan,* A. Mukherjee & Co., Calcutta, 1363 B.S.

Das, K., *Rabindra Pratibhar Parichaya,* Puthighar, Calcutta, 1360 B. S.

Dasgupta, S., *Upanisader Patabhumikaya Rabindra Manas,* Calcutta, 1368 B. S.

Gangopadhyay, S. and others, *Rabindradarshan,* Visva-Bharati, Calcutta, 1375 B.S.

Ghosh, T. K., *Rabindranather Dharmachinta,* Calcutta, 1369 B.S.

Gupta, N.K., *Rabindranath,* Aurobindo Patha Mandir, Calcutta, 1368 B.S.

Mukhopadhyay, P.K., *Rabindra Jivani O Rabindra Sahitya Praveshak,* Vols. I-IV, Visva-Bharati Granthalay, Calcutta, 1340-56 B.S.

Mukhopadhyay, A.K., *Rabindrachetanaya Upanishad,* Calcutta, 1382 B.S.

Nandi, S.K., *Rabindradarshan Anvikshan,* Sribhumi Publishing Company, Calcutta, 1960.

Roy, N.R., *Rabindra Sahitya Bhumika,* Book Emporium, Calcutta, 1315 B.S.

Roy, P., *Rabindranather Dharmadarshan,* Gopa Prakashani, Calcutta, 1383 B.S.

Sarkar, S., *Rabindra Kavye Trayi Parikalpana,* Kanailal Sarkar, Calcutta, 1348 B.S.

Sengupta, S.C., *Rabindranath, N.C. Sarkar and Sons Ltd.,* Calcutta, 1359 B.S.

In English:

Aronson, A., *Rabindranath through Western Eyes,* Kitabistan, Allahabad, 1943.

Das, S.K., *Tagore and the Perennial Problems of Philosophy,* Rabindra Bharati University, Calcutta, 1971.

Banerjee, H., Rabindranath Tagore, Pub. Div., New Delhi, 1971.

Dasgupta, S.N., *Rabindranath–The Poet and the Philosopher,* 1948.

Ghosh, S.K. (tr.), *Tagore Rabindranath-Biography,* (Probhat Kumar Mukhopadhyay, Life of Tagore), 1975.

Mukherjee, A.K., *Upanishad–In the Eyes of Rabindranath Tagore,* Dasgupta & Co., Calcutta, 1975.

Narvane, V.S., *Rabindranath Tagore–A Philosophical Study,* Central Book Depot, Allahabad, 1961.

Narvane, V.S., *An Introduction to Rabindranath Tagore,* Macmillan, India, 1977.

Radhakrishnan, S., *The Philosophy of Rabindranath Tagore,* London, 1919.

Rhys, E., *Rabindranath Tagore: A Biographical Study,* Macmillan & Co., London, 1917.

Roy, B.G., *The Philosophy of Rabindranath Tagore,* Progressive Publisher, Calcutta, 1970.

Sen, S., *The Political Thought of Tagore,* 1947.

Sengupta, S.C., *The Great Sentinel: A Study of Rabindranath Tagore,* A. Mukherjee & Co., Calcutta, 1948.

Tagore, S., *Rabindranath Tagore and Universal Humanism,* Standard Vacuum Company, Bombay.

Thompson, E.J., *Rabindranath Tagore: Poet and Dramatist,* 1926.

Thompson, E. J., *Rabindranath Tagore: His Life and Works,* Calcutta, 1921.

Winternitz, M., *Rabindranath Tagore: Religion and Weltanschauung des Dichters,* Pages, 1936.

Other Works

In Bengali:

Anirvan, *Divyajivan Prasanga,* Sri Aurobindo Ashram, Pondicherry, 1971.

Bhattacharya, H., *Hinduder Devdevi, Udbhav O Karmavikash,* Vols. I and II, Farma KLM, Calcutta, 1978.

Chattopadhyay, D.P., *Rup, Ras O Sundar (Nandantattver Bhumika),* Riddhi–India, Calcutta, 1981.

Marx, K. and Engels, F., *Rachana Samkalan,* Vols. I and II, Pragati Prakashan, Moscow, 1971-72.

Nandi, S.K., *Nandantattva,* Paschim Banga Pustak Parishad, Calcutta, 1979.

Roy, S., *Bharater Vaiplabik Sangramer Itihas,* Vol. I, DNBA Brothers, Calcutta, 1970.

Sen, A.C., *Upanishad,* Vols. I and II, Haraf Prakashani, Calcutta, 1974.

Sen, K.M., *Bharater Samskriti,* Visva-Bharati, Calcutta, 1352 B.S.

Sen, K.M., *Madhyayuge Bharatiya Sadhanar Dhara,* Calcutta University, Calcutta, 1930.

In English:

Bahm, A.J., *Axiology: The Science of Values,* Albuquerque, New Mexico, USA, 1980.

Banerjee, N.V., *The Conept of Philosophy* (K.C. Bhattacharya Lectures, 1964), University of Calcutta, Calcutta, 1968.

Bhadra, M.K., *A Critical Study of Sartre's Ontology of Consciousness,* University of Burdwan, 1978.

Blackham, *Six Existentialist Thinkers,* R. & K. Paul Ltd., London. 1961.

Bosanquet, B., *The Principles of Individuality and Value,* Macmillan, London, 1927.

Bradley, F.H., *Appearance and Reality,* Clarendon Press, Oxford, 1962.

Chatterjee, P.B., *Studies in Comparative Religion,* Calcutta, 1971.

Chatterjee, P.B., *Philosophy of Josiah Royce,* Dasgupta & Co., Calcutta, 1968.

Chardin, T.D., *The Phenomenon of Man,* 1959.

Cherrington, C., *Man on his Nature*, 1953.

Complete Works of Swami Vivekananda, Vols. I to VIII, Advaita Ashram, Calcutta, 1963.

Comte, A., *General View of Positivism,* translated by J.H. Bridges, Trubner & Co., London, 1865.

Conford, F.M., *The Republic of Plato,* Clarendon Press, Oxford, 1961.

Cultural Heritage of India, Ramkrishna Mission Institute of Culture, Calcutta, 1970.

Cunningham, G.N., *Problems of Philosophy,* Chuckerverty-Chatterjee & Co. Ltd., Calcutta, 1956.

Das, A.C., *A Modern Incarnation of God,* G.P. & P. Ltd., Calcutta, 1958.

Dasgupta, S.B., *Obscure Religious Cults,* Calcutta, 1962.

Dasgupta, S. N., *History of Indian Philosophy* (Vols. I to IV), Camb. Univ. Press, 1951-55.

Ducasse, C. J., *A Philosophical Scrutiny of Religion,* Ronald Press, 1953.

Dutta, D. M., *The Philosophy of Mahatma Gandhi,* University of Calcutta, Calcutta, 1968.

Dutta, D. M., *The Chief Currents of Contemporary Philosophy,* University of Calcutta, Calcutta, 1961.

Eddington, *Science and the Unseen World,* 1929.

Edwards, D. M., *The Philosophy of Religion* (Indian Edition), Progressive Publishers, Calcutta, August, 1960.

Foulquie, *Existentialism,* London, 1948.

Formm, E., *Man for Himself,* New York, 1947.

Galloway, *The Philosophy of Religion,* T. & T. Clerk, 1914.

Gandhi, M. K., *Ethical Religion,* S. Ganesan, Madras.

Gandhi, M. K., *My Religion,* Navaranjan, Ahmedabad, 1958.

Gangopadhyay, S., *Tradition Modernity and Development: A Study in Contemporary Indian Society,* Macmillan, India, 1977.

Greene, M., *Dreadful Freedom,* Chicago, 1948.

Hartmann, N., *Ethics* (all Vols.), Allen and Unwin, London, 1950.

Hiriyana, M., *Outlines of Indian Philosophy,* Allen & Unwin, London, 1967.

Huxley, A., *The Perennial Philosophy,* London, 1947.

Harper, R., *Existentialism: A Theory of Man,* Cambridge, Mass, 1948.

Holt, E. B., *Freudian Wish and Its Place in Ethics,* Moffat, New York, 1916.

James, E. O., *Comparative Religion,* Methuen, London, 1938.

Jaspers, K., *The Future of Mankind,* Chicago, 1961.

Kant, I., *The Critique of Judgement,* 1952.

Leibnitz, *Philosophical Writings,* tr. M. Morris, SC 8. 316, EV'man S, 13/6 Dent.

Lewis, H. D. and Slater, R. L., *The Study of Religions,* Pelican Book, 1969.

Martineau, J., *A Study of Religion: Its Sources and Contents,* Clarendon Press, Oxford, 1926.

Marx, K., *Capital,* Vol. I, New York, 1967.

Marx, K. and Engels, F., *Selected Works* (in one Vol), Moscow, 1970.

Moore, G. E., *Principia Ethica,* Cambridge U. Press, London, 1965.

Moore, G. E., *Some Main Problems of Philosophy,* London, 1962.

Nagaraja Rao, P., *Contemporary Indian Philosophy,* Bharatiya Vidya Bhavan, Bombay, 1970.

Nandi, S. K., An *Enquiry into the Nature and Function of Art,* University of Calcutta, Calcutta, 1962.

Paton, H. J., *The Moral Law: Kant's Groundwork of the Metaphysics of Morals,* Hutchinson University Library, London, 1972.

Pattison, P. and Seth, A, *The Idea of God in the Light of Recent Philosophy,* 2nd Edn. (reprint), 1967.

Pitcher, G., *The Philosophy of Wittgenstein* (Indian reprint), New Delhi, 1972.

Pearson, N., *Sri Aurobindo and the Soul of Quest of Man,* Allen & Unwin, London, 1952.

Radhakrishnan, S., *Eastern Religions and Western Thought,* Humphrey Milford, 1940.

Radhakrishnan, S., *Recovery of Faith,* Orient Paperbacks, India, 1967.

Radhakrishnan, S., *Religion and Culture,* Orient Paperbacks, India, 1968.

Radhakrishan, S., *The Bhagavad Gita,* Allen & Unwin, London, 1971.

Radhakrishnan, S., *The Creative Life,* Orient Paperbacks, India, 1975.

Raju, P. T., *The Idealistic Thought of India,* Allen and Unwin Ltd., London, 1953.

Rolland, R., *Swami Vivekananda,* translated by E. F. Malcolm Smith, Advaita Ashram, Almora.

Royce, J., *The World and the Individual,* Dover Publications Inc., New York, 1959.

Russell, B., *History of Western Philosophy,* Allen & Unwin, London, 1967.

Sarkar, A. K., *Whitehead's Four Principles: From West-East Perspectives,* Bharati Bhavan, Patna.

Sarkar, A. K., *Changing Phases of Buddhist Thought* (3rd Edn.), South Asia Publications, New Delhi, 1983.

Sarkar, A. K., *Dynamic Facets of Indian Thought,* Vol. I, Manohar Publication, New Delhi, 1980.

Seal, B. N., *Comparative Studies in Vaishnavism and Christianity,* 1899.

Sharma, C. D., *A Critical Survey of Indian Philosophy,* Motilal Banarasi Das, Delhi, 1964.

Sinha, D., *Phenomenology and Existentialism,* Progressive Publishers, Calcutta, 1974.

Sinha, J. N., *Moral Idealism and Theism,* Jadunath Sinha Foundation, Calcutta, 1978.

Sri Aurobindo, *The Riddle of this World,* lst Edn.

Sri Aurobindo, *The Life Divine,* Vols. I and II, 2nd Edn., Dec. 1944.

Sri Aurobindo, *The Idea of Human Unity,* 2nd Edn., 1950.

Zbavitel, D., *Bengali Folk-Ballads from Mymensingh and the Problems of their Authenticity,*University of Calcutta, Calcutta, 1963.

Srivastava, R. S., *Contemporary Indian Philosophy,* Munshiram Manoharlal, Delhi, 1965.

Smith, N. K., *Immanuel Kant's Critique of Pure Reason,* Macmillan, London, 1964.

Taylor, A. E., *Elements of Metaphysics,* University Paperbacks, Methuen, London.

Thily, F., *A History of Philosophy,* New York, 1963.

Underhill, E., *Mysticism* (4th Edn.), Methuen, London.

Edited Works

In Bengali:

Banerjee, H., *Rigveda Samhita,* Vols. I and II, Haraf Prakashani, Calcutta, 1976.

Bhattacharya, D., *Rabindranath,* East Light Book House, Calcutta, 1368 B.S.

Ghosh, A.K., *Rammohan Rachanavali,* Haraf Prakashani, Calcutta, 1973.

Goswami, B., *Yajurveda Samhita,* Haraf Prakashani, Calcutta, 1977.

Goswami, B., *Athrvaveda Samhita,* Haraf Prakashani, Calcutta, 1977.

Thakur, P., *Samveda Samhita,* Haraf Prakashani, Calcutta, 1975.

In Bengali:

Andrews, C. F., *Thoughts from Tagore,* 1929.

Bottonrore, T. B., *Early Writings,* K. Marx, New York, 1967.

Chatterjee, R., *The Golden Book of Tagore,* Golden Book Committee, Calcutta, 1931.

Conybeare, F. C., *Outlines of a Philosophy of Religion* by H. Lotze, Calcutta, 1954.

Encyclopaedia Britannica, Vols. II and XI, Encyclopaedia Britannica Inc., William Benton, 1969.

Hastings, J., *Encyclopaedia of Religion and Ethics,* Vol.VI, T. and T. Clark, Edinburgh, 1955.

Mahadevan, T. M. P. and Cairns, G. E., *Contemporary Indian Philosophers of History,* World Press, Calcutta.

Mohanty, J. N. and Banerjee, S. P., *Self, Knowledge and Freedom,* World Press, Calcutta, 1978.

Radhakrishnan, S. and Muirhead, J. H., *Contemporary Indian Philosophy,* Allen & Unwin, London, 1956.

Ryazanskaya, S., *The German Ideology-Karl Marx and Frederick Engels,* Moscow, 1964.

Solomon, R. C., *Phenomenology and Existentialism,* Harper & Row, 1972.

Sri Aurobindo and Rabindranath Tagore, Sri Aurobindo Ashram, Pondicherry, 1961.

Some Important Articles and Journals

In Bengali:

Bharati, Agrahayan, 1291 B. S.

Desh, Calcutta, 14th Magh, 1384 B. S.

'Patradhara', *Prabasi,* 1339 B. S.

Prabasi, Vaisakh, 1341 B. S.

'Prajna', *Bangiya Darshan Samsad Patrika,* Vaishak-Asar, 1381 B. S.

'Rabindrachetanaya Manavdharma' by S. N. Chatterjee, *Darshan,* Dacca University, 1977 and Proceedings of 3rd General Conference, Bangladesh Darshan Samiti, Chittagong, 1977.

Sahitya, 3rd Edn., 1361 B. S.

Visva-Bharati Patrika, Shravan-Ashvin, 1359 B. S.

In English:

Anviksiki, Banaras Hindu University, 1966, 1968.

Inaugural lecture of D. Sinha, Rabindranath Tagore Lectureship Foundation, Toronto, January, 1979.

International Review of Missions, 1914.

Memorandum of Association, Visva-Bharati.

Modern Review, August, 1913.

'Philosophy & History: Essence & Existence', Presidential address by S. P. Banerjee, History of Philosophy Section, Indian Philosophical Congress, 1977.

'Spiritualism not anti-Humanistic', by K. D. Bhattacharya, *Bulletin of the Ramakrishna Mission Institute of Culture,* Vols. xxix, Nos. 6-11, Calcutta, 1978.

'The Vedanta Concept of Man', by T. M. P. Mahadevan, *Religion and Society,* Vol. VII, Nos. 3 and 4, 1960.

'The Concept of Alienation in the Philosophy of Karl Marx', by S. P. Banerjee, *Journal of the Indian Academy of Philosophy,* July, 1969.

The Nation, 16th Nov., 1912.

Visva-Bharati Quarterly, Tagore Birthday Number, 1941.

Visva-Bharati Quarterly, Vol. XVIII, Part IV, 1953.

Rabindranath Tagore, Address on Education Week, 1916.